PRAISE FOR G

ON THE NATURE OF HIGHER CONSCIOUSNESS AN.

"I can think of no one else who has provided such remarkable insight into the psychology of consciousness. At this juncture in human evolution it is imperative for us to take note of his insights and embrace new thinking if we want Homo sapiens to have a long future."
— **Donald Johanson, Founding Director, Institute of Human Origins, author of** *Lucy: The Beginnings of Humankind*

"A magnificent exploration of ancient versions of religious beliefs combined with Ornstein's original views of transcendental consciousness...a legacy of unmatched wisdom."
— **Philip Zimbardo, Stanford University, author of** *The Lucifer Effect*

"In a compelling blend of solid psychological science and surprisingly universal religious practice, *God 4.0* reveals rarified insights into a uniquely human form of consciousness. It is mind blowing, indeed."
— **Robert Cialdini, author of** *Influence* **and** *Pre-Suasion*

"A stunning tour de force of erudition...a brilliant, guided expedition through reams of archeological and neurological research, highlighting the important discoveries and developments in our perennial quest for meaning and purpose."
— **Lisa Alther, author of** *Kinflicks*

"Using rigorous, rational, scientific analysis Ornstein shows that the spiritual impulse is innate, a human ability that from the Ice Age forward has been essential to problem solving. He lays out how this capacity to reach beyond the everyday can, cleared of cobwebs and seen afresh, be part of preparing humanity to confront today's staggering global problems."
— **Tony Hiss, author of** *Rescuing the Planet*

"Opened my mind — and my heart — to new possibilities."
— **BJ Fogg, Stanford University, author of** *Tiny Habits*

"Ornstein has combined the latest research from a number of domains to create a new spiritual literacy that offers an understanding of the transcendent nature of consciousness...allows us to truly see God. Humbling, profound and, ultimately, transformative."
— **James R. Doty, Stanford University School of Medicine, author of *Into the Magic Shop: A Neurosurgeon's Quest to Discover the Mysteries of the Brain and the Secrets of the Heart***

"Makes you rethink what God, religion, consciousness, and the human experience of them are. What if God were not a disembodied spirit? What if God were an altered state of consciousness, an inborn network of the human brain which can be accessed and help us today? This landmark book shines new light on things we thought we understood."
— **Charles Swencionis, Yeshiva University, author of *The Healing Brain Reader***

"A visionary fusion of true spirituality and neuroscience. The authors forcefully argue for 'consciousness evolution,' a shift away from self-centeredness that releases enhanced perceptual capabilities. This shift can profoundly influence epigenetic expression, health, and perhaps even influence the epigenetic inheritance of future generations."
— **Kenneth R. Pelletier, UCSF School of Medicine, author of *Change Your Genes, Change Your Life***

"A timely invitation to explore a latent, intuitive faculty we all share – one that can move us beyond belief, faith, and doctrine to a wider perception of who we are and who we could become."
— **David S. Sobel, Stanford University School of Medicine, author of *Healthy Pleasures***

"There is no question that Ornstein had the rare gift of combining rigorous scientific methodology with the whimsy and humor of a Sufi storyteller. This, his final book, takes the exploration to a new level – to the very boundary where human consciousness touches the divine."
— **Jeffrey Mishlove, host of *New Thinking Allowed***

GOD 4.0

*On the Nature of
Higher Consciousness and the
Experience Called "God"*

Robert Ornstein

with Sally M. Ornstein

MALOR
BOOKS

By Robert Ornstein

THE BRAIN, MIND AND CONSCIOUSNESS

God 4.0: On the Nature of Higher Consciousness and the Experience Called "God" (with Sally M. Ornstein)

The Psychology of Consciousness

The Evolution of Consciousness: The Origins of the Way We Think (with Ted Dewan, illus.)

Multimind: A New Way of Looking at Human Behavior

The Right Mind: Making Sense of the Hemispheres

The Roots of the Self: Unraveling the Mystery of Who We Are (with Ted Dewan, illus.)

MindReal: How the Mind Creates Its Own Virtual Reality (with Ted Dewan, illus.)

The Nature of Human Consciousness

Symposium on Consciousness

The Mind Field

On the Psychology of Meditation (with Claudio Naranjo)

Meditation and Modern Psychology

The Amazing Brain (with Richard Thompson and David Macaulay, illus.)

On the Experience of Time

Psychology: The Study of Human Experience (Third Edition with Laura Carstensen)

Psychology: The Biological, Mental and Social Worlds

Common Knowledge: or Can of Foot Powder Elected Mayor of Ecuadorian Town

THE MIND AND HEALTH

The Healing Brain: Breakthrough Discoveries about How the Brain Keeps us Healthy (with David Sobel)

Healthy Pleasures (with David Sobel)

The Healing Brain: A Scientific Reader (with Charles Swencionis)

The Mind & Body Handbook: How to Use Your Mind & Body to Relieve Stress, Overcome Illness and Enjoy Healthy Pleasures (with David Sobel)

OUR FUTURE

The Axemaker's Gift: Technology's Capture and Control of our Minds and Culture (with James Burke)

New World, New Mind (with Paul Ehrlich)

Humanity on a Tightrope: Thoughts on Empathy, Family, and Big Changes for a Viable Future (with Paul R. Ehrlich)

FOR YOUNG ADULTS
ALL ABOUT ME Series

Foreword by Robert Ornstein (with Jeff Jackson, illus.):

Me and My Feelings: What Emotions Are and How We Can Manage Them (by Robert Guarino)

What's the Catch? How to Avoid Getting Hooked and Manipulated (by David Sobel)

Me and My Memory: Why We Forget Some Things and Remember Others (by Robert Guarino)

What We See and Don't See (by Robert Guarino)

The illustrations on pages 13, 32 and 48:

Figure. 1: The drawings from Joseph E. Bogen, "The Other Side of the Brain, I," *Bulletin of the Los Angeles Neurological Societies* 34, no. 3 (July 1969).

Figure. 2: The images of the "Sorcerer" taken from publicly available and open resources.

Figure. 3: The three stages of altered consciousness: possible examples that might be experienced by a Westerner. This image taken from *The Shamans of Prehistory: Trance and Magic in the Painted Caves* by Jean Clottes and David Lewis-Williams, Harry N. Abrams, Inc., 1996, p. 14.

Robert Ornstein, the award-winning psychologist and pioneering brain researcher, authored more than 20 books on the nature of the human mind and brain and their relationship to thought, health, and individual and social consciousness. His books have sold over six million copies. They have been translated into dozens of languages and used in more than 20,000 university classes worldwide.

His groundbreaking books *The Psychology of Consciousness* and *The Evolution of Consciousness* introduced the two modes of consciousness of the left and right brain hemispheres and a critical understanding of how the brain evolved. Ornstein considered these, along with *God 4.0: On the Nature of Higher Consciousness and the Experience Called "God,"* his most important writings. The three books together provide a fundamental reconsideration of ancient religious and spiritual traditions in the light of advances in brain science and psychology, exploring the potential and relevance of this knowledge to contemporary needs and to our shared future.

Dr. Ornstein taught at the University of California Medical Center and Stanford University, and lectured at more than 200 colleges and universities in the U.S. and overseas. He was the president and founder of the Institute for the Study of Human Knowledge (ISHK), an educational nonprofit dedicated to bringing important discoveries concerning human nature to the general public. Among his many honors and awards are the UNESCO award for Best Contribution to Psychology and the American Psychological Foundation Media Award "for increasing the public understanding of psychology."

Ornstein's trailblazing research and writing on the specialization of the brain's left and right hemispheres, on the multiple nature of our mind and its untapped potential for solving contemporary problems, have advanced our understanding of who we are, how we got here and how we might evolve to the benefit of ourselves and our planet.

For more information and access to the complete works of Robert Ornstein, visit **robertornstein.com**.

For M.B., with love and gratitude always

Some Acknowledgements

In writing this book we read so very many exceptional books on science and religion, and are indebted to the many great authors who wrote them. Among the most notable are Karen Armstrong and Robert Wright, Nicholas Wade, Jesse Bering, Stephen Sanderson, Elaine Pagels, Bart Ehrman and the late Marvin Meyer, as well as the invaluable works by the late Idries Shah and the magnificent series by David Lewis-Williams and his associates — and, more recently, books by Ara Norenzayan and Tanya Luhrmann that deal with the development of the concept of God, the different gods in our civilization and the gods in others. And there are books about why we have faith, about the conceptions of God in Medieval times, about the beginnings of the three Abrahamic religions, about the differences between those three religions, about how belief in God affects our behavior — and countless others.

There are far too many people whose research work has contributed to this book, for us to thank them all here, but among them are Erika Bourguignon; Mircea Eliade; the Reverend John Shelby Spong; the members of the Leakey family; Frans de Waal; Matthew Lieberman; Robin Dunbar; Roger Sperry and Joseph Bogen, who first discovered the different functions of the brain's two hemispheres — and, more recently, Brick Johnstone and the others who have worked on the connection between the right hemisphere and selflessness, as well as the discoverers of how insight works in the brain and those who discovered mirror neurons, the brain's idling system and default-mode network, and the neural changes that lead to inspiration and insight.

We are indebted to the Will J. Reid Foundation for its continuing support of our work during this long period of writing.

Very special thanks to all those who read, reread, edited and encouraged us to complete this work. To Phil Zimbardo for his early encouragement and enthusiasm. Denise Winn for her tireless research and for her sanity, amazing support, friendship, encouragement as well as editorial genius in completing the book. Similar thanks to David Sobel, Mary Ann Cammarota, Charlie Swencionis, Tony Hiss, Ann Bowcock, George Kasabov, Dan Sperling, Jonathan Scott, Willa Moore, and Lance Ternasky for all their comments and suggestions. To Shane DeHaven for her constant, quiet attention to all the tiny details, and to her and Bob Dunkle for giving me (SMO) and our two cats a home and place to write for more than a year. My deepest thanks to Jonathan and Saori Russell and to all those dear friends who have helped me through this time. They know who they are.

Contents

Preface by
Robert Ornstein

This book is about what it means to go beyond the ordinary perception of reality and to understand why, throughout our human history almost all of humanity has had the concept of transcendence and connection to "the other" — to "the spirit world," to "God" or to "the One behind it all" — whether the society has a formal doctrine of it or not.

◆ ◆ ◆

In 1972, I wrote *The Psychology of Consciousness*, which received a lot of attention for its delineation of the functions of the two sides of the brain (a reviewer in *The New Yorker* said, "...this was the book I had been waiting for"). That book spelled out how modern psychologies, the (then) new discoveries about the workings of the brain aligned with spiritual traditions, since both describe our ordinary consciousness of the world and of ourselves as a construction, or sometimes, as an "illusion."

Twenty years or so later, one reviewer said of the second book in this series, *The Evolution of Consciousness*, that "this could be the first work of a new Bible, to be read again and again by those seeking a wise and intelligent future."*

This current book is, I guess, a sequel, in that it sets out a new way to understand what's been called "spirituality" and what it means in modern terms. It points toward a new unity of science and the spiritual.

New findings in psychology and neuroscience, in genetics, in paleontology, and the many post-war discoveries of ancient religious texts, have stimulated a new view, one shorn of misunderstood metaphors, or scientific reduction and smug dismissal. The data assembled here have yielded the answers to many puzzles, such as: Why do those seeking higher consciousness do such weird things? Why is religious or spiritual experience called "high," anyway? How has the search for transcendence affected the development of society? What is the relationship between creative inspiration and "spiritual" insight? And why are people who tend to be strongly politically conservative also more religious?

There's enormous and continuing interest in the topic: More books and articles are published daily than could be read in a month (trust me, I know). Then why take the trouble to add a shard atop this mountain?

It's because the years since the early 1970s have produced unprecedented progress and have generated more information regarding human nature and consciousness, and about our own religions' histories, than perhaps has been discovered in all the years before. It is thanks to this modern research — from archeology to anthropology to religious studies, genetics and especially to psychology — that, by combining these findings with my own work, there is now a new understanding of how the brain produces a transcendent shift in consciousness, which many have called "seeing God."

---

*Stuart Whitwell, *Booklist*.

The data taken together nudge us to a radical conclusion: that what we have experienced as "God" is a development and extension of consciousness. This has been misrepresented in history, due to ignorance of how the brain and nervous systems work. So the experience was ascribed by the ancients, and continues today in our religions to be ascribed to metaphorical beings. This is what these "Gods" — which I think should be thought of as God 1.0 to 3.0 — were about.

Obviously, there's an enormous amount to consider, but this book isn't an exhaustive, exhausting look at all of human history in detail. It is a short read, and it traces a new path along the constant nature of the concern with the transcendent. Through different areas of research, it coalesces what might seem diverse and unconnected concepts, methods, myths and results. New ideas take time to absorb, and this book weaves together many threads from different disciplines, practices and eras, and provides a different way to look at them as a whole. As the pieces and shards of the mosaic fill in, I hope this leads to connections from different areas of research and to the beginning of a new spiritual literacy.

This book is for the inquisitive and open-minded reader — a person who reads the newspapers, history, biography and science; one who finds that there's "something missing" in all of these disciplines as he or she genuinely tries to understand life and meaning. For such people, an involvement with God, as they've encountered It, may be thought to be retrograde nonsense, or may be narrowed to fish on Friday or a once-a-year visit to a house of worship.

Neither an academic tome nor a religious treatise, *God 4.0* is addressed to people who seek more out of life than they find in it at this moment. They find themselves spectators in their religious life, where they may well see themselves at the bottom rung of an archaic, distant and sometimes corrupt hierarchy. If they could, they might welcome knowing the first steps to move beyond rather than just to look on.

It is also now almost a lifetime after that review of *The Psychology of Consciousness*. With all the research that has expanded our knowledge since then, I'll now adopt *The New Yorker's* 1972 comment, more than four decades later, as my own:

"This is the book I was waiting for."

Robert Ornstein
Los Altos, California
November 2018

Preface by
Sally Ornstein

Bob and I connected on April 29, 1981, in London. He spoke at a conference on "The Psychology of Consciousness and Health" and, being on the "take-care-of-the-speakers" committee, I was designated to drive him to his hotel. It was pouring, the rain pelting down. But he wanted to go for a walk on Hampstead Heath. So we did.

I don't remember what was said, but I know that after that walk, both of us knew we were on the same journey, that we wanted, or needed, exactly the same things out of life.

We both had an insatiable curiosity and a determination to find answers that had bugged us both since adolescence: Who are we? What are we here for, if anything? What makes sense, and why does so much not — in our behavior, in our priorities and in our beliefs? Finding answers to such questions was a priority for us both. That is what had led me — and I'm sure, so many of Bob's readers — to his work. As he said to a friend in an email I found just recently, "Truth has always been an obsession with me. It's nothing commendable, I'm just built that way."

That was his life.

I must confess, I was somewhat in awe of Bob's ability to absorb and synthesize information. He never stopped searching. He was always asking, always open and learning, always assimilating anything and everything that caught his attention, and from multiple fields — as he says, from archeology to anthropology to religious studies, to genetics and especially to psychology; and I would add: from cultural history, current affairs, art, fiction, poetry, and on and on. Anything of interest, he would store in his remarkable memory and pull out to connect with other ideas at some point when they made sense.

Perhaps most remarkable about him was that no matter your background, if you were genuinely asking questions on any topic with which he was familiar, he saw his job as explaining in words devoid of academic jargon, but without warping or simplifying complexities, his understanding thus far. This gift is reflected in *God 4.0*.

Our relationship at first was a bit like *Educating Rita*, for those who remember that movie, only he was not my professor but my love, my best friend, and would become my partner for 35 years.

Our backgrounds couldn't have been more different, which I think made ideas and insights richer for both of us in writing *God 4.0*. A British middle-class white female, daughter of colonial parents, I had been through the mill of a Roman Catholic boarding school and come out the other side with many more questions than answers. I loved to paint and write poetry, but, since that didn't pay the rent, I'd worked in London and West Africa in business and in publishing.

It was Easter sometime in the mid-1990s, and I was up in my studio here in Los Altos painting, when I heard the Catholic Mass on the radio. I hadn't planned to listen to it, but it just came on — the words *"Take this, all of you and eat of it: For this is my body, which will be given up for you."*

— and I still, after so many years, felt a strong emotional pull. It didn't make any sense, but it made me remember something my friend and mentor Idries Shah had told me many years before, and though the following quote may not be word-perfect, this is as I remember it: "You cannot free yourself from the hold that beliefs have over you until you understand where those beliefs come from." Much of what I found out is now included in the website The Human Journey (humanjourney.us), in the section "Ideas that Shaped our Modern World." This website is something Bob, I and others have developed over a number of years, under the umbrella of the nonprofit The Institute for the Study of Human Knowledge (ISHK). Our research informs the chapters of this book dealing with God 1.0, 2.0 and 3.0.

Bob was uncompromising and courageous in his work and amazingly intuitive. I recently re-read the works that, along with *God 4.0*, he considered his most important: *The Psychology of Consciousness* and *The Evolution of Consciousness*. I came across a sentence from the latter, published in 1991, that struck me as an example of his intuition, patience and foresight. He wrote, "Within religious traditions, however encrusted they are now, is a different perspective on life, could we but connect it with the rest of modern knowledge." More than a quarter of a century later, in *God 4.0* he was able to do this. It was, indeed, as he said, the book he had been waiting for.

This was the first book we planned to write together. Now that Bob is no longer with us, I am privileged to see it come to light as he wished and as I promised.

Sally Ornstein
Los Altos, California
March 2021

Introduction

Originally you were clay. From being mineral, you
became vegetable. From vegetable, you became animal,
and from animal, man. During these periods man did
not know where he was going, but he was being taken
on a long journey nonetheless. And you have to go
through a hundred different worlds yet. There are a
thousand forms of mind.[1]

— JALALUDDIN RUMI*

For scores of millennia, human beings have tried to transcend normal existence in search of answers to our perennial questions about the meaning of life and death. In every society we looked at, we found that people have been, and still are, interested in altered states of consciousness and transcendence — sometimes described as "self-transcendence" — most in the hope of a clearer understanding and connection to our purpose on this planet.

---

*Born in Balkh (present-day Afghanistan) in the 13th century, Rumi was a Sufi mystic and poet. His *Masnavi-i-Manawi* (Spiritual Couplets) is considered one of the greatest poems of the Persian language.

Our normal consciousness is just a narrow range of our ability to be alert and aware. Geared to survival, it demands a level of awareness of the external and internal world that allows us to respond rapidly, taking the shortest route to survive physically and do well in the world.

But whenever we've wanted to get outside this narrow range to reach an altered state of consciousness, we've had to disconnect from our normal consciousness. To do this, it appears that we've had either to overload the brain with rituals, marching, dancing, drumming, drugs, extreme physical effort and suffering, etc., or reduce the load on the brain through meditation or sensory deprivations such as prolonged sitting in dark caves.

We now know and use many of these activities, not as a trance mechanism in our search for meaning, but for emotional satisfaction, pleasure or entertainment. Taken up in this way, these methods no longer work for us as tools for understanding our place in the world. As the well-known historian of world religions Karen Armstrong emphasizes, "...the truths of religion require the disciplined cultivation of a different mode of consciousness." She goes on to note that "human beings are so constituted that periodically they seek out *ekstasis*, a 'stepping outside' the norm. Today people who no longer find it in a religious setting resort to other outlets: music, dance, art, sex, drugs, or sport."[2]

Our search for meaning has continuously needed revision to make it viable, for over time avenues to the deautomization of consciousness have been blocked or become deteriorated by erroneous descriptions and excessive use of techniques. The word "spiritual" today is often confused with "deep feeling." But it originally meant "of the spirit or soul," an alternate awareness or perceptive capacity — the sense that we use here.

Metaphorically, we live from day to day under a cloudy sky that interferes with our seeing the subtle signals that can guide us

— like the stars in our everyday world, which have guided people across the Earth and enabled us to settle everywhere. Initially, our priority was to harmonize and maintain a balance between the spirit world and our world, and thus to ensure survival; but as populations increased, control by the few over the many became imperative. Consequently, almost all societies fell to prematurely organizing those "points of light," creating percepts such as the Mayan Corn God, who wants you to sacrifice the people you have captured; or the Christian God, whose representative on earth (the Pope) commands that you go on a crusade to free the holy city from the infidels.

The first part of this book deals with how people have achieved changes of consciousness to connect with the "other" worlds — from the shamans to the prophets, from the Paleolithic era to the Axial Age, and to the latest manifestations of the major monotheistic religions that many of us have been brought up on. It includes a look at how our search for meaning has repeatedly been derailed, and for what reasons.

Throughout this book we will frequently refer to Sufism, which is an extraordinary and quite important approach to the problem of understanding and developing human consciousness. Sufism describes the experience of life through an alternative higher perception — in *God 4.0* we have termed this higher consciousness.* As one Sufi master said, "Sufism is truth without form,"[3] thus it has no historical beginning but represents the

---

*Note that by "higher" or "raised" consciousness, we are not referring to the ordinary sense of "consciousness raising," as in raising awareness about something or elevating it in our minds' queue, for example, about social injustice or racism. We are talking about change in the structure of consciousness itself, its becoming "raised" or "higher" in the sense of encompassing more — the activation of a latent state of perception in which formerly unseen connections are perceptible, as when looking down on a scene from a higher place.

continuous line of transmission of the inner Truth of every religion. The contemporary Sufi educator and scholar Idries Shah writes, "The Sufis claim that a certain kind of mental and other activity can produce, under special conditions and with particular efforts, what is termed a higher working of the mind leading to special perceptions whose apparatus is latent in the ordinary man. Sufism is therefore the transcending of ordinary limitations."[4] It is not a body of thought in which you believe certain things and don't believe other things. It is an experience that has to be provoked in a person, and once provoked it accesses an intuitive skill, rather as a person masters an art.

Neither of us claims any authority or exclusivity in presenting this approach. We simply offer a short perspective on its role in the Middle Ages, thoughts from some of its outstanding exemplars, and ideas and methods that might be useful.

As we'll describe later, there are certain identifiable brain processes that are activated when people are experiencing altered states of consciousness. Shamans travel outside their bodies; seers, prophets and saints — from Zoroaster, Isaiah and Muhammad to St. Paul, Teresa of Avila and Joan of Arc — are all reported to have had celestial visions. The Old Testament acknowledges this: *"If there be a prophet among you, I the Lord will make myself known unto him in a vision, and will speak unto him in a dream."* (Numbers 12:6, King James Version [KJV])

In order to begin to get beyond our normal consciousness toward a greater understanding, we need to distinguish the experience of higher consciousness that results from directed study and disciplined effort from the kind of hasty organization into "God" that people have employed and later codified into religion. We have to distinguish between people who really have developed a stable higher consciousness and have attained transcendence, and those experiencing temporary "mystical" states — some of whom have become part of the hierarchy of an organization, with communities who follow them.

Many of the techniques used to develop an alternate higher consciousness are those that involve the diminution of the self. Qualities such as generosity, humility, gratitude and, above all, service to others are emphasized in almost all traditions. The Gospel of Mark says "... *whoever wants to become great among you must be your servant, and whoever wants to be first must be slave of all.*" (Mark 10:43-45, New International Version [NIV]) In a similar statement, Tirmizi, a Sufi of the 8th century said, "*He who does not know about service knows even less about Mastership.*"[5] Mark's gospel text goes on to remind the followers of Jesus: "*For even the Son of Man did not come to be served, but to serve, and to give his life as a ransom for many.*" The Prophet Muhammad is quoted as saying "*Do you love your Creator? Love your fellow beings first.*" Saadi, a 13th-century Sufi and one of the major Persian poets, wrote that "*The Path is none other than service of the people.*"[6] We will reflect on and explicate virtue, not only about its possible function in society, but particularly in its role in the enlargement of an individual's consciousness. From a psychological point of view, "service" directs attention away from the individual, and that again moves consciousness away from the self to experience the unity of the world and, at the same time, to understand one's place in it.

> In order to know the relationship between the drop
> and the Sea, we have to cease thinking of what we
> take to be the interests of the drop.
>
> — HAJI BAHAUDIN, DERVISH OF BOKHARA[7]

SECTION ONE:

Why "God 4.0"?
An Overview

1

A New Beginning

The Second Network

There's a new understanding about how human beings have been trying to "seek God" from the time of the Paleolithic to now, from Boston to Tasmania.

Countless research findings reveal the existence of a second network of cognition that transcends everyday consciousness. It is what people have tried to activate, from the earliest shaman-sages to Moses 3,500 years ago, to Jesus 2,000 years ago, to Muhammad 1,400 years ago, all the way up to the myriad of contemporary seekers.

To understand when, how and why this activation can happen, we begin with what humanity was doing during all this time, and coalesce findings on the origins of humanity, the ancient temples, the Neolithic revolution and the origins of our modern religions. We consider how people have achieved these changes of consciousness over three historical phases that we call God 1.0, God 2.0 and God 3.0 — from the shamans to the prophets, from the Paleolithic era to the Axial

Age and to the origins of the major monotheistic religions. These religions have, as is the way of all institutions, changed very much from their inception, so we are not presenting a portrait of contemporary Christianity or Islam, but — as near as possible — of the original spiritual experiences and insights and the ways those insights have been misinterpreted and have led to their current manifestations.

What has been thought of traditionally and described metaphorically as "knowing God" is a special mode of perception, a development of cognition that opens an extra dimension usually dormant in consciousness. Unfortunately, the heritage of this "second network" activation is more than a bit muddled, as our society is left with the followers of the original sages who through countless generations, have interpreted, reinterpreted, distorted and even replaced the prophets' transcendent insights with sets of rules made up in the cultures of many different eras. As a result, dogma and bureaucracy have replaced the original innovation and insight. This has created needless conflict and destructive hostility between different sects, and between "science" (even its modern developments) and "spirituality."

Our ancestors lacked the accurate understanding of human nature, human cognition and physiology, so they did not have the knowledge base or the language to describe their experiences or attribute them correctly. Instead, religions and spiritual groups have used metaphors, as we do when we link stars together into a pattern, even though one star may be thousands or even millions of light-years from another. Although we see Orion as "the hunter," this is an illusion on many levels. For one thing, Orion's stars range from 243 to 1,360 light-years away from us, but we see them on a single plane, joined together as a unit. Other cultures see other forms in this constellation; for instance, the Lakota of North America see an outstretched hand, the Aboriginal people of Western Australia's Great Victoria Desert see a different hunter, Nyeeruna, pursuing the

Yugarilya (sisters of the Pleiades) but prevented from reaching them by their eldest sister, Kambugudha (the Hyades).

Identifying the experience some have called "God" as a conscious perception should not be understood as a reduction of "heavenly" experiences, but as a deflation of a fantasy (as is our imagination of the stars' arrangements). It is a correction of the many literal interpretations of metaphors that have dragged on for millennia, taking us along as passengers. It corrects our understanding of terms that have come down to us, such as "angels," "Heaven and Hell" and "Son of God," themselves metaphors based upon other metaphors.

Why a new version of God — that is, why God 4.0?

The transcendent experience has been misunderstood, mistreated and, very often, deliberately misconstrued for social and even sexual control, and for political ends. We simply have not had the framework to understand it until now, and whole societies have grown up around this fundamental lack.

Fortunately, since the end of World War II, we've gained a revolutionary amount of scientific understanding about our place in the universe, about our brains and minds, how they operate, and about our potential.

We now know how our "everyday" mind works as a device for selecting just a few parts of the outside reality that are important for our survival. We don't experience the world as it is, but as a virtual reality — a small, limited system that has evolved to keep us safe and ensure our survival. This small everyday world is what the prophets and teachers throughout history have advised us "to shun" — to go beyond.

There's always some skepticism surrounding the assertion that personal experience is central to knowledge. And there are also thoughtful, though mistaken, interpretations as to what the personal experience means. The studious but extreme religious conservative literalist, *New York Times* columnist Ross Douthat feels that ". . . the Gnostic/God within [point of view]

. . . make[s] every individual into his own Chosen Person, with his own private Yahweh somewhere deep inside."[1]

What, one wonders, would he say to someone who said that "the kingdom of God is within you"? (Luke 17:21 [KJV])

Douthat mischaracterizes what an authentic experience of conscious connectedness would offer. While of course there are some who are like his characterization of self-*ish* superiority, the genuine experience is the development of a self-*less* consciousness of the unity of life. The result is connection and solidarity with others — not an elitist "Chosen People" or egocentric monomania. It is not about possessing a personal Godlet or Godlette within, *but perceiving the without within.*

This is something different, and it is why we need the fresh start.

In fact, there is evidence that this sense of connectedness is the wellspring of human solidarity and of civilization as we know it. The knowledge gained from an extended "higher" perception (a "God within") is central. It is not the result of deduction, research and reason. It is not obtained from a neo-medieval doctrine that is taught to be memorized, recited or sung weekly, or from a dogma with which one is inculcated. Nor does it come from feeling deeply or emotionally what is really true. *It is what one perceives.*

Finding and knowing, rather than absorbing dictums, is what "deeper understanding" is. It is a conscious and direct perception of the unity of life, a removal of the mind's internal barriers to direct understanding and knowledge, and "seeing" truth on another level.

These concerns have all become almost hopelessly confused and, through the ages, have become bureaucracies and agents of privilege and domination. Douthat himself presents a myriad of examples of the contradictory and dismaying aspects of contemporary Christianity, which he rightly decries.[2] To help clear away the driftwood, we need to understand how and why we have the beliefs and traditions we have today. We need to distinguish between the original conscious experience of unity and connectedness by a great prophet, and the way it is then almost always altered or misunderstood by devoted followers, their descendants and the hangers-on.

So we'll trace some of the history and evolution of this quest to "seek God," and the attempts to answer such questions as "why," "how" and "when" it all started. Then we'll review what psychology, neuroscience and genetics now tell us in answer to these same questions.

It is time now to look forward to a new understanding that unites the recent scientific and the "sacred," to see what we've lost and how we lost it, and where we might go from here.

The Turn in Science: What We Didn't Know

What we consider "modern" religions developed five to 1.5 millennia ago, when the principals didn't know about weather systems or cosmology — what was in the sky — or the geologic age of the Earth. They didn't know that the brain is involved in thought and the control of the body, or that genes influence our development. What happened in the world was a great mystery.

For instance, one spectacular event, the Vela supernova, lit up the sky for months about 11,000 or 12,000 years ago. We now know that the source of that illumination was a star's explosion that took place 800 or so light-years away, but how could our ancestors understand that? With all we know today, it's still difficult to comprehend light traveling at the speed it would take to circle the Earth about seven times in one second — and sustaining that velocity for 800 years!

Two millennia ago, we didn't know the causes inside us of dreams, epilepsy or psychosis; or outside us, of cataclysmic lightning storms, meteors, fires, earthquakes or floods. Our ancestors back then did not understand our evolutionary history, our deep biological connection with other animals and our close similarity to apes.

It is no wonder, then, that our predecessors expressed what they could not understand in metaphorical terms — as the actions or influence of spirits, gods, angels, jinn, demons and so on.

A New Spirit of Science/A New Science of Spirit

A bit of long history. For more than 1,000 years, it was accepted by all Western philosophers and scientists that Ptolemy's sphere-based model of the universe was correct. There were spheres of earth, air, water and fire, with the Earth at the center of all; and Human Beings, considered to be God's Special Creations, were at the Center of the Universe. This concept informed our idea of our place in the larger scheme of things — that, in essence, the world, *everything*, literally revolves around humanity.

Since then, there has been a long process of what's called "decentration": the loss of humanity's self-assured, special, central position in the world. Considerations of humanity's place in the scheme of things had traditionally been the province of religion and of "spiritual" thinkers, priests and clerics who maintained that humans were the special creations of God. But for approximately the last 600 years, advances in science have encroached continually upon the realm of religion and have challenged the understanding of our essential and central role in the universe. Nicolaus Copernicus' demonstration that the Earth and the other planets orbit the Sun finished off the Ptolemaic universe. Galileo and Newton followed with a more precise explanation of its mechanical workings. Earth was just one of many planets, and the movement of these "heavenly bodies" was due solely to physical forces. Newton's mechanics also showed that inanimate objects move on their own according to physical laws, and are not "moved" by an "unmoved mover."

Biological and psychological discoveries also make us less unique creatures: Darwin's brilliant insight into how organisms could change over time* connected human life to the rest of nature; Freud demonstrated some of the "unconscious" determinants of thought and behavior; and Einstein showed the relativity of our understanding of space and time. And now we know that the "world" isn't just the Roman Empire and Asia, and that we live in one of at least two trillion galaxies in the Universe.

Human beings could no longer be seen as so special and central to the universe or the animal world — or even to the management, understanding and control of their own minds. This loss of specialness set off a loss of faith and put the two worldviews into incessant conflict.

This idea of decentration permeated the culture. For instance, Michael Pollan writes about Martin Amis' 1995 novel, *The Information*, which includes a character who aspires to write "The History of Increasing Humiliation," chronicling the overthrow of humanity from its position at the center of the universe.[3]

"'Every century we get smaller,' Amis writes. Next came Darwin, who brought the humbling news that we are the product of the same natural laws that created animals. In the last century, the formerly sharp lines separating humans from animals — our monopolies on language, reason, toolmaking, culture, even self-consciousness — have been blurred, one after another, as science has granted these capabilities to other animals."[4]

---

*He said it was through a process of random generation by the organism (although Darwin did not know of genetics) and selective retention by the environment; i.e., changes in an organism that, then, aided its reproducing and so were "selected" for the next generation, similar to the way animal breeders work.

Of course, nobody was really humiliated; this was just an exaggerated but fun dyspeptic view of the process. Now we understand how close we are to other animals, especially the great apes, in empathy, compassion, social organization and even learning (different chimpanzee groups in Africa have even passed down different techniques for getting food). At the same time we also know more about our uniqueness. The information we humans pass down is hundreds of thousands times greater in sophistication than that passed down by chimps. Their language isn't close to a human three-year-old's, let alone a writer's.

One can take a newborn human and place him or her high up in Chile's Atacama Desert at an elevation of approximately 13,000 feet or at sea-level in Bangladesh — or near the North Pole or somewhere on the Equator. In each case, the person (if given appropriate care) will learn a language and customs, adapt to the altitude and temperature, and survive. We human beings may not be the center of the universe at all, but we are not humiliated — funny as Amis' notion is. We are an extraordinary animal, one who routinely goes beyond its biological inheritance to create its own world. No other animal on Earth does that.

While science may have taken away some of our traditional religious beliefs about the centrality of humans, it has also given us new insights into the experiences of our ancestors, the evolution of consciousness and our essential connection to the world around us.

Discoveries in just the last century and a half have changed our view of human history and biology, and the rate of discovery has accelerated since the Second World War. As we'll see, the new knowledge about the human brain's workings and our biological and social inheritance contains the beginning of the resolution to the quandary and conflict between religion and science.

One major line of revolutionary evidence began in 1879 when a young girl, María Sanz de Sautuola, while exploring the back of the Altamira cave near Santander, Spain, called out to her father, "Papá, look at the painted bulls!" She had discovered Paleolithic drawings of animals she recognized as bulls on the cave's walls.

The idea that early humans could actually paint recognizable animals tens of thousands of years ago was so outrageous to the church-dominated worldview of the time that the girl's father, Marcelino Sanz de Sautuola, who owned the land where the cave was situated, was ridiculed for suggesting such a thing, and pilloried at scientific meetings for his assertions. He died in 1888 a discredited and broken man, but soon after his death, more Paleolithic paintings were found at two important sites in France: Les Combarelles and Font-de-Gaume. Paleolithic parietal art is sophisticated enough for the great 20th-century painter Pablo Picasso reportedly to note after visiting the caves at Lascaux, "We have invented nothing."

Another line of evidence had a similarly mundane origin when, in 1945, a Bedouin named Mohammad Ali, searching in the Egyptian desert for gold, came upon some old amphorae (ancient clay jars). They held a cache of papyri containing more than 50 texts, including a complete copy of the Gospel of Thomas, the Gospel of Philip and the Gospel of the Egyptians, previously lost writings that date from the early days of Christianity and that offer expanded insights into the original teachings of Jesus.

In East Africa in the early 1960s, members of the Leakey family discovered ancient bones that pushed back by millions of years our understanding of the time when our first direct ancestors emerged. Louis Leakey, the patriarch of the family, encouraged the young Jane Goodall to study chimpanzees in the wild, and her research revealed many striking similarities to human life and behavior. In the 1990s, scientists in Italy saw that cells in a monkey's brain respond to other monkeys' intentions and movements.

Over the past several decades, the ability to analyze ancient DNA has allowed us to track our evolution from ape to *Homo sapiens*, and to map biological, physiological and behavioral changes more accurately than ever before.

When the surgeon Joseph Bogen divided the brain hemispheres of an epileptic patient in 1962, the way was opened to understanding different modes of consciousness in the brain and the special role of the right hemisphere. There have been many new discoveries since that address the real nature, working and function of the brain, leading to a deeper understanding of consciousness and spirituality, formerly the exclusive domain of religion.

Consciousness of Connection – the Roots of Human Solidarity

Suppose that you are examining a multitalented animal, one that can, immediately after its birth, recognize the facial expressions of its parents and mimic them. It's an animal with separate mind/brain systems to detect the details of close events and to gain an overall view from a higher perspective; and it has special brain cells that respond to and connect with other animals of its kind.

This animal can form flexible connections with other such animals to accomplish things that no single one could do on its own; as a consequence, it has become the dominant animal on Earth. Animals of this species can unite to work together in ever-changing groups of different sizes, and for different purposes. How do they do this? It is a matter of an inherent and embryonic cognitive ability, one that can be developed further.

It is this cognitive process that gets enhanced in spiritual thinkers. The process is not like memorizing information in books and not like intellectual learning, nor does it involve deepening an emotional feeling. It is a change of conscious perception toward a higher organization, seeing things that seem separate as together — a "higher" (if you will) perspective in which happenings that seem disconnected "down low" on ground level are experienced as part of a larger, organized whole. One basic example:

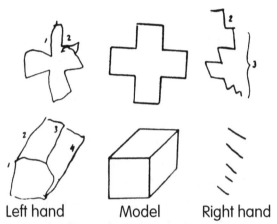

Left hand   Model   Right hand

Figure 1. A split-brain patient is asked by Joseph Bogen to copy shapes with left and right hand.

When Joseph Bogen surgically split the two hemispheres of the human brain (the famous "split-brain" operation), the patient's ability to connect objects to a whole was gone in one side.[5] Consider the drawing in Figure 1. The left hand (controlled by the right hemisphere), although it is a poor draftsman, is clearly able to copy the whole figures in their entirety. All sides are attached and connected. The right hand, controlled by the left hemisphere, without the ability to see the figure whole, produces a group of lines that are not the least bit organized, are in no way connected together and don't make up a whole.

While this is a simple example, it delineates the basis of the cognitive process of going above and beyond the ordinary: When things are connected, they are attached, they become a part of each other, a whole, and they operate in unison. Connectedness yields wholeness and unity, important aspects of consciousness. In this basic example, the set of single lines isn't a square, and the set of unconnected, isolated corners isn't a cross.

One side of the brain — the right hemisphere in most people — is highly involved in producing and maintaining this overall comprehensive outlook.

This makes the right hemisphere better, for example, at avoiding fake news. One innovative research study used electrical stimulation to temporarily inactivate either the left or right hemisphere.[6] With one side of the brain or another knocked out, the researchers presented a fake syllogism to the subjects.

An example:

"Winter is cold in tropical countries.

Thailand is a tropical country.

Is it cold in Thailand in winter, or not?"

With the brain's right hemisphere inactivated, causing the person to operate in what the researchers called the "left self" mode (with the left hemisphere in control), the solutions were limited to the internal consistency of the syllogism rather than its correspondence to external reality. In our example above, the subject would insist that it is cold in Thailand "because it says so."

By contrast, when the left hemisphere was inactivated, the same person, but now operating in the "right self" mode, would reject a similar syllogism as wrong because "everyone knows that tropical countries don't have cold winters." There is a sense of an overall perspective and context that's activated in one side of the brain, and something closer to a localized, step-by-step analysis of the text alone is activated in the other.

The best way to think about the relationship between the brain's two hemispheres is as one between the *text* (the literal statement itself, alone) and the *context* (the meaning, taking in all the information as a whole).

That perception of a larger whole is the wellspring of humanity's solidarity in tribes, societies, teams, nations, religions. It is not the possession of any religion or sect, and it is not a delusion. The complement of brain structures and social development necessary for this group solidarity forms the deep basis of a sense of something beyond and, sometimes, of a "God." This universal capacity is responsible for humanity's success on the planet. There is evidence now that the first massive gatherings for worship stimulated the development of agriculture about 11 millennia ago, changing human life forever.

This capacity for understanding is what makes human lives singular and distinct from the lives of all other animals. While it often doesn't seem like it — especially these days — almost all of human life is based upon cooperation and connection. Many animals do, of course, show both minor and elaborate cooperation: Wolves and lions do so in the hunt; dolphins work together to chase, corral and scoop up schools of small fry; and ants are legendary in their organization. But humans are flexible in cooperating in countless pursuits, and with different partners: with a single collaborator, with a few or with many; with a large workgroup, a sports team, a political party or a country. All of these are changeable and flexible connections — which is not the case with other species.

Human beings evolved to go beyond the individual, to transcend the "self" and to connect in a manner that no other organism can — and this is the basis of our planetary success. Understanding the centrality of "connecting up" yields a different outlook on human nature and on the development of societies. It reveals the foundation upon which our cognitive ability for higher consciousness is developed.

So the human brain seems to be equipped for connection to others and has evolved in ways that facilitate this. Recent research has shown that the more personal connections one has

— in this case, measured by the size of a person's social circle — the bigger the brain's orbital prefrontal cortex.[7]

As the anthropologist and evolutionary psychologist Robin Dunbar put it, "Understanding this link between an individual's brain size and the number of friends they have helps us understand the mechanisms that have led to humans developing bigger brains than other primate species. The frontal lobes of the brain, in particular, have enlarged dramatically in humans over the last half million years."*[8]

We see the importance of connection clearly in daily life. We become depressed when alone too long; solitary confinement is the most punishing of penalties in incarceration. When we are just sitting at rest, with our brains just idling, it is most often our personal social connections that occupy our minds. The widespread popularity of computerized "social networks" embodies this drive to connect. For many people, the experience of social distancing in response to the COVID-19 pandemic brought this into stark relief.

Psychiatrist and author George Vaillant noted how import-ant connection to others is for the emergence and survival of hu-manity itself. While humanity is certainly dominant on Earth now, we forget that our early human ancestors were scrawny and scarce. Living in isolated bands of a few dozen, they needed to bind into communities to help them survive predators and climate fluctuations. It is most probably the case that human beings have thrived as a species because of sophisticated social bonding, attachment to others, forgiveness and gratitude.[9]

A genuine higher transcendence of the "small world" self began with the long bonding and attachment of the mother

---

*Our "cognitive load," the mental capacity of managing information, appears to limit our social relationships to about 150 people, a number established by Robin Dunbar and known as "Dunbar's number." This is by far the largest social network of any animal, and almost three times larger than that of our nearest hominid relative, the chimpanzee.

and child, and of different individuals into a society; and it is the *consciousness* of that connection to others that is the basis of human solidarity and a cooperative society. This is the foundation upon which our innate "second system," a connection to higher consciousness, can develop.

A Second System of Cognition, Inspiration and Insight

> There is no cause for fear. It is imagination,
> blocking you as a wooden bolt holds the door.
> Burn that bar. . .
>
> — Rumi[10]

Almost nothing has been the subject of more concern and conflict than the conception of God. But God is everywhere, in the sense that every known society has a religious practice and a concept of God. This is true even among individuals who are part of traditions that don't officially "believe." It is the promise of transcending beyond the everyday limited world, of attaining a consciousness of reality above and beyond the norm.

Like other universals in human nature, such as color vision and basic emotions, there is regularity in our "higher" experiences. The Yale anthropologist Erika Bourguignon and her colleagues studied 488 societies, including the ancient Egyptians, Greeks, Hebrews and 41 others in the Mediterranean. When they reviewed the ethnographic data, they found that "altered states of consciousness" existed in virtually all of them.[11] Bourguignon observed that "societies which do not utilize these states clearly are historical exceptions which need to be explained, rather than the vast majority of societies that do use these states."[12]

Prehistorian Jean Clottes and archeologist David Lewis-Williams, in their book *The Shamans of Prehistory*, make a similar observation: "Indeed the potential to shift, voluntarily or involuntarily, between different states of consciousness is a function of the universal human nervous system. All people have to cope with different states of consciousness in one way or another."[13]

Individuals have tried to comprehend and interpret this expansion of consciousness for millennia, beginning long before we had any idea of who we are and where humanity comes from. Their interpretations gave rise to the metaphors that have come erroneously to be taken literally.*

Seen in this light, one can understand several sayings of Jesus, Moses, Muhammad and others in a new way. In the Gospel of Thomas, Jesus says, "*It will not come by watching for it. It will not be said, 'Look, here it is,' or 'Look, there it is.' Rather, the father's kingdom is spread out upon the earth, and people do not see it.*"[14] In other words, "It's not what you believe, it's what you perceive" — a most important maxim, to which we'll return.

These sayings also remind us that attainment of a wider perception is much, much closer to everyday experience than most people believe. A companion of Muhammad recorded: "*We were with the Prophet on a journey, and some men stood up repeating aloud, 'God is most great'; and the Prophet said, 'O men, be easy on yourselves and do not distress yourselves by raising your voices; truly, you do not call to one deaf or absent, but truly to one who hears and sees; and He is with you; and He to whom you pray is nearer to you than the neck of your camel.'*"[15]

This understanding of what the nearness and universality of "higher" experience really means — that it is inside ourselves and a capacity we can develop — may possibly, in time, diminish

---

*Once oral literature was written down, interpretation of it became less flexible. Stories could be "wrong," or they could be "the truth." This fostered a literal understanding, especially after the advent of printing in the 15th century.

the divergence between science and religion, and could reconcile many cultural and religious conflicts.

But there are many problems to address.

Religion, Spirituality and Transcendence

There are plenty of reasons why bright, intellectually oriented people reject or ignore the "transcendent." For one thing, we've outgrown the language. Many words used in antiquity no longer have the same meaning. As we wrote in the introduction, the word "spiritual" traditionally meant "of the soul" (referring to a higher perceptive capacity); today it is often confused with "deep feeling." Some words have a diaphanous, and sometimes weird, feeling. The word "transcendence" itself can evoke the idea of escaping from life and its difficulties, floating away to a warm and fuzzy safe space. But transcendence really means shifting one's state of consciousness to achieve a new insight, perceiving the connections between formerly unrelated happenings, objects and events.

We usually conceive of a common connection between spirituality and religion, but there is a clear separation between the two — in concept, in practice and even between their practitioners. Spirituality more often entails the person leaving her received doctrine behind to search for something "beyond," while religion most often involves following a received tradition and its rules laid down for established behaviors. As we uncover the history and development of both, we'll see that there are even different genetic dispositions related to these two different belief predispositions (which do seem to make them irreconcilable for the individuals involved).

"Mysticism" sounds a bit strange, too. The word itself derives from the church's medieval "mystery plays." "Metaphysics," which also sounds like something filmy and beyond the realm of reality, is just Aristotle's name for the next book in a sequence he was writing, the one "after" physics: "meta-physics," whence he took on these issues.

It's imperative to either rescue or do away with these archaic terms and to clarify the importance and the reality of the phenomena they describe. Otherwise, it is as if we were to hear a thunderstorm being described as a god's angry voice and then believe that if we went outside, we wouldn't get soaked.

There's also a lot of oddity to try to put together and to understand. Why do people all over the world have "high" experiences? Why do they build soaring structures to stimulate awe? Why do people, in transcendent moments, have such similar experiences of timelessness, spacelessness, placelessness and a sense of nothingness? What could those terms mean, and why are they universal?

And, why do people do and say crazy, incomprehensible things? All over the world, people seeking higher experiences might focus on a sound, phrase or image for an hour; they might dance to exhaustion; synchronize spinning movements; endure deprivation and pain; fast; stimulate a trance state; put ash on their faces; or wear clothes suitable for a Middle European winter in the sweltering heat of a Jerusalem summer. We hear the statement "The world is an illusion" and have little idea what that might mean. It's all too easy to dismiss, if you don't know what the speakers are talking about (and, all too often, they themselves don't know).

We all possess inherent cognitive biases ranging from reliance on strict, sequential methods of examining information (often called, mistakenly, rationality) to an all-at-once manner of thought involving diffuse and loose associations. Where we are on this continuum underlies how open we are to new ideas and experiences, versus being tethered and fixed to doctrinaire interpretations of the saying of venerated ancestors. These biases affect everything from our idea of God, to our religious and political affiliations, to our preference for open versus closed borders of our country. As we shall see in Chapter 10, people who adhere strongly to one or another cognitive style have a genetic predisposition to do so. People who abhor social, religious or political change are somewhat prewired (though not hardwired) to be fundamentally conservative: to keep things as they are or as they believe they were in the paradisiacal Muhammadan Caliphate, in the church of the Council of Nicaea, in the colonial world of the original Constitution, or even in the days of late 1950's European royalty. We observe this cast of mind all over the world today.

The public discussion of spirituality is often dominated (as it is in politics) by the extremes: One side maintains that "the whole thing is an illusion — an old-fashioned superstition," while the other side maintains that "God is everywhere, always, and sees and guides everything." Transcendence, then, seems alien and a waste of time to the minds of many. To those with very ordered minds, people interested in the possibility of transcendence can seem flakey, prone to magical thinking and less able to use structured logic. And there is, in truth, a strong association between an individual's interest in spirituality and a certain fluidity of thought — too much of which can be maladaptive, just as too much rigidity can lead to obsessive-compulsive disorder and the like.

Transcendence has had a much greater role in the development of society than mechanistic thinkers believe. Archeological evidence at Göbekli Tepe, a settlement 11,000 years old in what is now southeastern Turkey, shows that gathering together for transcendent insight actually stimulated the need for agriculture and the rise of modern organized society. We'll come to that later.

Neither extreme is the answer. The optimum is a balance between what William James called "tender-mindedness and tough-mindedness."[16] A precise, mechanistic, "engineering" approach to comprehend the world's workings may provide consistency and repeatability that's great for technical progress, but it can foreclose on our openness to new experiences and new ideas.

What Kind of a System Is the "Second System"?

It's not a physical organ or a specific set of cells in the brain that underlies, for example, the ability to speak a language. But it is evidently present. The "second system" is a quiescent faculty; accidents can activate it, as can certain procedures, such as meditation, isolation, fasting, overstimulation, prayer and the use of drugs which have appeared in every known society. They all involve a breakup or a bypass of normal cognition, and the opening of "another world," as it has been called metaphorically.

We now know how the mind and brain do this, and for the first time, we can explore how this innate mode of cognition can be activated in a way relevant to the rapidly changing modern world.

The capacity for this development is a part of everyone's natural endowment. All of us possess a nascent, intuitive sense which is the basis of an expanded consciousness; but it is not fully developed in most of us, just as a lot of other human capacities lie embryonic and untrained. All human beings can speak and understand language, but to write it and read it demands a lot of teaching, and to write like a James Joyce requires a rare combination of talents. Similarly, all human beings can understand the concept of "one, two and many" but to learn arithmetic, algebra, geometry and calculus is not, as we all know, natural. It takes work.

And beyond that, from time to time, a prodigy comes along. As a child in rural India, Srinivasa Ramanujan somehow learned, almost on his own, to do advanced mathematics. Mozart composed music on a level considerably more advanced than that to which he had been trained. Einstein somehow developed a conception of the universe far beyond anything conceived of by his predecessors or contemporaries (or even by us today) and worked out specific predictions about the laws of physics, which were confirmed years later.

Consciousness changes continually within each of us, and does so radically each day. It shifts from the hallucination of dreaming sleep, to the fluid thought that is experienced in hypnagogic states, to narrowly focused workaday full alertness — and to everything in between.

The fluidity of our minds makes a possible change in consciousness closer to our daily experiences than we usually assume. It is a further development of what we experience when we get an insight into the workings of a machine, or into how another person is thinking, or when we suddenly discover the solution to a problem. Areas inside the brain temporarily shut off normal thinking to make way for a new insight or new level of understanding.

The activation of this more inclusive consciousness is sometimes called "wisdom," "perspective," "second sight," "the sight of the seer" (*an da shealladh* in Gaelic), "deep" or "direct perception," or "seeing God." These are all traditional terms that can seem strange and off-putting, and they don't offer practical steps forward. But the widespread similarity of such descriptions, in all areas of the world and in all ages, indicates that the experience of altered states of consciousness is universal.

Fortunately, the neuropsychology of altered states is now becoming better understood, which opens up the possibility of developing this "higher" consciousness to many of us rather than to a select few.

What happens is that the normal step-by-step, moment-by-moment way of dealing with the world — which is useful for crossing the street or cutting up carrots — gets bypassed, shoved aside. And inside the brain, what's called the "default mode" switches from an everyday "small world" of limited connections to one in which connections are expanded.

It's a shift (as some describe it) away from an egocentric world into a selfless one in which, as many studies show, the brain changes to a more right-hemisphere mode. With this expanded connectedness, individuals can sometimes get new insights. When this happens, there's a specific shutoff of brain activity in the area of the right hemisphere that maintains the sense of self. This deactivation of the self is necessary for a holistic system of cognition to emerge. We need this expanded perception now, because as our view of consciousness and its possibilities changes, so too will our understanding of religion and science — something that could have far-reaching effects on our common human future.

Barriers that Cloud the Mind

Barriers to connection and communication are everywhere. There are barriers within us, barriers between ourselves and others and barriers between our groups and outsiders. We all build invisible barrier walls within to keep out irrelevant or difficult thoughts and experiences; and we wall ourselves off socially and psychologically — and even physically, from "invaders" to our own society.

The first step towards an expanded perception is to get around, in some way, the barriers of the everyday mental system and preoccupations. As Rumi said "burn that bar." The way to do this is to begin at the beginning, to establish where the barriers are, how they change and how we can change them.

So think of it this way, in a metaphor (which will remain a metaphor).

It's a few thousand years ago. You are at sea, along with others of your tribe. But there are no stars by night; the fog clouds have covered them. The wind is taking your boats aimlessly one way then another, one strong gust after another. Whether you realize it or not, you are lost.

Then the clouds partially clear, and for a moment you get an insight into what has been hidden but was always there, behind the fog — there are faint stars there! You might be dazzled and confused by this breakthrough, perhaps a bit destabilized in your life following this new sight of something "beyond." Some fellow travelers might imagine beings in the Milky Way, or soldiers calling them to war; some might conjure up images of freedom, or commandments. Others might deny that there's anything relevant in what they've just seen. Some sight-impaired travelers may only see what is right in front of them and are unable to see the stars at all. Some will stop at a first glimpse, as it yields a measure of peace, perhaps a reduction of anxiety or the shedding of an addiction. Others will travel on and can navigate home.

In an individual life, the quick breaking up of these internal barriers to perception can, in some cases, cause confusion, even derangement. But breaking through them, or even slightly opening them up, can allow one to get a first glimpse of faint, ever-present signals. We believe it's better to think about the aim of spiritual and religious efforts this way: as developing another — an extra — dimension of consciousness, and "seeing" a reality coexisting along with, but above and beyond, the narrowly focused, survival-centered reality of our everyday world.

There have been different metaphors used by different traditions and different authors to describe this experience, but beyond the surface differences, one can see a common focus. One metaphor is the distinction between 3-D and 2-D perception; another, color vision versus black-and-white. The experience has also been likened to awakening from sleep, opening a new "eye" or bypassing the "reducing valve"[17] of the senses. All of these bespeak a development of perception and an extension of consciousness beyond the norm.

Given our current understanding of what really is going on inside us, we prefer the metaphor of clouds at night. Clouds are permeable barriers that vary during the day in their thickness and color, and sometimes we can peek into an existence of a different realm behind them; and then it all "clouds" over and shuts down again. So this metaphor gives more of a sense of the evanescence, the shifting rather than fixed nature of our real internal barriers to the perception of these "two worlds" (which is itself a metaphor).

Crossing these barriers is by no means the whole story of transcending everyday consciousness. It is just the beginning. But with practice and under the right circumstances, one can see things from a more complete, "higher" perspective and begin to understand that those faint signals convey valuable information: you can "navigate home." One anonymous mystic wrote, "When the clouds of thoughts and emotions disappear . . . You experience Reality as it is."

A New Phase of Religion

The "4.0" in the title of this book indicates that our understanding and worldview have gone through (to simplify things greatly) three earlier configurations, all striving for transcendence to a deeper or "higher" knowledge of reality which many have called "God." — "God 1.0" refers to the spirit world of our Stone Age ancestors; "God 2.0," to the multi-god religions of Egypt, Mesopotamia and elsewhere; and "God 3.0," to the monotheistic religions of today: Judaism, Christianity and Islam.

We focus on these three "Abrahamic" traditions for the most part because their adherents constitute more than half of humanity. Almost all of this majority are Christian and Islamic, with close to two billion people each. While Jews are miniscule in number — less than two-tenths of a percent of all peoples, or about 14 million — they are an important part of this history.

It is now almost a millennium and a half since the emergence of Islam, two millennia since the birth of Christ, and almost four millennia since the purported birth of Abraham and the beginning of Jewish history. We're in dire need of an update.

We now know that many experiences that have formerly been attributed to external, mystical entities are, in truth, mental phenomena based on brain processes, and we'll expand on this later. The Andalusian Sufi scholar and poet Ibn el-Arabi intuitively recognized this, writing, "Angels are the powers hidden in the faculties and organs of man."[18] Idries Shah says of el-Arabi: "He also speaks of God as the name given by man to the impulse which originates all kinds of developments, rendered in customary terms as the deity which most people associate with that word; but none the less important by reason of his referring to it in what we would today call scientific terms – and this in the thirteenth century." [19]

Knowing the biological basis of experiences does not explain them away or reduce them, just as understanding the brain mechanisms of language and the universal regularities of syntax doesn't diminish or deny that we understand what's being said to us — which when you think about it, is quite a marvel.

The higher reality — metaphorically presented as "seeing God," being "born again" and "entering the light," among many other images — has not changed. But it is now possible to connect the dots to understand these metaphors and the progression for attaining a higher insight, both neurobiologically and psychologically. It's time for a new conceptual framework, a framework based on a foundation of current knowledge — one without the restrictions, accumulations and clannishness of contemporary religions; one based on an understanding of the capacity for expanded consciousness inherent in us all. It is time for God 4.0.

FOR FURTHER READING

How Many Friends Does One Person Need? Dunbar's Number and Other Evolutionary Quirks, Robin Dunbar, Faber & Faber, 2010.

The Gnostic Gospels of Jesus: Definitive Collection of Mystical Gospels and Secret Books about Jesus of Nazareth, Marvin Meyer, Harper Collins, 2005.

The Psychology of Consciousness, Robert Ornstein, Malor Books, 2021.

Religious Evolution and the Axial Age: From Shamans to Priests to Prophets, Scientific Studies of Religion: Inquiry and Explanation, Stephen K. Sanderson, Bloomsbury Publishing, 2018.

The Shamans of Prehistory: Trance and Magic in the Painted Caves, Jean Clottes and David Lewis-Williams, Harry N. Abrams, 1998.

SECTION TWO:

God 1.0, God 2.0 And God 3.0

2

God 1.0 – Our Inheritance, The Caves And The Shamans

The desire to cultivate a sense of the transcendent
may be *the* defining human characteristic.

— KAREN ARMSTRONG[1]

The Caves

The ground is damp and slimy, we have to be very careful not to slip off the rocky way. It goes up and down, and then comes a very narrow passage about ten yards along through which you have to creep on all fours. And then again there come great halls and more narrow passages.

. . . The tunnel is not much broader than my shoulders, nor higher. . . . With our arms pressed close to our sides, we wriggle forward on our stomachs, like snakes. The passage, in places, is hardly a foot high, so that you have to lay your face right on the earth. I felt as though I were creeping through a coffin. You cannot lift your head; you cannot breathe. . . . And so, yard by yard, one struggles on: some forty-odd yards in all. Nobody talks. The lamps are inched along and we push after. I hear the others groaning, my own heart is pounding, and it is difficult to breathe. It is terrible to have the roof so close to one's head. . . . Will this thing never end? Then, suddenly, we are through, and everybody breathes. It is like redemption.[2]

This description by the paleontologist Herbert Kühn, from his book *On the Track of Prehistoric Man*, goes on to describe how the group, oxygen-deprived and exhausted, finally arrives inside "a colossal hall" whose walls portray layer after layer of amazingly vivid, lifelike beasts.[3] They are standing in the "Sanctuary" at Les Trois Frères, a cave in the Ariège region of southwestern France, surrounded by animals that roamed that area between 10,000 and 30,000 years ago. Looking upward, seemingly higher than any person could reach, they see a painted mythical figure, part-man, part-animal: the famed "Wizard" of Les Trois Frères, also known as the "Sorcerer," who watches them from approximately 13 feet above their heads.

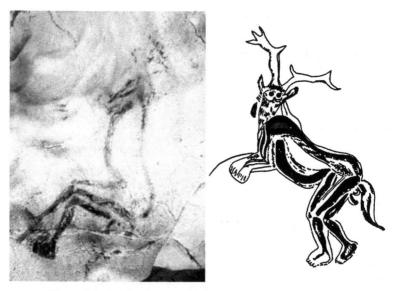

Figure 2. Left side: photograph of the "Wizard" or "Sorcerer" cave painting at Les Trois Frères. Right side: rendered drawing of the "Sorcerer," by 20th century French prehistorian Abbé Breuil.

A similar almost intolerable rite of passage must be carried out when entering many of these ancient caves. It will be echoed in later Greek temples designed and constructed in a way that mimics the cave experience. In one modern discovery of an ancient cave, speleologist Eliette Brunel Deschamps (selected in part because of her slender size) squeezed through a very narrow tunnel to arrive at a ledge that overlooked a large chamber at least 10 meters below. The team needed a ladder to reach the deeper, richly embellished chambers of what is now known as the Chauvet cave, where they found some of the oldest European figurative cave paintings made by *Homo sapiens*. The well-known paleontologist Andre Leroi-Gourhan describes the journey into the Etcheberriko-Karbia cave, high in the mountains of the Basque region of France:

> The entrance to the cave is huge and would seem admirably suited for a fine set of wall decorations; but to reach the sanctuary a veritable expedition with full speleological equipment is required. One must toil for more than an hour, crossing little lakes, moving along narrow ledges, and climbing over slippery stalagmites several yards long, before reaching a low entrance that opens on a very narrow tunnel; the tunnel ends at a sheer cliff more than six feet high with no handholds. The sanctuary begins only on the other side of this cliff! It is even hard to get to the end: beyond the first composition, one must climb down a stalagmite fifteen feet high, skirt the edge of a precipice, and work down a twenty-seven-foot cleft to find the next composition. The last composition, a horse painted at the bottom of the cleft, is so placed on the edge of a sheer drop that we can only suppose that a colleague was holding the artist by the back of his garments over the void.[4]

Not all sites are so deliberately inaccessible, and much of the art that was more exposed to the outside air and elements may well have disappeared. That notwithstanding, these paintings were placed far inside deliberately, and one can't help but ask why these people would undertake such difficult journeys to find dark, inaccessible, oxygen-deprived, noxious, gaseous caverns deep inside the earth and decide that this would be a great place to create art of such astounding beauty, accuracy and abundance.

A closer look at the images they created reveals some unusual characteristics. Without grass or any other background, the animals appear to float in mid-air along these cave walls. Their hooves are undefined or left hanging, or a leg appears to end with the underside (a hoofprint) showing. Sometimes, as in the Axial Gallery at Lascaux, the paintings float upward and create what archeologist David Lewis-Williams called "a tunnel of floating, encircling images."[5] Many images take advantage of the uneven walls; for example, a protrusion in the rock surface becomes a horse's head looming out into the cave, or an edge or curve in a rock wall evokes — with just a few lines — a bison, lion or auroch emerging from the wall. Some images are engraved, others painted with fingers or charcoal. The animals depicted are those our ancestors knew, presumably selected for their importance to the community as a source of food or power. Then there are multiple handprints — the majority of which appear to be of female hands[6] — both negative (where the pigment is blown around a hand pressed against a wall) and positive (where the hand has been dipped in pigment). Animals fly, swim or charge and are sometimes depicted wounded or dead. Dots, grids and patterns appear in places, and mysterious figures which combine animal and human characteristics, like the "Sorcerer" mentioned above, watched those who, long ago, entered these dark spaces carrying flickering tallow lamps.

The most intense prehistoric artistic activity appears to have occurred just as the Ice Age (approximately 40,000 to 15,000 years ago) was its most severe. From about 40,000 years ago, and for approximately the next 25,000 years — a period 12 times longer than the Common Era — the artistic expression of early modern humans exploded and spread all over Europe, Asia and Siberia, and also appeared in Australia and Africa.

As people moved into Western Europe, they carried with them statuettes, figurines and pendants, mostly created from mammoth bone, depicting the same animals that they painted on their cave walls. One such object is the famous *Löwenmensch*, a 32,000-year-old lion-headed upright human figurine found in Holenstein, Germany. From the way they were created and from where they were found, scholars feel that these pieces were of special significance, highly valued and not part of daily use.

Like the Paleolithic parietal art found in more than 300 European cave sites, such works required enormous effort, skill and craftsmanship, so they had to be of some practical use — but what? Who were these artists, and how and why did they make the extraordinary leap in imagination that allowed them to "see" and "create" two- and three-dimensional images in the first place?

The Evolution of Our Consciousness

To grasp why we have the beliefs and traditions we have today, we look first at early human beings in their ancestral environment, long before humanity settled and dominated the entire Earth. Any evidence of their early beliefs, practices and situations will help clarify why and how we worship, and how we think of "gods."

Human consciousness evolved over hundreds of thousands of years, until a heightened awareness of self eventually separated us from the rest of the animal world. The earliest portable representations of the human figure date from a period before modern humans. A small quartzite figurine from Morocco, known as Tan-Tan, dates from between 500,000 and 300,000 years ago. It is at least 99-percent created by nature and may well have been safeguarded by our hominid ancestors, who, because of their emerging self-consciousness, were able to recognize that it resembled the female form and hence was most likely infused with meaning that was of a magical or religious significance. Though largely natural, a tiny piece of volcanic rock known as the Venus of Berekhat Ram, was found in Israel's Golan Heights. It was deliberately modified to represent the female form about 230,000 years ago.

In 2014, an international team of scientists discovered what, to date, is the earliest known example of a deliberate pattern made by ancient humans. The etched zigzag-patterned shell was carbon-dated to as far back as 540,000 to 430,000 years ago. The shell was originally found on the Indonesian island of Java in 1891 by the Dutch paleontologist Eugene Dubois, at the same site at which he discovered "Java Man," now known as *Homo erectus*.

These finds are at least four times older than the oldest previously known etchings made in a sample of ochre found in South Africa's Blombos Cave (70,000 BCE). They push back the origin of our capacity for abstract symbolic thought by 300,000 years or more.

By at least 35,000 years ago, our ancestors were by all measures modern human beings, able not only to experience different states of consciousness but also to remember and talk of them. People in small bands were linked across vast distances, communicating and developing social relationships that would be advantageous at a time when food resources were limited or depleted in specific areas. Language allowed them to plan and, most likely, to discuss their internal states and the external world; to think and speak about things in the abstract; and to refer to the past, the present and the future. Settlements, where bands probably united for rituals commemorating rites of passage and other significant events, have been located. Burial sites found at Sungir in Russia show that around 34,000 years ago people appear to have had rich beliefs about death. Some people, at least, were buried with thousands of mammoth ivory beads and other ornaments, and with spears, presumably to aid them in their next life.

There is good reason to believe that during this Upper Paleolithic Era, which dates from 50,000 to about 12,000 years ago — a period comprising most of human history — humans manifested mental abilities that are latent and less obvious in modern man. There were only a small number of people in existence then. One study suggests that the human population in Europe ranged from about 130,000 at its lowest point to about 410,000 during the severe cooling episode in the last glacial period about 13,000 years ago. The mean population density in the inhabited area varied between 2.8 and 5.1 persons per 100 square kilometers.[7] (Compare that to an estimated 748 million in Europe in 2021, with a density of about 3,400 people per 100 square kilometers.)

Moving in their small groups, these early people endured unimaginable hardships including numerous predators and erratic climatic conditions. Given all that was against us, it's hard to believe we could have survived solely by trial-and-error experiments. Our ancestors would have had to rely much more on their senses — including intuitive senses — than we do today.

Today we have to learn almost everything — even metaphysics — through language. One spiritual teacher, the Sufi mystic Simab, explained, "…you cannot think without words. You have been reared on books, your mind is so altered by books and lectures, by hearing and speaking, that the inward can only speak to you through the outward, whatever you pretend you can perceive."[8]

Our ancestor's brains, though structurally the same at birth as our own, developed differently. Although they certainly had language, it would have been less dominant than it is today. Areas of the brain that are now taken up with the vocabularies of more than 50,000 words — and our ability to read them, as well as deal with spreadsheets, online banking, ever-changing technology and speed limits — were likely used to acquire different capacities that enabled them to survive.

Even today, some remote tribespeople have an amazing capacity to navigate through the jungle or on the open sea. A contemporary Muskogee Creek Native American shaman, Bear Heart, discusses the early days of his people: "The environment was our starting point in learning as much as we could from what was around us — the seasons, the things that grow, the animals, the birds, and various other life forms. Then we would begin the long process of trying to learn about that which is within ourselves. We didn't have any textbooks, we didn't have great psychiatrists who lived years ago and presented theories in this and that. We had to rely on something else, and that was our senses. Rather than through scientific investigation, we sensed those things within and around us."[9]

Bear Heart goes on to say that "children were encouraged to respect all inanimate and animate objects. Trees, for example, were their tall-standing brothers who emit energy all the time." He describes one exercise where the children would be instructed to love the meeting place they were in; they were told to "put your heart into it." Then they would be blindfolded and taken into the woods and required to find their way back. He writes that "the only way they could find their way back was by experiencing the love they felt before they went out."[10] These children were expected to master the difference between "looking" and "seeing." Paleolithic cave painters that we'll consider next definitely understood that difference.

Shamans – a Contemporary Representation of Our Original Religion

A look at contemporary hunter-gatherer peoples can provide a window into the lives of our early ancestors. Paleolithic humans likely lived close together in largely egalitarian bands, much like today's hunter-gatherers, such as the Ituri pygmies in the Democratic Republic of the Congo and the San peoples of southern Africa.

They were animists, so they experienced a vital spirit inherent in all things everywhere: humans, animals, plants, rocks, mountains, rivers and the weather. As Robert Wright wrote in his book *The Evolution of God*, "... if you asked hunter-gatherers what their religion is, they wouldn't know what you were talking about. The kinds of beliefs and rituals we label 'religious' are so tightly interwoven into their everyday thought and action that they don't have a word for them. We may label some of their explanations of how the world works 'supernatural' and others 'naturalistic,' but those are our categories, not theirs."[11]

David Lewis-Williams spent years studying the San peoples. His work with them included accumulating ethnological data, neurophysiological research and studying their rock art in depth. He noted that "about half the men in any San camp are shamans and about a third of the women." He pointed out that "for the San, and for other shamanistic societies as well, shamanism is not an optional add-on to daily life: rather, it is the essence of all life."[12] So it is very likely that for the Paleolithic people too, the spirit world and the shamanic experience were at least as present and essential as the world of everyday life, if not more so.

The word "shaman" comes from *saman*, a Siberian Tungus word meaning "ecstatic one." Practicing shamans have been found in all hunter-gatherer societies on record. Shamans believe in supernatural beings or spirits with whom they can communicate; by entering ecstatic states of consciousness, they travel to "other worlds," where spirits can enter their bodies and speak through them.

Described most classically and comprehensively by the religious historian Mircea Eliade as the specialists in the use of "techniques of ecstasy" ("ecstasy" in the meaning of "outside oneself"), contemporary shamans are not necessarily central to a society's belief system, but often coexist with its priests or tribal leaders.[13] All shamanic cultures around the world (including the Samoyed of Siberia, the Aboriginal people of Australia, the Maya of Central America, the Huichol of Mexico and the Tucano of the Amazon) experience altered states of consciousness, or vision journeys.

The Shamanic Vision Journey

The vision journey is essential to shamans. While on it they encounter spirits in the form of animals such as wolves, bears and birds which might then become helpers that, in deep trance, integrate into the shamans' self-experience and become part of them.

Shamans in all cultures and in all countries undergo remarkably similar training and perform generally similar practices wherever they are found. A potential shaman can be alerted to his or her calling in a number of ways: through heredity, because of a striking physical feature or experience, through a disorder such as epilepsy, as a consequence of an unexpected recovery from a severe illness, or through omens and dreams. Anthropologists often describe the shaman's natural disposition as schizotypal or deeply neurotic, or at least manifesting the extreme qualities that we often associate with an artistic temperament.

When David Lewis-Williams and Jean Clottes analyzed how people became shamans, they found that all initiates had similar experiences that they either experienced involuntarily or took positive steps to induce. A Native American apprentice shaman might go on a vision quest and, through hunger, pain, intense concentration and isolation from society, induce a trance state in which his spirit animal helper appears to him and he is filled with its supernatural potency. A South African San man or woman who wishes to become a shaman might dance with experienced shamans until he or she achieves a trance state.

It is this inner world of visions, dreams and spirits that be-stows a supernatural power on the initiate and enables him or her to function as a shaman. Common privations such as fast-ing, exposure to extreme heat or cold, dangerous situations and extended periods of isolation, and practices such as chanting, re-peated rhythmic movements, hyperventilating, intense concen-tration and ingesting hallucinogens are selected and combined in various ways to induce this state. "For successful candidates," the psychiatrist and anthropologist Roger Walsh notes, "these climax in culmination experiences, which indicate that a degree of shamanic mastery has been attained."[14]

That the vision journey is an integral part of shamanic life is one thing; but interestingly each journey, no matter where in the world it takes place, follows a similar pattern. Since their resemblance to each other cannot be accounted for by communication or migration, it must be that the experience is always generated anew in the mind of the shaman. If based on a shared neurological activation, this same pattern would be found in most, if not all, cultures and throughout history — and indeed it is.

Shamanism has been found in Australia, Siberia, Malaya, the Andaman Islands, Africa and in all the Americas. It is en-countered in some of the world's most remote regions — among the Ona of Tierra del Fuego at South America's extreme tip, among the Inuit of the Arctic, among the Tucano of Colombia and among the San of southern Africa. Its influence has been identified in cultures throughout history, including ancient Mayan society, Norse mythology, Greek mythology, religion, and philosophy.[15]

The shamanic scholar Michael Winkelman compared magico-religious practices in 47 societies spanning almost 4,000 years, from the Babylonians of 1750 BCE to the present. He noted that all of these cultures, prior to the spread of Western influence, used altered states of consciousness for religious and healing practices, and he concluded that "the primordial role involving the manipulation of consciousness was that of the shaman."[16]

Altered states of consciousness are extremely common. Of the 488 societies studied worldwide by Bourguignon and her team, 77 percent engaged in possession trances, where the practitioner is temporarily changed through the presence in or on her, of a spirit entity or power.[17]

For our early ancestors, shamans were diviners, predicting the best times to hunt or move on; they were likely the first astronomers, able to understand the heavens, predict weather patterns and provide directions; they were healers, who came back from their vision journeys knowing the source of a malady and, if permitted by the spirits, able to cure it; and among them were almost certainly our first storytellers. As the scholar and Paleolithic archaeologist Alexander Marshak notes:

> The storytelling skill, then, helped [Paleolithic man] to see and recognize process and change, to widen his references and comparisons, to "understand" and to participate in them in storied terms, and it enabled him to tell and foretell them. One assumes, then, that the kind of stories a man tells...helps him to unify the extraordinary diverse phenomena and processes of his life; and since a story is an *equation*, a cognitive form for abstractly structuring and dealing with process and relation, the uses and complexities of the story form would change as the culture became more complex. For us the important thing is to recognize that the innate, evolved *Homo sapiens* capacity for storied thinking has probably not changed significantly in the last 40,000 years.[18]

The Caves and the Shamanic Experience

In 1995, Lewis-Williams and Clottes began a collaboration to study examples of Paleolithic parietal art in 12 French caves, art dating from the earliest Gravettian period (c. 26,000 to 20,000 BCE) to the ancient, Middle and Upper Magdalenian (c. 12,000 to 9,000 BCE). Lewis-Williams' research had shown that San rock art was created as part of shamanic rituals. The two men felt without doubt that many of the Paleolithic images created deep inside the caves were as well.

Creating two-dimensional representational art is not an innate human ability, as illustrated by the well-known story originally told by the French archeologist and historian Salmon Reinach, about the Turkish officer who, as a Muslim, was entirely unfamiliar with representational two-dimensional art and was incapable of drawing a horse "because he could not move round it."[19] Similarly, the Paleolithic artist him- or herself would not have sought realism or understood why that was something valued. When questioned, writes Lewis-Williams, "the painter might have replied, 'that is not a real bison: you can't walk around it; and it is too small. That is a "vision," a "spirit bison." There is nothing "real" about it.' For the makers, the paintings and engravings were visions, not representations of visions — as indeed was the case for the southern African San and the North American shamans."[20]

Some images seem to have been created by spitting ochre and charcoal onto the cave wall. The prehistoric art specialist Michel Lorblanchet, who has himself reproduced ancient art in this way, feels that this spit-painting, common among Aboriginal people today, may have had a symbolic significance. "Human breath, the most profound expression of a human being, literally breathes life onto a cave wall. The painter projected his being onto the rock, transforming himself into the horses. There could be no closer or more direct communication between a work and its creator."[21]

Lewis-Williams points out that the images these people painted were not their inventions, they were manifestations or re-creations of what they recently saw on their vision journeys. He suggests that they were "reliving" their experience. For, like the San, he says, "Art and cosmos united in a mutual statement about the complete nature of reality. The walls of the shelters thus became gateways that afforded access to realms that ordinary people could not visit — but they could glimpse what it was like in the realm as painted images filtered through and shamans, such as K"au Giraffe, described their journeys."[22]

Lewis-Williams notes the "fluidity of shamanic experiences,"[23] and points out the extreme unlikelihood of a shaman being in a deep trance while executing these images. Instead, the visions were likely "fixed" while the practitioners were in a light trance state in which they were experiencing the visions but were still aware of their surroundings. At some point, there probably occurred a further stage where the shaman, revisiting the cave in which he or she had experienced a vision journey, would recreate that journey, calling it forth from memory. Then, much later, once the images had become familiar and their stories celebrated, there would be those who, although they had never experienced an altered state, were familiar enough with the images to replicate them.

A cave's very structure mirrored humanity's deeply held notion of a three-tiered cosmos, a belief that we will turn to next. It meant that once inside a cave people would experience a profound and immediate connection with the spirit worlds above and below. The overall effect created was of a multisensory experience: "through dancing, music, imitation of animal sounds and dramatic revelation of already existing paintings, vision seekers stocked their minds with emotionally highly charged mental images. The caves were alive with the sounds and visions of potent spirit animals."[24]

Our Three-Tiered Cosmos

The religion of the San of southern Africa is built around the belief in a world above, where the spirits reside, and another world underground or underwater, which is below our everyday world. Entering an underworld or experiencing supernatural flight to a spirit world above are found in shamanic tales throughout the continents of America, Africa and Australia, as well as in Siberia and Central Asia. The Tungus shamans of Central Asia descend to the underworld through a narrow hole to cross three streams, where they encounter the spirits. The South American Tapirapé shamans change into birds and fly through the cosmos; the Tupinamaba shamans of Brazil and the Carib shamans of Guyana take hallucinogens so that their souls leave their bodies and they can fly. The North American Inuit shamans transform from humans into birds and then fly. The shamans of Panama's Cuna tribe send spirits back into the sky.

As we will see, the neurological underpinning of a three-tiered cosmos is common to all human beings, so the interpretation of it is consistent: Along with our normal, everyday world, a dangerous Underworld and a limitless, light-filled, "heavenly" Overworld are envisaged in almost all cultures, from Paleolithic times to now.

That same cognitive pattern is evident — whether in Greek myths, in Christian prayers or in the adventures of our modern popular heroes. Mircea Eliade observed this and concluded that "probably a large number of epic 'subjects' or motifs, as well as many characters, images, and clichés of epic literature, are, finally, of ecstatic origin, in the sense that they were borrowed from the narratives of shamans describing their journeys and adventures in the superhuman worlds."[25]

The arched roof of the cave, the narrow passageway and the deep cavern below were part of, and built into these people's idea of, and belief in, a tiered cosmos. Many of our contemporary places of worship, with their domed ceilings and underground crypts, reflect the spaces within which humanity took the first steps in its search for transcendence: the caves of our Upper Paleolithic ancestors.

Shamanic Training and Practice –
Suffering, "Death" and Rebirth

Shamanic journeys, like near-death experiences, frequently include being immersed in radiant light. Mircea Eliade mentions that "clearly, the 'inner light' that suddenly bursts forth after long efforts of concentration and meditation is well known in all religious traditions."[26]

A sense of dying and being born again is one held by shamans in common with other, more recent, religious traditions. As we'll see later on, the idea of "death" and rebirth in many religions really describes the dissolution or breaking-up of the normal, everyday cognitive barriers to transcendence. To be born again does not refer to a physical rebirth but to a spiritual rebirth, more accurately translated from the Greek as "born from above" or "born anew." In Christianity, we are spiritually dead when apart from Jesus (Ephesians 2:1-5, Colossians 2:13). To become spiritually alive, we need to be "born again."

The anthropologist Richard Katz found that, when a Ju/'hoan (!Kung) San ritual specialist falls to the ground in deep trance, he is said to have "died." That "death" is thought to be, in its essence, identical with physical death: The spirit leaves the body and journeys to the spirit world. Pushing his San informant, Kau Dwa, Katz asked "Does that mean really die?" Kau Dwa answered, "Yes . . . it is the death that kills us all. . . . but healers may come alive again."[27]

Katz concluded that "spiritual transition between a material world and a spirit world infuses the San concept of 'death.' It is not (so much) decay of the body after physical death that matters to the San. For them, 'death' is not annihilation but rather enhanced sight: the dead are seers. Around the world, ritual specialists' mastery of 'death' — their ability to return from the spirit world — gives them social status and respect and, in some instances, political influence." The social anthropologist

Peter Gow found the same thing in the Amazon: "Dying, in [Amazonian] Piro thought, is not the negation of life, but a further mode of ontogenesis."[28]

In Roger Walsh's book *The World of Shamanism*, a young shaman Inuit describes his journey: "Igjugarjuk declared that the strain of those thirty days of cold and fasting was so severe that he 'sometimes died a little.'" As a result of his experiences, Igjugarjuk concluded that "the only true wisdom lives far from mankind, out in the great loneliness, and it can be reached only through suffering. Privation and suffering alone can open the mind of a man to all that is hidden to others."[29] Many in all religious traditions and throughout the centuries have held a similar view. Shamanic Mayan rulers believed they could maintain legitimacy on Earth and connection with their gods by piercing their penis or tongue as part of a blood-letting sacrifice. In common with major religious figures, shamans are known to isolate themselves for days, or to undergo long periods of sensory deprivation. Christian devotees have subjected themselves to "mortification of the flesh" with self-flagellation, hair shirts and stigmata, believing that by this form of suffering they become closer to a Christ who himself suffered on the cross; self-flagellation rites are still carried out by some Roman Catholics — in the Philippines, for example.

According to Eliade, Inuit shamanism and Buddhist mysticism share as their goal "deliverance from the illusions of the flesh." And shamanism in general is shot through with "the will to transcend the profane, individual condition" in order to recover "the very source of spiritual existence, which is at once 'truth' and 'life.'"[30]

From Paleolithic times onwards, the disassembling and negation of self is viewed as the first step in getting out of the "fog" that clouds a view of the "beyond."

The contemporary Muskogee shaman Bear Heart describes death and rebirth in this way: "There are many kinds of death. It isn't necessary to leave the physical body in order to let a part of you die that doesn't serve you any longer. When you allow that to happen, you can be reborn into a new and better life."[31]

The cultivation of detachment aids both the shaman and the saint in the mission of service. Bear Heart tells of constructive empathy; that is, empathy that eludes the intrusion of emotion: "You can be of greater help if you are strong enough to lift that person's spirits up and not allow your emotions to get in the way. It's called empathy — you put your mind in that person's situation, but only your mind, while you stand in a safe place and try to bring that person to the same point of safety you are at."[32]

Like the saints and prophets of later religions, the shaman's goal is to come back from these journeys able to be transparent within themselves and thence of service to their community. Bear Heart writes, "I began to see that, when it comes right down to it, we are nothing until that nothing becomes so dedicated that it is like a vessel through which good things can move, an instrument for receiving knowledge and sharing it with others who might be in need."[33]

The Three Stages of Altered Consciousness

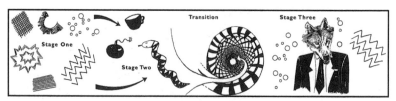

Figure 3. The three stages of altered consciousness: possible examples that might be experienced by a Westerner[34]

Lewis-Williams and Clottes note that there are three overlapping stages of altered consciousness experienced (though not everyone experiences them all) and that neurophysiological studies of the trance state have shown that these three overlapping stages can be identified.

In the first stage, people "see" geometric forms (you'll recall that we noted dots, grids and patterns on some of the walls of Paleolithic caves) that can be brightly colored and may flicker and pulsate, all constantly enlarging, contracting and blending with one another. In the second stage, the geometric forms morph into objects of religious or emotional significance. In the third stage a shaman's spirit leaves his body and he or she becomes completely withdrawn from the outside world. This stage appears similar to what we know of many near-death experiences. The participant is drawn into a vortex, hole or tunnel at the end of which is a bright light. The sides of the vortex often include the same geometric imagery of the first and second stage, but now the imagery forms and floats on surfaces that have themselves become animated. Often people feel that they are flying and changing into birds or animals — becoming one with their hallucination, so to speak.[35]

Just as different cultures have different conceptions of the constellations in the night sky, so do societies give varied meanings to these geometric forms. What subjects "see" in the second and third stage is determined by their cultural background as well as by their state at the time. As in Figure 3, a thirsty person might "see" a cup of water, whereas someone in a fearful state might "see" a bomb. A shaman might "see" an animal spirit; a Christian mystic, her favorite saint.

Lewis-Williams notes that these and other phenomena are "a neurological bridge" to the Paleolithic mindset. He cites studies showing that in induced trance states, the human optic system generates the same types of visual illusions in the same three stages, differing only by culture, whatever the stimulus — drugs, music, pain, fasting, repetitive movements, solitude or high carbon-dioxide levels (a phenomenon that is common in confined underground chambers) — and that these stages seem hard-wired in the nervous system.[36]

Our ancestors exploited the natural world — in this case, the way each cave was structured. The topography, passages and chambers of these caves reflected, and helped to induce, these shamanic experiences. Speaking of the vortex or tunnel experienced by the shaman in the second stage mentioned above, Clottes and Lewis-Williams note that:

> The vortex creates sensations of darkness, constriction, and, sometimes, difficulty in breathing. Entry into an actual hole in the ground or a cave replicates and is a physical enactment of this neuropsychological experience. . . . But entry into a cave does not only replicate the vortex; it may also induce altered states of consciousness. . . . During the Upper Paleolithic, entry into an actual cave may therefore have been seen as virtually the same thing as entry into deep trance via the vortex. The hallucinations induced by entry into and isolation in a cave probably combined with the images already on the wall to create a rich and animated spiritual realm. A complex link between caves and altered states seems undeniable.[37]

Contemporary Shamanic Experiences

As we've seen, shamanic traditions are universal and very likely reflect humanity's early spiritual practices, ones that predate all known religions.[38] So studies of the shamans practicing today can provide a link to, and insights into, our original religious procedures and practices.

The participant in one contemporary study of shamanic research, Corine Sombrun, was born in 1961 in Draguignan, in southeastern France, and spent her childhood in Ouagadougou, the capital of Burkina Faso. When she was six, she experienced a spontaneous trance state and was recognized as having an inclination toward this mode of consciousness. Eventually, after a varied career, she moved to London in 1999 and worked as a reporter for BBC World Service. In 2001, during a report she was filing on Mongolian mysteries, the sound of a shamanic drum induced a violent state of consciousness in her in which she could no longer control her movements.

A shaman of the Dakhad people (one of the 31 ethnic Mongolian groups) acknowledged Sombrun's shamanic potential and invited her to apprentice for shamanic training.[39] Sombrun traveled in Mongolia near the Siberian frontier for the next eight years, being taught shamanic practices by a local shaman. In 2009, Sombrun became the first Westerner to achieve the status of *ugdan* (female shaman) in the Mongolian tradition.

She describes her trance experiences:

> It was a very light trance, because I was asked not to move a lot. My nose began to tremble as it used to do in the beginning of each trance (now I am able not to move at all). Then my hands and my arms started shaking lightly. An inner vision of a wolf face, very close to my face, came soon after. Then an owl (two close representations are joined). I have to add that these visions were not seen as precisely as they are with our eyes. It may happen that the visions are quite similar to how we see with our eyes, but sometimes it's more like the feeling of a presence than the image of it. But despite the fact that I don't really see it, I 'know' what or who it is. During that trance too, I perceived some soft sounds and a bit of a song that I didn't know.
>
> I find myself in a completely dark place (I don't know if it is the reason why the shamans call it 'black world'). The first impression is the loss of time perception, like being in a timeless space. My strength is increased a lot (I can hold and beat the drum, which weighs 8 kg, for hours without any difficulties). My perception of pain is considerably reduced. For instance, at the beginning of my practice, my body hurt a lot because I had to manipulate the drum made of thick wood. But amazingly each trance was painless, while when I was back to my normal state, I felt a lot of pain in every part of my body. Another effect of the trance is the loss of the perception of cold and heat.
>
> My eyes (closed during every trance) have visions like geometrical patterns, places or entities called spirits by the shamans. They can appear to me as men, or women, or animal patterns, that

I can suddenly speak with. I feel like I can also detect discords in my environment. When discord is present, my nose can 'smell' it. Or, I guess, it is not the odor but the information at the root of the odor. My hands act like they are responding to these discords by performing gestures that I have absolutely no control over. I also can feel forms (more often like balls) in the air. My hands can turn around; try to soften them or to move them gently. I sing songs I have never sung or even learned, I speak unknown languages, and I perform very complex sounds that I am unable to perform in my normal state.

My sense of self seems to be receding because I don't feel like I am myself anymore; I lose the perception of who I am, or who I used to be. I suddenly feel like the animal or the entity I am supposed to be possessed by. As I am a wolf, for example, I can feel paws in place of my hands and a muzzle in place of my nose. I don't speak anymore but howl like a wolf. About the emotional changes, I'd like to say that I can feel I am incredibly at peace but at the same time possess the strength of 'a fierce warrior' when it happens that I have to fight what I see as a harmful entity.[40]

Sombrun continues to investigate shamanic trance with many other scientists. After her training in Mongolia, she went to Professor Pierre Flor-Henry's Clinical Diagnostic and Research Centre at Alberta Hospital in Edmonton, Canada, to help research the physiological mechanisms underlying her ability to induce a shamanic trance. She is one of the unusual people who can enter a trance state at will, allowing a simultaneous personal and physiological study to take place.

When Sombrun was in a "normal" state, no difference in brain activity was found between her and others who were in a normal state; but when she was in a trance state, important brain changes in the right temporal and right parietal lobes were found. The study's authors (who include Sombrun) note that "the novel contribution of this study is our cardinal observation of the right and posterior right shift in the transition to shamanic trance state . . . Previous observations identify right temporo-parietal junction as a specific substrate in maintaining a coherent sense of one's body ('me' vs. 'not me')."[41]

This provides both real-time evidence of a sense of selflessness and of an extraordinary experience with a person who can shift back and forth between that and our everyday state of consciousness. It also gives us an idea of the brain states recorded in the right parietal lobe, which underlie this shamanic experience. We will have much more to say on this in later chapters.

Sombrun's ability to enter and leave the trance state is rare. While breaking through the barriers that constrain the normal routes of our consciousness seems to be one major prerequisite to a greater vision and understanding, doing so can often take a mind out of control — which can be perilous. As another modern Westerner who reached the above-mentioned "transition" stage (identified as the "vortex" by Lewis-Williams) later said:

> I approached what appeared to be a very sharp, pointed piece of stainless steel. It had a razor blade quality to it. I continued up to the apex of this shiny metal object and as I arrived, I had a choice, to look or not look, over the edge and into the infinite abyss....I wanted to go all in but felt that if I did, I would possibly leave my body permanently.[42]

Storytelling, Mythology and Belief

From the somewhat limited selection of animals repeatedly depicted on cave walls and in carved images, it seems very likely that participants entered the caves already believing in the special role of certain animals that were part of their myths, and this predetermined "theology" created expectations of what they would experience.[43]

The images of these animals likely depicted a narrative shared by the whole group. Revised and retold throughout human history, such stories, illustrated by figurines and statues and painted on cave and church walls, become, if not "the truth," then the "guiding narrative" for the group. A story is told and retold, revised and adapted to enhance cooperation and fulfill contemporary needs. Stories would travel with the shaman, storyteller, bard, priest and prophet. For more than 35,000 years, stories have been an essential way we have understood our world and our place in it.[44]

Although some members of a community have no personal experience of the intense shamanic journey, the stories, insights and methodologies of the shamans are accepted and become part of each culture's narrative — describing their origin and history, encapsulating their values, aspirations and potential. Believers accept a tiered cosmos and believe that shamans travel its levels; they respect the images and the tales that describe these journeys, because they help to satisfy their need for meaning, and because this world of journeys into the cosmos was already somewhat familiar to them in their legends. They "know" because, as we have said, they share the same nervous system, and have very likely experienced evanescent glimpses of these realms accidentally or in dreams.

Shamanic Prophets

The sociologist Max Weber noted that there was certainly shaman-like behavior among some of the early Hebrew prophets. "They described visual and auditory hallucinations and abnormal sensations of taste and feeling of diverse sorts.... They felt as if they were floating ... or borne through the air, they experienced clairvoyant visions of spatially distant events like, allegedly, Ezekiel in Babylon at the hour of Jerusalem's fall.

... They saw hallucinatory blinding flashes of light and in it the figures of superhuman beings."[45]

Saints and seers throughout history have changed their lives and those of many others because of such experiences. Zoroaster, St. Paul and the Prophet Muhammad come readily to mind as examples.

Sociologist Stephen Sanderson claims that "Christ was the most 'shaman-like'" of all the prophets.[46] He notes some similarities between Jesus and the shamans, among them that shamans go into isolation to undertake intense practice, while Jesus spent those 40 days alone in the wilderness; that shamans enter in the spirit world, while Jesus was one with God; and that like shamans, Jesus was a healer and ascended into the sky after death.

We will expand upon this further, but it is important to distinguish between the shamanic ecstatic experience and the higher consciousness attained by prophets and genuine spiritual teachers.

From Shaman to Priest

The cave and surrounding ceremonial sites at which people gathered when ritual events took place would likely have been selected by shamans. The Pont d'Arc, for example, is an imposing natural bridge that is still today an impressive landmark. Above the bridge, affording a clear view of it, is the entrance to the Chauvet Cave which holds some of the finest and most ancient Paleolithic cave paintings. Recent radiocarbon calibration estimates indicate that the oldest carbon drawings there were created 36,500 years ago, and the most recent paintings between 32,000 and 28,000 years ago.

Scholars have suggested that some images at cave sites such as Lascaux represent ancient zodiac mapping, showing that these early humans used their knowledge of the night sky to keep track of time and changing seasons by watching how stars moved throughout the year.[47] The researchers postulate that some images were placed by the artists to mark significant astronomical events, such as comet strikes. Given the lapse of time and the plenitude of images, it is hard to establish this with certainty. But we will see clear evidence of the science of astronomy in the next Neolithic period.

But by at least 13,000 years ago, there is evidence that the shaman's high status had been established, and his or her role was, at least in part, to "stage manage" participants' experiences. The "Sorcerer" at Les Trois Frères whose image we included in Chapter 2 (Figure 2) was placed "four metres above the floor in an apparently inaccessible position, *only to be reached by a secret corridor climbing upwards in a spiral*" [italics ours].[48]

By the time the Ice Age ended and populations increased, the experience of the shamans, as well as their art, stories and predictions, would set them apart from the rest of society. Over time, the shamans' role would become more priestlike, but they would remain a specialized group destined to travel a unique path in humanity's search for deeper understanding and transcendence. They held the key to meaning for these very early communities and would do so — in one guise or another — for many millennia.

FOR FURTHER READING

The Mind in the Cave: Consciousness and the Origins of Art, David Lewis-Williams, Thames & Hudson, 2002.

Nyae Nyae !Kung Beliefs and Rites, Lorna J. Marshall, Peabody Museum of Archaeology and Ethnology, Harvard University, 1999.

The Rock Art of Southern Africa (the Imprint of Man), J. David Lewis-Williams, Cambridge Univ. Press, 1983.

The Shamans of Prehistory: Trance and Magic in the Painted Caves, Jean Clottes and David Lewis-Williams, Harry N. Abrams, 1996.

Shamanism: A Biopsychosocial Paradigm of Consciousness and Healing, 2nd Ed., Michael J. Winkelman, Praeger, 2010.

Shamanism: Archaic Techniques of Ecstasy, Mircea Eliade, Princeton Univ. Press, 2004.

The Strong Eye of Shamanism: A Journey into the Caves of Consciousness, Robert E. Ryan, Ph.D., Inner Traditions Intl., 1999.

The Wind is My Mother: The Life and Teachings of a Native American Shaman, Bear Heart (with Molly Larkin), Berkeley Publishing (Penguin), 1998.

The World of Shamanism: New Views of an Ancient Tradition, Roger N. Walsh, M.D., Ph.D., Llewellyn Publications, 2007.

3

God 2.0 – From Many Spirits To Many Gods, Gods For Everything

... [the] ice age was so climatically unstable that each time you had the beginning of a culture they had to move.... Then comes... ten thousand years of very stable climate. The perfect conditions for agriculture.... Civilizations in Persia, in China, and in India start at the same time, maybe six thousand years ago. They all developed writing and they all developed religion and they all built cities, all at the same time, because the climate was stable. I think that if the climate would have been stable fifty thousand years ago it would have started then. But they had no chance.

— PALEOCLIMATOLOGIST J.P. STEFFENSEN[1]

From Cave to Temple

The change in climate at the end of the Ice Age ushered in the Neolithic Era, which is sometimes called the "Neolithic Revolution" because it marked the change from small nomadic bands of hunter-gatherers and foragers to farmers and settlements. It also marked a dramatic change in popular understanding of the spirit world, spawning what we now identify as religion and religious ideas, as belief began to replace direct experience.

Once populations rose into the hundreds, some form of hierarchy was perhaps inevitable given the need to maintain a community's coherence and continuity. The shaman's position changed from that of a specialist facilitator who was part of an egalitarian group, to a more prestigious role, with greater control over the participants' experiences, beliefs and worldview.

Neolithic shamans were no longer limited by the natural topography of caves, but could now design and direct the building of gigantic stone structures to replace them. Under the control of these shaman-priests and elite chiefs, people likely understood that an enormous communal effort was required to assist and impress the spirit world above and below and, in so doing, maintain earthly and cosmic harmony — sometimes called, a bit grandly, "cosmic maintenance." This effort shaped the beginnings of organized religion, agriculture and science. Reflecting the new earthly hierarchy, it quite possibly created the first more distant divine beings, or gods, and the many religious beliefs and rituals associated with them — traces of which are still with us today.

Experiential methodologies became the exclusive property of the shamans, passed on only to those they chose to initiate, and kept secret from the majority. Shamans now began to modify aspects of their vision journeys in order to share them selectively with the community at large to ensure social cohesion and compliance.

Images and sound, light and darkness, drums and chanting, would now be used in orchestrated ritual ceremonies attended by hundreds of people. Continuity here was dependent upon connection with the dead ancestors who, buried under both temple and domestic structures, were most likely seen as intermediaries to the gods. Again, only through the expenditure of enormous effort by hundreds of people, both living and dead, could these gods be reached. In their book *Inside the Neolithic Mind*, David Lewis-Williams and David Pearce express it this way:

> In unprecedented and innovative ways, groups of Neolithic people manipulated cosmology and the states of consciousness that provided them with the fundamental building-blocks for religious experience, belief and practice. Seers thus gained political power and economic influence as well as religious domination. Therein lies the real, innovative essence of the Neolithic: expression of religious cosmological concepts in material structures as well as in myths, rather than the passive acceptance of natural phenomena (such as caves), opened up new ways of constructing an intrinsically dynamic society.[2]

The First Temple and the Birth of Agriculture

As our ancestors carried their worship rituals and practices with them out of the caves at the end of the Paleolithic era, they created a New Stone (the literal meaning of "Neolithic") world.

Göbekli Tepe (which means "Potbelly Hill") is situated in southeastern Turkey, on the northern edge of the Fertile Crescent. Known as "the first temple,"* these stone structures were erected about 11,000 years ago — approximately 7,000 years before the completion of the final stage of Stonehenge. Klaus Schmid, the late German archaeologist who led the Göbekli Tepe excavations, described the temple's pillars as once standing together on the hillside "like a meeting of stone beings."

Using only flint tools, our ancestors carved these massive pillars from a limestone quarry, then transported them from as

---

*In 2012, a settlement at Boncuklu Tarla, also in southeastern Turkey, was discovered. It is 1,000 years older than Göbekli Tepe and includes several T-shaped temple structures.

far as a quarter of a mile away without the aid of wheels or beasts of burden. This was an enormous undertaking. A complex of about 20 circles was created by T-shaped megalithic pillars that are each up to 20 feet high and weigh about 10 tons.

For some decades, the conventional conception of human progress has been that the development of agriculture stimulated worship, since it provided a stable base for sustained actions by large numbers of people. But the evidence at Göbekli Tepe, indicates that the reverse was true. One circular building alone would have needed the coordinated engagement of hundreds of laborers, craftsmen and builders. Once completed, it would have attracted large numbers of worshippers all needing food provisioning. Since einkorn wheat, a wild precursor of modern domesticated wheat, has been found in the Karacadağ hills nearby, scholars feel that participants taking grain to Göbekli Tepe for food likely dropped wild seed along the way, which grew and eventually became domesticated. "First came the temple, then the city," Schmid concluded. At least at Göbekli Tepe it was the need to transcend normal consciousness and connect to the spirit world that stimulated the beginning of agriculture, and not the other way around.

Göbekli Tepe's limestone pillars, each shaped like a capital T, stand as stylized human beings. Their "heads" the horizontal line on top of the letter, have "bodies" with relief carvings, some indicating arms, hands, belts and animal skin loin-cloths; others are decorated with animals then native to the area: bulls, foxes, cranes, lions, ducks, scorpions, ants, spiders, and snakes.

The pillars were placed to form circular or oval shapes ranging from 30 to 100 feet in diameter, each pillar standing an arm span or so apart connected to the next by a stone wall or bench; two larger pillars stand within the center. Scholars suggest that these structures may originally have supported domed roofs; their semi-sunken pillars are load-bearing. If left uncovered, the limestone would too easily have been damaged by rain and wind.

These pillared buildings would have been visible from a very long distance, yet there is no sign of habitation, so it seems certain that this was a meeting place used for religious and ceremonial purposes only. From the many animal bones that have been found at the site, it seems likely that when pilgrims arrived at Göbekli Tepe, they made animal sacrifices. A statue of a human, sculptures of a vulture's head and a boar have also been excavated there, and recently several human skulls, some with chiseled markings, have been uncovered.

It is likely these substantial sites were used for multiple ceremonies of birth, initiation to adulthood, burial, ancestor veneration and shamanism; and to ensure, through ritual, magic and sacrifice, the collaboration of the spirit world and perhaps also of the people's newly conceived gods of nature including the sun, moon and sky.

The limestone caves in the Taurus Mountains of southern Turkey are thought to have been the initial homes of a hunter-gatherer society that, once the weather improved, moved and settled about two days' journey away. There in about 7,000 BCE, some 2,000 years after the founding of Jericho, they built a Neolithic settlement known as Çatalhöyük. Over the next 1,000 years, people continuously inhabited this site, which for a period accommodated an average of 6,000 to 8,000 people.

There were no streets or paths in Çatalhöyük; instead honeycombed rectangular houses of mud brick were joined together by common walls, their flat roofs providing walkways and an area where much of daily life took place. Entry into each home was via a ladder that descended through the ceiling from an opening in the roof. Once inside, moving between rooms was possible only by passing through small openings 28 to 30 inches high, so people were obliged to crawl or bend low in order to move deeper into the structure. As David Lewis-Williams and David Pearce explain:

> In effect, the roofs of the town created a new land surface, probably, we argue, a replication of the cosmological level on which people lived their daily lives.... descent, limited light and the need to crawl through small openings between chambers are akin to the experience of moving through limestone caves.... The cosmos and its animals were embedded in the house.[3]

The Ice Age shamans of Altamira and Lascaux often used the cave walls' natural irregularities to create a part of a spirit auroch, horse or bison, so that the animal appeared, in torchlight, to float in and out of the rock surface. In the Neolithic settlement of Çatalhöyük, wild rams' heads and breast-like shapes loom out of the walls into rooms, creating a focal point, an altar where the act of worship is apparent. These wall reliefs included animal remains — the plastered skulls of bulls — as well as clay representations.

Death and the spirits of ancestors played an important part in the lives of Neolithic peoples. We know this because their dwellings also housed the dead, who were probably believed to intervene with the spirit world on behalf of their living descendants and, in return, were honored by the living. Skeletons were found under dwellings at Çatalhöyük. Plastered skulls and figures, their eyes emphasized with black bitumen outlines or inset with shells, were deliberately placed beneath house floors at the Near Eastern sites of 'Ain Ghazal in Jordan and Jericho in Palestine. We can only speculate, but their eyes could well have represented the 'enhanced sight' acquired by the dead and by shamans on their vision journeys.

Ian Hodder, the excavator of Çatalhöyük, says "The ability of the shaman or ritual leader to go beyond death and return gives a special status, and would be especially important in a society in which the ancestors had so much social importance. By going down into a deep room in which the dead were buried, the ritual leaders could travel to the ancestors through the walls, niches and floors."[4]

Images etched on the limestone pillars at Göbekli Tepe were by then understood in a more iconographic way, reminding participants of remarkable events or of the stories and myths already current at that time, as does a totem or a statue in a modern church or temple.* Sites as far as 100 miles away from Göbekli Tepe shared some of the same imagery, and people more than likely shared the same or similar stories, beliefs and ideas associated with them. Smaller but similar pillars — some with the same imagery — dating 3,000 years after Göbekli Tepe were found at Nevali Çori, a settlement 20 miles away; at Karahan Tepe, 23 miles away; and at other sites in the region.

Archeologist Trevor Watkins of the University of Edinburgh writes:

> The great advantage of all this symbolic reference through physical artefacts was that, unlike speech, dance or ritual enactment, which is transient, the physical symbolism with which they surrounded themselves was always there, always reminding them, teaching their children. They had learned what the psychologist Merlin Donald (1991, 1998) has called 'external symbolic storage' . . . Above all, these ideas about their world were systematic, categorical, discriminating, ordered. Such a systematic and symbolically rich world-view was ideal for providing the cultural underpinning that could be shared by all those in the community, for they lived in and by and through the symbolic references in their settlements. And finally, such a systematic and readily symbolised world-view was infectious, readily communicated and easily learned by others who had the same cognitive skills and the same need to cope with their new way of life.[5]

Beliefs and customs then journeyed with these early farmers. Now they could travel not only with their families, but taking with them their animals, their rituals and beliefs. Some travelled

---

*See Addendum: Chapter 3

east, their descendants ending up in present-day India. Others moved westward, settling around the Danube River; and others went southwest to Italy and surrounding areas. Around 4500 BCE, they arrived in Brittany, western Portugal and Holland, eventually journeying on to Britain and Ireland.

The many megaliths these people left behind help us trace their voyage. At some point, a tribe's ancestors would be buried on land they had worked year after year, possibly giving rise to the concept of land ownership. A social hierarchy would become established as populations increased and settlements and farming expanded. The imposing stone structures not only honored the ancestors but established a tribe's presence by indicating that "this land is ours; our ancestors are here too, and we will protect it." The dead were now regularly buried along with the everyday things they had used in life — ornaments, weapons, pottery — which presumably might be needed in the next world.

The experience of transcendence had become more remote and the rituals around it more organized. The concerns and questions were the same: How long will life as we know it last? And how do we maintain it? What is death? How do we know or ensure that the Sun will continue to come up? The idea of a tiered cosmos held fast, and it seems certain that in the minds of our ancestors, communication with the spirit world was still the only way to solve these problems and answer these questions.

The Birth of Science

As the climate grew warmer communities grew larger, and people spent more time outside, where the vast horizon and immense heavens would have made the spirit world seem much more distant. But the early priesthood was up to the task: In their hands, the ubiquitous and unpredictable spirit world was morphing into a hierarchical pantheon of gods, whose images and significance could be established, replicated and used for collaborative worship, ritual and sacrifice by the whole community.

Cosmic maintenance — ensuring that the Sun would rise and set, and that the seasonal cycles would continue — meant that a connection to the cosmos via worship was vital. This not only was important for the regularity of harvests in the face of droughts and floods, but also because it led to the beginnings of science, with emphasis placed on careful observation, measurement and recording of the natural world.

Like the caves and temples, these structures likely served multiple functions. They were religious centers, burial sites, meeting places, and territorial markers. They also served as astronomical observatories where the movement of the Sun was ritually monitored and ceremonies held to celebrate the spring and autumn equinoxes and the winter and summer solstices.

Oracles "spoke," sometimes thanks to the extraordinary acoustic properties of temple rooms, such as in the subterranean multistory Hal Saflieni Hypogeum in Malta, where the bones of some 7,000 humans were found.

Hidden rooms and stairways, oracular openings and doors designed to keep people out rather than lock them in are evident in Tarxien, Hagar Qim, Mnaijdra and Ggantija, other Maltese temples constructed between 3800 and 2500 BCE. These findings indicate that although the quest for insight and understanding stimulated what we know today as science, it, too, was the exclusive provenance of the elite — the chiefs and the shamans or priesthood — and was used to control the masses.

As people migrated, this knowledge traveled with them. Every December 21st (the winter solstice) at Newgrange in Ireland, a transom opening above the entrance lets in light from the rising Sun, whose beams illuminate the entire 60-foot passageway straight down into the heart of the mound to an artificial cave, a corbelled-roof chamber where the ashes and bones of ancestors were placed.

Megalithic structures — round mounds, long mounds, dolmens and passage tombs leading to covered chambers — were all evocative of the cave experience. The arched roof, the narrow passageway and the deep cavern below were built to echo the three-tiered cosmos — an underworld, our everyday world and a world above — and continued to induce, or remind people of the shamanic experiences and the possibility of transcendence.

To quote the shaman Bear Heart again, on entry into the sweat lodge, "The secret is humility. When we come into the [sweat] lodge, the opening of the doorway is so small that we must crawl through that door on our hands and knees. That's the first lesson right there — humbling ourselves before the Great Being as we come in."[6] In Chapter 13, we will take a closer look at the role of virtues, such as humility, in the search for transcendence.

Replicating the Cave Experience

At the beginning of the third century BCE, in what is now part of Turkey, a Greek temple dedicated to the god Apollo was built on the sacred site of Klaros, which dates back to at least four centuries earlier.[7] John Hale, an archeologist who has specialized in its study, recreates the experience of those seekers more than two millennia ago, in terms that seem strikingly similar to reports of entering the Paleolithic painted caves. He tells us that such was the reputation of Klaros in the second century CE, that people came from as far away as Britain and North Africa to have their (unspoken) questions answered. On arrival, they first provided their name and underwent a purification ritual. Then they were led down a long, dark staircase into the bowels of the Earth, through a passageway so low that they had to crouch, and so narrow that their shoulders rubbed against both sides. Descending lower and lower through a labyrinth that ran under the temple, they at last walked out into a vaulted chamber — a cave. Completely disoriented, they were instructed to sit and wait. They did so.

One by one, they had to stand and face the hallowed space before them. Their name was spoken. Then, out of a dark opening in the wall opposite them, the disembodied voice of the god Apollo answered their unspoken question. The answer was heard and the individual returned to a bench to sit and wait, as each of the others went forward to hear the oracle.

When everyone had received an answer, they left, squeezing through a different set of dark tunnels and eventually emerging together into the cool, clear night. Each one's life had been changed by this experience. The question that burdened each one had been answered. None of them would ever forget that night in the temple of Apollo at Klaros.

Hidden deep in the crypt, a sacred spring bubbled up from under the earth, and from this cleft, a magical power was released in the form of gases called "pneuma" ("breath" or "spirit") that Apollo's medium would breathe. Only Apollo's prophet was permitted to enter this spot and stand in the god's presence, near the omphalos ("navel" stone) that represented him. Breathing the gases and drinking the sacred water, the medium reached an altered state of consciousness that allowed Apollo to take over and, through her, to speak.[8]

Many oracle sites were built around places where such rock fissures occur. Dating from the Greek Mycenaean period (from the 14th to the 11th centuries BCE), the Oracle of Delphi became the most important shrine in Greece and survived until Christianity supervened, around the fourth century CE. During the time when the oracle was in operation, pneuma were not only released into the space above, but were also in the water and travertine rock. Plutarch, who was once a priest at Delphi, tells us that the priestess would sit on a tripod over the cleft. Breathing in the gases — now thought to be intoxicating light hydrocarbon gases such as methane, ethane and ethylene — she would fall into a trance that enabled Apollo to speak through her.[9] She would mutter incomprehensible words that would be interpreted by the priests for those who had submitted their questions. Professor Hale notes that although the religious conviction and fervor may have been sincere, sites such as Delphi were created, and rituals "stage-managed," to produce an illusion of where one was and what was happening:

> The temple is set on a high stone podium a long way above the rock where the fissure is. When you go in the door you go down a deep ramp into what the ancients describe as 'a cave' created by the temple rising around you. You feel as if you are at the heart of mother earth, which seems to be at the heart of so many religious experiences.[10]

From the moment our ancestors could build outdoor structures, right up until the present day, humans have continually erected edifices that, in many ways, resemble the cave experience: in Turkey, Göbekli Tepe and, later, temples such as Nevali Çori, as well as settlements such as Çatalhöyük; in Palestine, Jericho, where the remains of a very large early-Neolithic settlement of circular mud brick homes with domed roofs has been found; in ancient Greece, where sanctuary temples such as at Delphi and Klaros were built; and in the Roman world, where the Temple of Mercury and other domed buildings were erected. In the Middle Ages from the fifth to the 15th centuries, architects continued to replicate cave-like spaces with great cathedrals, temples and mosques — the Hagia Sophia and Blue Mosque in Turkey, Chartres Cathedral and Notre-Dame in France, the Mosque of Cordoba in Spain, Canterbury and Wells Cathedrals in England.

We continue to build structures designed to produce in the beholder a sense of awe similar to what our ancestors experienced deep inside the vaulted caves 30,000 years ago. One of these long underground caves, with an entrance to a high clearing — the Chauvet Cave in France — has been called the "Sistine Chapel of the Paleolithic;" but the actual Sistine Chapel in Rome could perhaps be called the "Chauvet Cave of the Renaissance."

Once populations increased and city-states sprang up, competition for limited resources altered the modus operandi of communities. Specialization of skills contributed to an ordered hierarchy in which control by the priesthood brought belief and dogma. Shamanic experiences, were kept secret, accessible only to the elite. The idea of mystical secrets, hidden from the populace by "those who know," may have had its origin at this period in our history.*

Mesopotamia – Many Gods, Gods for Everything

> The divine mind is remote
> Like the utmost of the heavens
> Knowledge of it is arduous,
> People are uninformed.

> — GUDEA, CYLINDER B, CIRCA 2144 TO 2124 BCE. (Gudea was a ruler of the state of Lagash in Southern Mesopotamia, four millennia ago.)

The Mesopotamians believed that human beings were created to relieve the lesser gods of all the hard work involved in making and maintaining the Earth, so understandably, the gods in their pantheon demanded a lot of worship, festivals, sacrifice and

---

*Traditionally, "secret" refers to the inability of the unenlightened to understand the experiences of enlightened prophets and sages. "Speak to everyone in accordance with his degree of understanding," a saying attributed to the Prophet Muhammad, refers to this.

work. Gods were involved in every aspect of people's lives. They had gods for everything from brickmaking to brewing — even a Lord of Livestock Pens.[11]

Mesopotamians believed that a divine transcendent power was behind everything. It manifested in a hierarchical pantheon of gods who were present in all aspects of the natural world. It was present in the statues of those gods, in the temples dedicated to them and in the people chosen to represent them in rites and religious festivals. Kings were created by the radiance of gods and, through that radiance, made powerful and godlike. The three most powerful gods were Ea or Enki, god of wisdom, magic and water; Enlil, the god of air, who also decreed the fates; and Anu, the divine personification of the sky and source of all authority. Each city-state had its own patron god or goddess that belonged to this pantheon. For example, Anu was the patron god of Erech (Uruk), and Der Enlil (Bel) the patron deity of the city of Nippur.

There were also demons, agents of the gods, who could be either good or (usually as punishment) evil. They could bring disease, cause miscarriages or death, and enter one's dreams. Some gods protected people against these demons. According to the Department of Ancient Near Eastern Art in New York's Metropolitan Museum of Art, "A deity depicted with the body of a lion and the head and arms of a bearded man was thought to ward off the attacks of lion-demons. *Pazuzu*, a demonic-looking god with a canine face and scaly body, possessing talons and wings, could bring evil but could also act as a protector against evil winds or attacks by *lamastu*-demons [associated with the death of newborn babies]. Rituals and magic were used to ward off both present and future demonic attacks and counter misfortune. Demons were also represented as hybrid human-animal creatures, some with birdlike characteristics."[12]

Initially, in the fourth millennium BCE, Mesopotamian religious worship focused on survival. People worshipped the powers of fertility and plenty to ensure cosmic maintenance. Then, in the third millennium BCE, as territories expanded along with the ensuing problems of security, the concept of the ruler god was added. And finally, in the second millennium BCE, as Thorkild Jacobsen, a historian of the ancient Near East, has pointed out, "the fortunes of the individual increase in importance until they rival those of the communal economy and security,"[13] and the personal god is added.

Mesopotamians believed that everything — nature, objects and actions, including poetry and literature — all manifested a supernatural power, an "in-dwelling spirit" without which it could not exist. Gods were present in objects and caused them to be, to thrive and to flourish. The Sumerian word for both the "Sun" itself and for the invisible, august and powerful deity was "Utu," and the moon god was named "Nanna," which was also the word for "moon."[14]

Like the gods of ancient Greece, Mesopotamian gods all bore human characteristics, but on a larger-than-life scale. Gods were taken to visit each other, and could die but could also come back to life. Human existence depended and revolved around these gods and the temple area where they resided on Earth. The temple area was a special part of the city, devoted to its patron god and, to a lesser extent, to other great or satellite gods. Almost all social, economic and political activities of the cities were concentrated around this vast area. Built in the center of each city-state, it included courtyards, storage rooms, bathrooms and living quarters. The most important part of the complex was the ziggurat, a massive, pyramid-like structure that was the sacred dwelling place of the patron deity and ensured that he/she remained close to the people. As the "mountain of God" or "hill of Heaven," a ziggurat connected Heaven and Earth, with the rest of the city-state built around it.

To the Mesopotamians, a god literally dwelt in a shrine at the top of the ziggurat. The only people allowed inside this sacred space were the king and the priesthood, who were responsible for caring for the god and attending to his/her needs.* They entered via a series of ramps on one side of the structure, or via a spiral ramp from the base to the summit.

Both statues representing gods, and participants chosen to act as gods in religious festivals and annual cult dramas, actually became the gods. They were believed to be literally present and, in the words of Thorkild Jacobsen, were able to "fulfill the divine will with all its beneficent results for the community."[15]

As kings conquered and absorbed city-states, their gods, too, were acquired and added to the pantheon or absorbed into other gods, their characteristics and qualities merging. And as monarchs became more and more powerful, one or two began to see themselves as deities, a step that bolstered and consolidated their power. The first Mesopotamian ruler recorded as having declared himself divine was Naram-Sin of Akkad, who reigned over the Akkad Dynasty in the 23rd century BCE. He apparently referred to himself as the warrior-husband of the goddess Ishtar, emphasizing her warlike, not her love aspect. The trend of the powerful to assume or be awarded godlike stature is one that will show up again and again in our history.

The bridging of the cosmic world of the gods and the personal god of the individual is first recorded in Mesopotamia toward the end of the second millennium BCE. A personal god was concerned with the individual's good or bad luck and his success or lack of it; the Akkadian term to describe luck and

---

*One practical function of the ziggurats was that they provided a high place on which the king and priesthood could escape the rising water that annually inundated lowlands and occasionally flooded everything for hundreds of miles. Another practical function of the ziggurat was to provide security. Since the sacred shrine at the top was accessible only by means of ramps, a small number of guards could prevent anyone else other than the chosen few from entering.

good fortune was "to acquire a god." A father and son might well have the same personal god, who dwelt in one's body, protected one from evil and, to quote Jacobsen, "served as a psychologically possible bridge to the great and terrifying awesome cosmic powers."[16] Ordinary people depended on a relationship with their own personal god for protection and to intercede for them with the great deities.

The idea of a personal god and a personal religion would be taken up again in the Old Testament where it would grow from the personal to the national realm, overseeing the whole nation. Intercession, previously seen in ancestor worship, would be taken up again and again in religious life: To this day, the Virgin Mary and other saints are called upon to intercede for many in the Catholic faith. Many nations, towns and activities have patron saints.

During the reign of Hammurabi in the 18th century BCE, Babylon became the principal city of southern Mesopotamia. The god Marduk, an important local deity, gradually grew in status and absorbed the qualities and characteristics of more than 50 deities to become head of the pantheon and Babylon's patron god. The Babylonian creation myth *Enûma Eliš* was probably written about this time. It tells of Marduk's rise to power, eventually becoming the creator-God of the Heavens and the Earth. This myth was chanted and reenacted on the fourth day of every New Year in the Ésagila, a temple dedicated to Marduk.[17] His ascension is one of the first indications of a move toward monotheism.

FOR FURTHER READING

Göbekli Tepe: An Introduction to the World's Oldest Temple, Rev. Ed., Avi Bachenheimer, Birdwood, 2018.

Inside the Neolithic Mind: Consciousness, Cosmos and the Realm of the Gods, David Lewis-Williams and David Pearce, Thames & Hudson, 2009.

The Leopard's Tale: Revealing the Mysteries of Çatalhöyük, Reprint Ed., Ian Hodder, Thames & Hudson, 2011.

Mesopotamia: Writing, Reasoning, and the Gods, Jean Bottéro, Univ. of Chicago Press, 1992.

Stonehenge – Exploring the Greatest Stone Age Mystery, Mike Parker Pearson and the Stonehenge Riverside Project, Simon & Schuster, 2012.

The Treasures of Darkness: A History of Mesopotamian Religion, Rev. Ed., Thorkild Jacobsen, Yale Univ. Press, 1976.

4

God 3.0 – Monotheism

The Fate of Religions and Other Institutions

There is an unavoidable cycle of innovation in all of our all-too-human institutions — inspiration, creation, growth, extension and then decay. This pattern was perhaps best summed up by the investor Warren Buffett: "All institutions have three 'I' stages . . . first the Innovators, then the Imitators, then, finally the Idiots."

Religions are no different. Enlightened individuals seek to initiate a new approach or radically reform an existing one. Then in a consolidation stage, a hierarchy is built up. And finally comes a sclerotic stage, in which the bureaucracy works for itself, and practices are hidebound — even tipping over to scandal and brutality. Ripe for a revolution, the cycle then begins anew.

The development of conscious insight is what the great religious and spiritual teachers have always taught. But the spiritual path is not easy. People who may start with good intentions become invested in their own authority, power or enrichment — the "temptations of the world" — and the innovator's insights get taken over by the fanatics and bureaucrats. This succession leaves behind little more than a legacy of adherence to a set of rules that the originator did not include and a simplified, literal, and often selective understanding of the words and acts attributed to him.

When encountering the ritualized, bureaucratic, formal, dogmatic religions of today, people who are likely to be interested in the original intent — spiritual understanding with an emphasis on direct experience — are at best flummoxed. It's often said that Jesus himself wouldn't be acceptable to many, or perhaps any, of the modern Christian churches.

In the centuries since their inceptions, our contemporary religions have diverged from their original transformative intention and, at least in the way they are publicly proclaimed, are all too often firmly in the grip of the last two of Buffett's "three I's." If we were to view these faiths only in terms of their current façades, we would miss their initial — and still real — meaning.

So our main focus is on the very first stages: the original insights of the sages and their understanding of God.

The Axial Age – No Other God

As the name given to it by the German philosopher Karl Jaspers connotes, the Axial Age, usually considered to have extended from approximately 800 BCE to 200 BCE, was a pivotal time when human beings all over the world began to reflect en masse about the meaning and purpose of life and death. Just before and during that era, human populations became much, much larger, forcing communities and tribes from very different, formerly isolated backgrounds to come into close contact. Differences in customs, beliefs and values became increasingly pronounced; conflict, war, disease and death became more frequent.

For the first time, individuals in countries from India to China to Greece all came to see themselves as separate from each other and responsible chiefly for their own actions. Life, one's actions and reactions, were no longer left to the spirit world, but were also up to oneself: What I do affects who I am and those around me. As a consequence, as Karen Armstrong points out, "Increasingly the gods were seen as symbols of a single transcendent Reality."[1]

Although the prophet Zarathustra, known to the Greeks as Zoroaster, is thought by many to have lived about 300 years before the Axial Age, aspects of what he taught transformed Indo-Iranian (Aryan) beliefs in a way that anticipated monotheism and the Axial prophets.

Zoroaster's revelation was that the purpose of humankind is to assist in maintaining *Rta asha* (or *aša*) — literally, "truth." Uniquely for a thinker of his time, he believed in individual responsibility and free will. One could choose or not choose to assist *Rta asha* through one's every deed and action, one's every choice and thought. According to the *Gathas*, which are the 17 inspired hymns attributed to Zarathustra, it is only through "good thoughts, good words, good deeds" that *Rta asha* can be maintained.

Zoroaster was convinced that Ahura Mazda was more than the lord of wisdom and justice; he was not only the benevolent Creator but also the one uncreated Supreme God. Ahura Mazda existed before everything, and "has left to men's wills" the choice between doing good and doing evil (bad thoughts, bad words and bad deeds).

Zoroastrianism most certainly influenced the Jewish, Christian and Islamic monotheistic worlds. It echoes the same legends as do both Judaism and Christianity, and includes the same concepts: a transcendent creator-God, a contrast and fight between good and evil, and salvation by a coming savior whom the Zoroastrians call Saoshyant, meaning "One Who Will Bring Benefit," who will lead humanity in the final battle against evil. Followers of Zoroaster came to believe that this Saoshyant would be born of the prophet's own seed that had been miraculously preserved in Lake Kazaoya, where a virgin would bathe and become pregnant. Zoroaster was, to quote the scholar Mary Boyce, "the first to teach the doctrines of an individual judgment, Heaven and Hell, the future resurrection of the body, the general Last Judgment, and life everlasting for the reunited soul and body."[2]

The people of Israel certainly did not have only one God in the time of Moses (thought to be around 1300 BCE). We're told that while waiting for Moses to come down from Mount Sinai, "*They have melted down gold and made a calf, and they have bowed down and sacrificed to it. They are saying, 'These are your gods, O Israel, who brought you out of the land of Egypt.'*" (Exodus 32:8, New Living Translation [NLT])

But who actually were all these "other gods"? It seems that the ancient Hebrews were initially animistic and then polytheistic. They worshipped stones, revered oak trees and "bowed down" to images. They worshipped the sun, the moon and the stars — "all the host of heaven" (2 Kings 17:16 [KJV]). As the 19th-century biblical scholar T.W. Doane pointed out, they "revered and worshiped a Bull called Apis, as did the ancient Egyptians. They worshiped fire, and kept it burning on an altar, just as did the Persians and others." They worshiped and burned incense to a "Queen of Heaven," the Assyrian goddess Mylitta. They worshiped gods such as Baal, a name attributed to the god Marduk (whom we met at the end of the previous chapter), the Canaanite deity Moloch, and Chemosh, a god revered by their Moabite neighbors east of the Dead Sea.[3]

Abram, later known as Abraham, who, according to Jewish tradition was born in Ur in Babylonia in approximately 1900 BCE, was the progenitor of the three major monotheistic religions known as the "Abrahamic religions." As historian Karen Armstrong has pointed out, Abraham initially worshipped "El, the local High God, and it seems that originally Yahweh was simply one of the 'holy ones' in El's retinue."[4] Yahweh even visits and eats with Abraham. Over time, Yahweh took on many more duties — from being the god of battles, to maintaining crops, to keeping the Sun going, and everything else. It took more than a millennium after Abraham for Yahweh to take over as the one God.

In spite of the admonitions of a string of prophets dating back to Moses, who all insisted that Yahweh was the only God, the Israelites would not become a truly monotheistic people until the late sixth century BCE, when King Jehoiachin of Judah and approximately 8,000 elite Jews were captured and taken to Babylon. It was while in Babylon that Jewish scholars began to collect, redact and retell the memories, stories and events — some from written sources and some from oral tradition — that would comprise what we know today as the Old Testament.

These influential Jews discovered that Yahweh was still with them while they were in exile. They became convinced that Yahweh could be worshipped away from the Temple in Jerusalem. He could be worshipped in the way they lived their lives wherever they were — even in a foreign land. Yahweh was both transcendent and personal. Morality and justice were imperative, but the essential element of religion was the individual's personal relationship with Yahweh. This relationship depended upon sincerity and, above all, upon Yahweh's help: *"I will put My law within them and on their heart I will write it; and I will be their God, and they shall be My people."* (Jeremiah 31:33, New English Translation [NET]) This passage encapsulates the idea of the "God within."

The Bible wasn't written in a vacuum. In Babylon, the stories and ideas of other cultures surrounded the Israelites. There are striking similarities between the creation stories in the biblical Genesis and the Babylonian tablets of *Enûma Eliš* mentioned in the previous chapter. These were originally written down circa

1800 BCE or earlier, but probably came from an oral tradition that was very much older. With Cyrus the Great, founder of the first Persian Empire, came the teachings of Zoroaster, which claimed Ahura Mazda as the one supreme true God. Under Cyrus, Zoroastrianism became the state religion of the Persian Empire and remained so until the rise of Islam in the seventh century CE. Cyrus was on good terms with the Jews: He was anointed Messiah for allowing the Babylonian Jews to return home to Judah after he took over.

Monotheism: Judaism, Christianity and Islam

The historic leaders of the Judeo-Christian-Islamic tradition were certainly involved in direct political activism and revolt, with a consequent need for protection of their community and the defeat of their enemies. Moses is depicted as fighting the Pharaonic regime, leading his people to flee out of Egypt. Jesus, living in an era of deep conflict between Israel and the occupying power, Rome, was killed. Muhammad was hunted like an animal because of his clashes with the Meccans and had to flee to Yathrib (now Medina); later, he came into conflict with the Jews and pagans who resided there. So it is certainly the case that violent clashes occurred in the lives of these three religious leaders, and that this is reflected in their holy scriptures. The Qur'an is by no means all milk and honey, any more than is, say, the Book of Leviticus or the Book of Deuteronomy.*

But our concern here is not with the political objectives and conflicts of these sages. It *is* about their having an ability to transcend ordinary consciousness amidst the chaos and disorder of their lives — a sense of God and spirituality and how to go beyond a tribal focus to a focus on humanity.

---

*See Addendum: Chapter 4

Early Christianity and Its Origins

Jesus taught at a time when, because of Rome's imperial domination, the Jewish experience of religious ideals melded with their politics. Rome instituted social stratification throughout society, leading to systematic injustice for the many people on the bottom rungs. Jesus, following the Jewish messianic tradition and eschatology, aimed to restore justice and peace in the kingdom. He taught through direct communication, to anyone who would really listen ("Whoever has ears to hear, should hear"[5]), that both society and the individual could be transformed. The Kingdom of God that Jesus spoke of was within us, achievable here and now through our own efforts, actions and thoughts.

It's important to remember one fact that is sometimes glossed over, ignored or forgotten: that Jesus, St. Paul, Mary, Jesus' brother James, Simon Peter, Matthew, Mark, Luke and John — as well as the apostles and others — were all Jewish. To quote *The Jewish Encyclopedia*, "Jesus was born a Jew and died a Jew. As far as can be determined, Jesus was a faithful and righteous Jew, teaching strict adherence to the Torah." Many Jewish scholars have observed that he taught and argued in parables like a Jewish rabbi. They note that it was not unusual for a radical Jew to be crucified by the Romans — it was considered an extremely shameful way to die. In 4 BCE, a reported 2,000 Jews were crucified by the Roman general Varus. Mass crucifixions were frequently held in Judea in the first century CE.

Jesus lived his entire life within Jewish society, and his concerns were about reforming and updating Jewish thinking. He proclaimed that his mission was to restore the spiritual nature and function of the Jewish faith, which had declined into empty ritual, worldliness and corruption. *"Think not that I am come to abolish the law or the prophets. I am not come to destroy, but to fulfill. For verily I say unto you, till heaven and earth pass away, one jot or one tittle shall in no wise pass from the law, till all be fulfilled."* (Matthew 5:17-18, [KJV])

Jesus was part of a continuing tradition of Jewish teaching that stretched all the way back to Abraham. Like the great prophets and teachers before him, Jesus' aim was spiritual revitalization — a "new kingdom" in which those who listened and followed could fulfill their potential and destiny.

Not much is known about the historical Jesus, since nothing was written down by him or about him during his lifetime. The best-known documented references are by the Jewish historian Josephus, who was born in 37 CE, shortly after the crucifixion. He refers to Jesus twice in his 20-volume *Antiquities of the Jews*, most prominently in a section known as the "Testimonium Flavianum," which deals with various actions of Pilate:

> Now there was about this time Jesus, a wise man, if it be lawful to call him a man, for he was a doer of wonderful works, a teacher of such men as receive the truth with pleasure. He drew over to him both many of the Jews, and many of the Gentiles. He was the Christ, and when Pilate, at the suggestion of the principal men among us, had condemned him to the cross, those that loved him at the first did not forsake him; . . . And the tribe of Christians so named from him are not extinct at this day.[6]

Immediately after the death of Jesus, his followers stayed in Jerusalem under the direction of his brother James. They, too, had no thought of starting or being part of a new religion. They wanted to have Jesus and his teachings included in the Jewish faith, as were the teachings of Moses, Isaiah, Hosea, Amos and other prophets.

We know enough about what was going on in the region at the time to imagine what Jesus' followers went through after the death of their teacher. There can be no doubt that those who loved him and wanted to learn from him were devastated. Then about 40 years later, further tragedy occurred when several members of a Jewish movement called the Zealots led a rebellion against the power of Rome. This "Great Revolt" (66 to 73 CE) was a disaster; it resulted in the destruction of the Jewish Temple and of Jerusalem itself, which was burned to the ground. The historian Josephus estimated that 1,100,000 Jews perished in the siege of Jerusalem alone. Galilee, where Jesus taught, was the home of the Jewish resistance and suffered badly — the Romans killed and pillaged without mercy. According to Josephus, "One could see the whole lake red with blood and covered with corpses, for not a man escaped."[7]

The Roman armies, in destroying Jerusalem and its Temple, effectively ended the revolt. By the time hostilities ceased with the fall of Masada in 73 CE, Judaism had lost its national home, its holy city, its Temple and its priesthood, and was struggling for survival. It had no spare capacity to put up with revisionist movements that would demand change and challenge the status quo.

By the year 65 CE, believers in Jesus and his message already lived in all the major cities of the eastern Roman Empire. Gradually separating themselves from the local Jewish communities, they formed their own separate groups. These early Christians met regularly in households of like-minded people, in a similar manner as was likely practiced by Jesus and his close circle of disciples. Apart from the practice of baptism, and the celebration of the Eucharist meal that probably took place in people's homes, they would have adhered to established Jewish customs. It's likely that they gathered together in small groups — each group initially centered around one of the apostles — to discuss the sayings and teaching of Jesus they could remember. As one contemporary study of this period suggests, "This early practice reflects an inner spiritual tradition still current in parts of the East, where, in addition to observing the external religious law, certain students also receive wisdom handed down through a chain of masters."[8]

These small groups — reminiscent, perhaps, of the Jewish *minyan* or the *halka* of the Sufis — developed independently, with the members' own memories of Jesus' teachings and stories of his life. Three centuries later, the New Testament Gospels we know today were deemed to contain the only authentic accounts of the life and teaching of Jesus. Suppression of documents outside this approved canon most probably led the early followers of Jesus to bury the more than 50 texts we mentioned earlier that were found in 1945 on a cliff at Nag Hammadi in Upper Egypt. Among these codices were other Gospels, such as the Gospel of Philip, the Gospel of Truth and the Gospel of Thomas. Most likely hidden by people who feared condemnation as heretics, they were not available in English until 1977.

Religious historian Elaine Pagels writes that the "living Jesus" of these texts "speaks of illusion and enlightenment, not of sin and repentance, like the Jesus of the New Testament. Instead of coming to save us from sin, he comes as a guide who opens access to spiritual understanding."[9]

The Gospel of Thomas contains no narrative, in it Jesus performs no physical miracles and fulfills no prophecies; yet it is invaluable for anyone wishing to get an idea of what Jesus taught. Some of the 114 Sayings in this gospel are similar to those included in the Synoptic Gospels but, as set down by Thomas, seem to have a more authentic voice. The concept of perceiving the "God within" and the "within without," which we've already spoken of, is expressed in the first two of these sayings:

> Jesus said, *That which you have will save you if you bring it forth from yourselves. That which you do not have within you [will] kill you if you do not have it within you."* (Saying 70)

> Jesus said, *If those who lead you say to you, 'See the kingdom is in the sky,' then the birds of the sky will precede you. If they say to you, 'It is in*

the sea,' then the fish will precede you. Rather, the kingdom is inside of you, and it is outside of you. When you come to know yourselves, then you will become known. And you will realize that it is you who are the sons of the living father. But if you will not know yourselves, you dwell in poverty and it is you who are that poverty. (Saying 3)

Jesus said, Recognize what is in your sight, and that which is hidden from you will become plain to you. For there is nothing hidden which will not become manifest. (Saying 5)

Jesus said, I shall give you what no eye has seen and what no ear has heard and what no hand has touched and what has never occurred to the human mind. (Saying 17)

Jesus said, There was a rich man who had much money. He said, 'I shall put my money to use so that I may sow, reap, plant, and fill my storehouse with produce, with the result that I shall lack nothing.' Such were his intentions, but that same night he died. Let him who has ears hear. (Saying 63)

Jesus said, Why have you come out into the desert? To see a reed shaken by the wind? And to see a man clothed in fine garments like your kings and your great men? Upon them are the fine garments, and they are unable to discern the truth. (Saying 78)

Jesus said, He who will drink from my mouth will become like me. I myself shall become he, and the things that are hidden will be revealed to him. (Saying 108)[10]

Saying 13 has a theme similar to Saying 108 but adds more to our understanding of the nature of Jesus' teaching. This translation is from *The Gnostic Gospels of Jesus*, by the late Marvin Meyer, an expert in the field:

Jesus said to his disciples, Compare me to something and tell me whom I am like.

Simon Peter said to him, You are like a righteous messenger.

Matthew said to him, You are like a wise philosopher.

Thomas said to him, Teacher, my mouth is utterly unable to say what you are like.

Jesus said, *I am not your teacher. Because you have drunk, you have become intoxicated from the bubbling spring which I have tended.*

And he took him, and withdrew, and spoke three sayings to him.

When Thomas came back to his friends they asked him, *What did Jesus say to you?*

Thomas said to them, *If I tell you one of the sayings he spoke to me, you will pick up rocks and stone me, and fire will come from the rocks and consume you.*

In this extract, only Thomas perceives and understands the unique and substantive quality of Jesus. In our terms, Jesus has higher consciousness; he is a transcendent "perfected man," able to live in both dimensions at the same time. Thomas knows that there are no words to adequately express this. Others have described it as equivalent to having, as it were, a separate organ of perception, a permanent "I," as being someone who is "awake" and has self-knowledge and through that clarity has knowledge of Reality. Jesus tells Thomas that he is not his teacher, because Thomas has understood and so developed this perceptive faculty himself: he, too, has knowledge of Objective Truth. They are "as one."

Pagels goes on to say: "This, I believe, is the symbolic meaning of attributing this gospel to Thomas, whose name means 'twin.' By encountering the 'living Jesus,' as Thomas suggests, one may come to recognize oneself and Jesus as, so to speak, identical twins."[11] As confirmation of this understanding and the way to it, Pagels includes an extract from the Book of Thomas the Contender, another text from the Syrian Thomas tradition also discovered at Nag Hammadi:

> *Since you are my twin and my true companion, examine yourself, and learn who you are. . . . Since you will be called my [twin], . . . although you do not understand it yet . . . you will be called 'the one who knows himself.' For whoever has not known himself knows nothing, but whoever has known himself has simultaneously come to know the depth of all things.*[12]

For students of higher consciousness, rules that are uniformly applied to everyone — for example, on feasting or fasting — are irrelevant and can even be counterproductive. One saying of Jesus, found in both the Gospel of Thomas and the Gospel of Matthew, sums this up:

> When you go into any land and walk about in the districts, if they receive you, eat what they will set before you, and heal the sick among them. For what goes into your mouth will not defile you, but that which issues from your mouth — it is that which will defile you. (Gospel of Thomas — Saying 14)[13]

> What goes into someone's mouth does not defile them, but what comes out of their mouth, that is what defiles them. (Matthew 15:11[NLT])

As we shall see in the next section, the transformative essence of Jesus' teachings went underground as Christianity moved westward.

Jesus' Message Moves West

To the West, Jesus' message — as understood by Saul of Tarsus (St. Paul) — was proclaimed as being universally applicable to all Gentiles, without regard to the strictures and customs of Jewish laws and traditions. Paul believed in a literal Kingdom of God on Earth, and that Jesus would return to it in triumph at any moment, or at least when enough people had entered the fold to be saved.

It is important to note that, as the Reverend John Shelby Spong has pointed out, very many Gentile converts lacked the Jewish background needed to understand the references or the context of many of the narratives in the New Testament.[14] The gospel stories include influences from traditions that were more familiar to the Jews, and were created and understood to be parables or metaphorical narratives.

Over time, these parables and narratives began to be taken literally — leading, many centuries later, to the great problem of literalism in the beliefs of many people today, especially in the U.S. So when, for example, the Gospel of John speaks of resurrection (meaning spiritual ascent), people took it literally, and, as sociologist Stephen K. Sanderson has pointed out, "things became considerably more complicated. If Jesus was God, and God was God, there would appear to be two Gods and thus a regression to a type of polytheism. How could this be? More than two centuries of debate ensued; there were many nuanced interpretations and many accusations of heresy. . . . To make a long story short, the view that won out was the doctrine of the Trinity that was formulated as the Nicene Creed in the early fourth century."[15]

The New Testament contains no explicit trinitarian doctrine, though it is thought that the concept was likely rooted in three aspects of Christian belief: in the Creator God of the Old Testament, in Jesus as the Resurrected One, and in Pentecost (when the Holy Spirit descended on the Apostles and other disciples following the Crucifixion). Some passages do refer to the Father, Son, and Holy Spirit as associated. For example, the command that Christians, "Go ye therefore, and teach all nations, baptizing them in the name of the Father, and of the Son, and of the Holy Ghost" (Matthew 28:19 [KJV]); and in the apostolic benediction: "The grace of the Lord Jesus Christ, and the love of God, and the communion of the Holy Ghost, be with you all." (2 Corinthians 13:13[KJV])

Early church fathers such as Basil, his brother Gregory of Nyssa, and Gregory of Nazianzus used the purposefully incomprehensible "Three as One "Trinity as a "teaching tool," an object of contemplation which helped early Christian initiates shift from the idea of God as a larger-than-life person, as were the gods of the ancient world, to the experience of *musterion* or divine mystery.[16] We'll expand on this later, but in our terms, meditation on the Trinity was used to activate the brain's second system, awakening a more comprehensive perception inaccessible through rational analysis.

Those Christian communities that had developed independently from the church of Rome, had beliefs and practices that were different, and a goodly number of gospels circulated, as noted by Bishop Irenaeus of Lyon, the leader of the Christian church at the end of the second century:

> The heretics boast that they have many more gospels than there really are. But really they don't have any gospels that aren't full of blasphemy. There actually are only four authentic gospels. And this is obviously true because there are four corners of the universe and there are four principal winds, and therefore there can be only four gospels that are authentic. These, besides, are written by Jesus' true followers.[17]

Makes sense — right? By the early fourth century, dogma and doctrine began to replace spiritual development. At the Council of Nicaea in 325 CE, the 27 books now included in the New Testament were first declared by the 300 bishops in attendance as being "God-breathed." Those 27 books, along with the 39 books of the Old Testament, make up the 66 books in the Holy Bible of today.

The earliest books in the New Testament are the Epistles of Paul, composed in the 50s CE — about two decades after the crucifixion. Scholars date Mark as the first Gospel, written around 70 CE — at least 35 years after Jesus' death. Then came the Gospels of Matthew and Luke which were composed independently in the 80s or 90s CE. Many of the narratives they contain were sourced from Mark; hence, the three are referred to as the Synoptic (Greek for "seen together") Gospels.

In spite of the Gospels' titles, their authors were actually anonymous, and they make no claim that they are writing literal eyewitness accounts or building on eyewitness testimony. What we would today view as plagiarism was common practice and perfectly acceptable at the time. The vast majority of people were illiterate, and stories were told, retold, embellished and absorbed into existing stories, with new ones added and subtracted to suit local circumstances, concerns and beliefs. We would thus expect the "Good News," or Gospels of the life and death of Jesus, to be similarly crafted. Scholars of the texts have pointed out that Matthew's Jesus resembles Moses, Luke's Jesus resembles a Greek philosopher, and John's Jesus embodies the Jewish ideal of Wisdom.

The Gospel of Mark, the first of the Synoptic Gospels, was probably written to strengthen the faith of the early Greek Christians in the face of persecution. As New Testament scholar Dennis R. MacDonald notes, "Its themes of travel, conflict with supernatural foes, suffering, and secrecy resonate with Homer's Odyssey and Greek romantic novels. Its focus on the character, identity, and death of a single individual reminds one of ancient biographies. Its dialogues, tragic outcome, and peculiar ending call to mind Greek drama. Some have suggested that the author created a new, mixed genre for narrating the life and death of Jesus."[18]

While the stories in the Synoptic Gospels are clearly related, only Matthew and Luke tell of the nativity of Jesus — though the two accounts differ considerably from each other. Mark tells nothing at all about the early life of Jesus. As Jesus scholars Marcus Borg and John Dominic Crossan explain, the birth stories are fictions. Each one acts as a "parabolic overture," a prologue of everything that is going to follow in that gospel. They were created independently and for entirely different audiences.[19]

Matthew's gospel was primarily for a Jewish-Christian audience. It echoes the best-known stories of the Hebrew Bible; for example, the story of the birth of Moses, in which Pharaoh orders that all children be killed, yet the infant Moses escapes. Matthew weaves a contemporary account — unsubstantiated elsewhere — in which the infant Jesus escapes Herod the Great's edict of infanticide. Matthew's "good news" is that Jesus is the new Moses, and the real King of the Jews — not Herod, who had been given that title by their Roman oppressors. Matthew is the only gospel to mention the wise men from the East who "saw his [Jesus'] star when it rose." (Matthew 2:2, [NIV]) Traditionally referred to as the Magi, these wise men would almost certainly have been understood to be Zoroastrian astronomer-priests.

The Gospel of Luke was written for the Gentiles living in the Greek cities of Asia Minor and in Greece itself, so the text is much more antagonistic toward the Jews. This gospel emphasizes the obligations of the rich to the poor, the outcasts and the marginalized. In this tale, the birth of Jesus is announced to nearby shepherds — a class of people who, Borg and Crossan point out, were ranked even lower than peasants in the social hierarchy.[20]

It's no surprise, then, that the genealogy of Jesus differs in these accounts. In order to establish that Jesus was the long-awaited Jewish messiah, the gospels of both Matthew and Luke say that he was "of the house of David," but they differ in the details from that point. They disagree on Joseph's lineage: Luke (3:23, [KJV]) describes Joseph as "the supposed father" of Jesus and as the son of Heli, whereas Matthew (1:16, [KJV]) describes Joseph as the "husband of Mary" and the son of Jacob. Both Matthew (1:18-25, [KJV]) and Luke (1:26-38, [KJV]) introduce the idea of a virgin birth, which if taken literally would create a problem. As biblical scholar Geza Vermes notes, Davidic descent is established through the paternal line, so "if in order to proclaim the virgin birth, they had to deny the real paternity of Joseph, they were unavoidably bound to undermine the royal messianic claim of Jesus.[21]

Paul, who wrote all of his epistles two or three decades before the Gospels of Luke and Matthew were written, never mentions the parents of Jesus, except to say that Jesus was "born of a woman" and "born under the law" (Gal. 4:4, [NIV]).

Christians may be familiar with the passage in *Isaiah* (7:14, [KJV]) that says *"Behold, a virgin shall conceive and bear a son, and shall call his name Immanuel,"* but they may well not know that the Hebrew word *ha'almah,* a feminine noun with a definite article, translates as "the young woman," not "a virgin." Most biblical scholars agree that it indicates "a young woman of marriageable age" (that is, old enough to bear a child), but has nothing to do with whether or not she is a virgin.

The Reverend John Shelby Spong's view is that the Gospel of John stems from a time when the excommunicated Jewish followers of Jesus had to define themselves, now that they were no longer part of the Jewish community. With all their norms disrupted, they are invited by John to look inward.[22]

In John events in the life of Jesus echo messianic images that any Jew of the time would have recognized. Moses parts the Red Sea; Jesus walks on water. Jesus even says *"For had ye believed Moses, ye would believe me: for he wrote of me"* (John 5.46, [KJV]) and, soon after saying this, he proceeds to multiply five barley loaves and two fishes so that they feed 5,000 people — with 12 baskets full of bread left over! It is a story reminiscent of Moses sustaining the children of Israel with manna in the Wilderness of Sin (Exodus 16:1-36).

"The Jesus John intends to illustrate," writes playwright and biblical scholar Tony Morinelli, "is nothing short of a mystical sage whose words and deeds are loaded with philosophical and theological implications. The Gospel of John is a work of metaphysics with Jesus as the enlightened sage."[23]

As Spong points out, John includes characters present nowhere else in the gospels. A prerequisite to higher consciousness is to "know thyself." Much like a number of the teaching stories of the Sufi tradition,[24] John's characters embody human foibles and can act as mirrors to encourage self-observation. John exhorts people not to use the scriptures to justify personal biases and behaviors, and not to believe in the literal interpretation of the many "signs" (miracles) he describes.

Spong suggests that the final edits to the Gospel of John occurred around 88 CE, once the followers of Jesus were excommunicated from the Jewish fold. Much like the change in thinking that occurred when the Jews were captive in Babylon, these early Christians, banished from their Jewish community, began to understand that their experience and understanding of Jesus and his message were both personal and of a transcendent, universal import. According to Spong, this more mystical approach enabled them to "pass beyond all tribal boundaries and to reach a new and transcendent sense of the reality of God."[25]

However, in the fourth century at Nicaea, the Christology question was adjudicated, the core dogma of the Christian faith determined and the concept of the Holy Trinity as the supreme deity officially adopted. The personal approach to wisdom was rejected, and Jesus became a literal part of the Godhead, no longer a human being.

Given the original message of the Gospel of John and the understanding of the original followers of Jesus, the agreed-upon Creed of Nicaea, after all the wrangling and intellectual arguments of those hundreds of clergymen, seems astonishing:

> We believe in one God, the Father, Almighty, maker of all things visible and invisible;
> And in one Lord Jesus Christ, the Son of God, begotten from the Father, only-begotten, that is, from the substance of the Father, God from God, light from light, true God from true God, begotten not made, of one substance with the Father, through whom all things came into being, things in heaven and things on earth, who because of us humans and because of our salvation came down and became incarnate, becoming human, suffered and rose on the third day, ascended to the heavens, will come to judge the living and the dead;
> And in the Holy Spirit.
> But as for those who say, 'There was when he was not' and 'Before being born he was not' and that 'He came into existence

out of nothing' or who asserts that the Son of God is of a different hypostasis or substance or is subject to alteration and change — these the Catholic and Apostolic church anathematizes.[26]

Just over a century later, in 431CE, the third Ecumenical Council of Ephesus attempted to seal shut the already closed door by declaring that "it is unlawful for any man to bring forward, or to write, or to compose a different Faith as a rival to that established by the holy Fathers assembled with the Holy Ghost in Nicaea."

Why Did Christianity Flourish?

So the question we asked ourselves in writing this book was: How did Christianity take the place not only of Judaism, but of the many pagan religions around at the time? It was a puzzle, as historian Wayne A. Meeks recognizes:

> Among the scores of religious sects that offered Eternal Hope or present ecstasy to the diverse peoples of the Roman Empire in the middle of the first century, Christianity was not conspicuous. An impartial observer asked which of these cults might someday become the official religion of the Empire, even a world religion, would perhaps have chosen Mithraism. He certainly would not have named the inconspicuous followers of a crucified Jew.[27]

But it did happen. Christianity grew rapidly during its first few centuries and has become one of the world's most successful religions today, with approximately two billion adherents. But what made it blossom in this unlikely soil? Many historians say that early Christianity had several selective advantages over its competitors — in short, it provided people with a "better offer."[28]

The Roman Empire's reach, influence and troops spread from modern Sudan in the south to the Scottish border in the north, from Morocco in the west to the Caspian Sea and Arabian Gulf in the east. It was a melting pot of cultures, each with its own stories, myths, legends and beliefs. Since religious expression was understood to be symbolic of a unified transcendence, a new sect or religion could be added, and any new ideas or rituals absorbed into their current beliefs. Numerous cults — such as those of Attis, Adonis, Dionysus and Venus — had their adherents. Greek and Roman gods mixed with the ancient gods of Egypt, and in the first century CE, Mithraism became extremely popular, particularly among soldiers.

Early Christians were skilled at adapting and absorbing the traditions and practices of their potential converts. Unlike Mithraism, Christianity was inclusive; it appealed to poor people who felt alienated from the mainstream religions, and to women (who were excluded from Mithraism).

Pauline Christianity was definitely a "better offer" than Judaism, which had then, and still has, many regulations and prohibitions that prospective Gentile Christians did not have to bother with or observe. Among those were the Jewish Law's stringent requirements: to read and be able to recite the Torah; to adhere to dietary restrictions, and to obey laws affecting one's person (even intimately, such as the circumcision requirement).

In contrast to the Old Testament with its sometimes wrathful, sometimes loving, often confusing and remote God, the early Christian scriptures were largely personal narratives about individual people and events in their lives; and since they were expressed plainly, they were easy to follow and to identify with. Christianity focused on a loving Son of God, who, although he performed miracles and was quite exceptional, was not a remote deity, but a personal savior, a role already familiar in the Mediterranean world.

Jews do not proselytize, and conversion to their religion is demanding, sometimes taking years of study. In contrast, Christians sought and welcomed converts. Anyone could become a Christian and by accepting Christ could enter the Kingdom of God. And there were real advantages: Christians believed that

Jesus' death and resurrection atoned for their sins and ensured their place with God, and that those who did not believe would go to Hell. Christians "knew" that they were right — and naturally tried to get others to believe too, and so be "saved."[29]

An important, but not often noted, factor was that Christians stressed nursing the sick, feeding the hungry, clothing the homeless and caring for the destitute. Just as they do today, early Christian societies set up orphanages, hospitals, almshouses, hostels and more, on a greater scale than did other religions. Because Christians nursed their sick, especially during major epidemics, their sick were perhaps more likely to survive, and this in itself could have motivated people to convert.[30] However, New Testament scholar Bart Ehrman suggests it's likely that the number of Christians who died from exposure to sickness because of these efforts would have decreased their overall population rather than increase it. His research leads him to understand that converts were attracted because "The Christians did amazing miracles." He notes that "Paul spoke of the 'signs and wonders' that he himself performed on the mission field (Romans 15:18–19); of the proofs of his message that came 'in demonstration of the Spirit and of power' (1 Corinthians 2:4); 'of the signs of a true apostle . . . performed among you with signs and wonders and miracles' (2 Corinthians 12:12)."[31] As Ehrman suggests, it's not that people had to personally experience these miracles, but that the repeated telling of miraculous deeds and happenings convinced outsiders that the Christian church was the best option, and led them to convert.

Saul of Tarsus, later named St. Paul, was certainly pivotal to the spreading of the early Christian faith among the Gentiles. Unlike the twelve Apostles, Paul never met Jesus, yet claimed a supernatural acquaintance with him, which he asserted gave him the authority to proselytize. Fueled by this conviction, Paul developed his own theology outside the Jewish-Christian community in Jerusalem.

Although Jewish by birth, Paul was instrumental in changing Christianity into a much less restricted, more cosmopolitan, outward-looking, proselytizing organization. He and others did this through relentless effort, skillful communication and affiliations, and a willingness to delete, adapt, compromise and absorb the traditions and predispositions of potential converts in order to save them.

In 391 CE, Theodosius the Great made Christianity the official state religion of Rome and completely banned worship at pagan temples, most of which were subsequently destroyed. This final, officially agreed-upon version of Christianity did not understand Jesus to be a living part of the continuum of reformers and inspired prophets — from Abraham, to Moses, to Hillel, to Jesus and later to Muhammad. Instead, the decision was to regard Jesus, after his death, not as an exceptional man of wisdom, a reformer and restorer of the original meaning of Judaism; in fact, not as a mortal human being at all, but as one who was God Himself. Instead of the (animal) blood sacrifices found in many religions, including the Judaism of Jesus' time, Jesus himself is sacrificed, so that his followers' sins might be expiated.

This is not to say that there have been no attempts at all at restitution and reform. St. Francis of Assisi reacted to the ecclesiastical and social corruption of his time by renouncing wealth, living a life of poverty and service. He sought to return to the example of Jesus, while remaining in the Church. The monk Martin Luther decried the supreme, unchecked authority of the Pope, the selling of indulgences, and other, even more awful, abuses of the 16th-century church. He was a rebel who decided that one did not need intermediaries, such as priests, in order to know God. Luther left the Church as it was — and, of course, we now have the Lutherans. And not all Protestants believe in a Trinity; Unitarians, as their name suggests, hold a monotheistic vision.

The long historical transition of Christianity from the "innovator's" life-changing spiritual pathway toward seeking God and thus Knowledge, to a bureaucracy bereft of deep understanding, offered enough perceived advantages to ensure its overwhelming success. Nevertheless, the search for and knowledge of the path to transcendence continued, though unremarked as a major historical event until the beginning of the seventh century.

On Consciousness in the Beginnings of Islam

The Arab world experienced a progression of belief — from worshiping multiple gods to worshiping One God — similar to that found in the Hebrew tradition. The Arabs' most important god, Allah, was always there, but was such a remote figure that He had very little influence in daily life.[32] Mecca was the place of their most important sanctuary, the Ka'ba. Its ancient origins are unknown, though the shrine was said to have been rebuilt by Abraham and his oldest son, Ishmael, from whom the Arabs claim descent. Since all accessible deities were represented in the Ka'ba, it was a place of annual pilgrimage for every Arab tribe. At one time there were said to be as many as 360 idols in and around the Ka'ba, including representations of religious figures such as Abraham, Jesus and Mary.[33]

For centuries, Arabs from all over the Arabian Peninsula had made annual pilgrimages to Mecca, performing their various traditional rites over a period of several days. The Quraysh, a leading tribe, controlled all of Mecca, including the Ka'ba, and established a nonviolent zone extending for 20 miles around the sanctuary that was *haram* (sacred, forbidden). This made Mecca a place that any tribe could enter without fear, and where everyone was free to practice both religion and commerce.

However, by the end of the sixth century CE, tribal conflict severely threatened the Arab world. Since the desert environment was so harsh, tribesmen traditionally shared their wealth — the Bedouin ideal was the *Karim*, the "Generous Hero" — but as opportunities for trade increased, an extreme competitiveness had taken over, with families seeking exclusive prestige and dominance. Those who fell behind were no longer protected, but were left exposed to destitution and misery. A state of mind prevailed that the Prophet Muhammad called *jahiliyyah* — which, according to Karen Armstrong, translates as "violent and explosive irascibility, arrogance, tribal chauvinism." This same word, *jahiliyyah*, would later be understood to mean the pre-Islamic historical period itself, often translated as the "Time of Ignorance."[34]

One response to this crisis was Hanifism, a practice that is equated with Sufism.[35] It arose in Mecca and spread throughout the Hijaz (western Saudi Arabia). Its members, as suggested by the definition of the word "hanif," "turned away from," or rejected, idolatry and sought *hanifiyyah*,[36] "pure religion." The myriad minor gods and idols that were in the Ka'ba needed to be destroyed. The true religion, the original monotheism of Abraham, the essential Truth that existed before the establishment of either Judaism or Christianity, had to be restored.

The Hanifs regularly spent time away from the pagan, polytheist environment, retreating to nearby mountains and hills to contemplate and pray, as did one of their number, Abū al-Qāsim Muhammad ibn Abd Allāh ibn Abd al-Muṭṭalib ibn Hāshim, who we know today as the Prophet Muhammad.

Muhammad was deeply troubled by *jahiliyyah*. Islamic tradition states that one day, when he was about 40 years old, he was alone and asleep in a cave on Mount Hira, when he saw before him, "like the brightness of the dawn," the Angel Gabriel, who commanded that he recite. Muhammad replied that he could not do so.

Then he took me and squeezed me vehemently and then let me go and repeated the order 'Recite.'

'I cannot recite' said I, and once again he squeezed me and let me go till I was exhausted.

Then he said, 'Recite.' I said, 'I cannot recite.'

*He squeezed me for a third time and then let me go and said:
'Recite in the name of your lord who created—*

From an embryo created the human.

*'Recite your lord is all-giving
Who taught by the pen
Taught the human what he did not know before*

*'The human being is a tyrant
He thinks his possessions make him secure
To your lord is the return of everything'* (Qur'an: 96:1-8)

From the traditional point of view, "God's words" were "spoken" directly to Muhammad, as they had been to the Old Testament prophets before him. A more modern understanding of his revelations might be that at those times, Muhammad experienced a transcendent state of higher consciousness that enabled him to understand a Reality "beyond words." "I cannot recite" would then indicate that the experience is impossible to put into words. As a Messenger of Allah, he would recite as much as he could through allegory and metaphor. Like Jesus, Muhammad saw a way to transform both society and the individual, and, through imagery and the richness of Qur'anic Arabic, he could address both. But, as Karen Armstrong has emphasized, "There was no question of a neutral simplistic reading of the scripture. Every single image, statement, and verse in the Qur'an is called an *ayat* ("sign," "symbol," "parable"), because we can speak of God only analogically."[37] Idries Shah suggests that the Qur'an is to be experienced on many levels, "each one of which has a meaning in accordance with the capacity for understanding of the reader."[38]

After his first revelation there was a gap of two years in which Muhammad received no further revelations, and he quite naturally doubted the veracity of the first one. After all, he was not from a distinguished clan, not a miracle worker, and not an impressive figure in the eyes of the Quraysh. Then a second vision occurred, this time revealing that those who experience the care of God have a duty to others "*. . . one who asks for help do not turn him away;*" (Qur'an 93.10) and Muhammad was clearly instructed to proclaim God's message: "*And the grace of your lord proclaim!*" (Qur'an 93.11).

As Muhammad experienced new revelations, people close to him learned them by heart, and those who were able to write them down did so, though these revelations would not be assembled into the Qur'an until 20 years after the Prophet's death.

In many traditional stories, there comes a point at which the protagonist, having gone through numerous hardships, continues to be faced with so many obstacles that he or she feels "all is lost." Then a breakthrough — either psychological or circumstantial — occurs. People working creatively on a challenging task of any kind have frequently reported experiencing despair prior to a breakthrough. This was so with Muhammad when, in 619, the "year of sadness," he lost not only his wife of 25 years, Khadija, but also his uncle and protector, the esteemed tribal chief Abu Talib. Not only was Muhammad devastated, but without his uncle's protection, he found himself in an extremely precarious situation. According to scholar Reza Aslan, "The results were immediate. Muhammad was openly abused on the streets of Mecca. He could no longer preach or pray in public. When he tried to do so, one person poured dirt over his head, and another threw a sheep's uterus at him."[39]

After Muhammad's first revelation, Khadija's elderly cousin Waraqa had warned him that his task would not be easy and that the Quraysh would eventually expel him from Mecca.

Muhammad had been dismayed at hearing this at the time, but almost 10 years later, it seemed inevitable. His message was dividing the families of Mecca, appealing above all to the young. Muhammad and his followers would have to take steps unheard of in the Arab world: They would have to leave their city, their tribe and their clan, leave their family ties and possessions, and go off into the desert to establish a new community.

Tradition states that one night, Muhammad was awakened by the Angel Gabriel and conveyed miraculously to the holy city of the Jews and Christians. The Qur'an refers only obliquely to this vision: *"Limitless in His glory is He who transported His servant by night from the Inviolable House of Worship (al masjid al-haram) to the Remote House of Worship (al-masjid al-aqsa) — the environs of which We had blessed — so that We might show him some of Our symbols (ayat)."* (Qur'an 17:1) Jerusalem is not mentioned by name, but later tradition associated the "Remote House" with the holy city of the "People of the Book."

Later Muslims, starting with the historian Ibn Ishaq in his eighth-century biography of Muhammad, began to piece it all together and create a more coherent narrative. Karen Armstrong suggests that "influenced perhaps by the stories told by Jewish mystics of their ascent through the seven heavens to the throne of God, [the writers] imagined their prophet making a similar spiritual flight."[40] According to the historian Tabari, Muhammad told his companions that he had once been taken by the angels Gabriel and Michael to meet his "fathers" — Adam (in the first heaven) and Abraham (in the seventh heaven) — and that he also saw his "brothers" Jesus, Enoch, Aaron, Moses and Joseph.[41]

Ibn Ishaq presents the event as a spiritual experience. He writes that Aisha, a later wife of the Prophet and daughter of the Prophet's companion Abu Bakr, said: *"The Prophet's body stayed where it was, but God transported his spirit by night."* Later historians such as Al-Tabari and Ibn Kathir describe the event as a physical journey, which many Muslims prefer to believe.

Whatever one's interpretation, the Night Journey of Muhammad is important. From his youth, the Prophet had been a unifier. Ibn Ishaq, in a memorable story, tells of the reconstruction of the Ka'ba when Muhammad was a boy. A quarrel broke out as to which Meccan clan should set the Black Stone into place in the eastern corner of the Ka'ba. The solution was to ask the first person who entered the sanctuary from outside to be the judge. The young Muhammad was the first to enter. He put the stone on a heavy cloth and had an elder from each clan take a part of the cloth to raise it and thus share in the task equally.

The Night Journey not only prepared the Prophet for the Hijra (the migration of the Believers from Mecca to Yathrib/Medina); more importantly, from this experience, he came to understand that the message he received from God was for all humanity. Muhammad was a unifier not only of the Arab tribes; but, as he proclaimed again and again, anyone who believed in the One True God could enter into a new community of unity among the Believers[42] and a unity with Him. "*[God] has established for you the same religion enjoined on Noah, on Abraham, on Moses, and on Jesus.*" (Qur'an 42:13).

The Qur'an addresses the challenge of diversity directly:

> *Unto every one of you have We appointed a different law and way of life. And if God had so willed, He could surely have made you all one single community: but He willed it otherwise in order to test you by means of what He has vouchsafed unto you. Vie, then, with one another in doing good works! Unto God you all must return and then He will make you truly understand all that on which you were wont to differ.* (Qur'an 5:48)

The Qur'an maintains that there is a unity of all the exponents of true spiritual insight, and an identical origin of each: "*. . . And there never was a people, without a warner having lived among them (in the past)*" (Qur'an 35:24). It calls on both Jews and Christians — "the People of the Book" — to unite in Truth: "*O People of the Book, let us arrive at a word that is common to us all: we worship God alone, we ascribe no partner to Him, and none of us takes others beside God as lords*" (Qur'an 3:64).

Muhammad worked to restore the original monotheistic faith of Abraham and the other prophets, whose messages had become misinterpreted or corrupted over time. His revelations confirmed that the God of the "People of the Book" was the one and only Allah, God of all humanity. The parallels between Islam and these older forms of monotheism reflect the continuation of the same revealed Wisdom that comes from the same God who "revealed His word" to Abraham, Moses, Jesus and other prophets. Humanity should honor Him and only Him in life and deed.

Reza Aslan observes that, since it is not possible to describe the transcendental experience in words, it is not surprising that there are, as he says, "striking similarities between the Christian and Qur'anic description of the Apocalypse, the Last Judgment, and the paradise awaiting those who have been saved." He points out that "these similarities do not contradict the Muslim belief that the Qur'an was divinely revealed, but they do indicate that the Qur'anic vision of the Last Days may have been revealed to the pagan Arabs *through a set of symbols and metaphors with which they were already familiar* thanks in some part to the wide spread of Christianity in the region [italics ours]."[43]

The Qur'an includes stories of Jesus that come from gospels banned from the New Testament canon in the fourth century and, for that reason, known as apocrypha ("things put away" or "things hidden"). They include the Gospel of Pseudo-Mathew, the Arabic Infancy Gospel, the Infancy Story of Thomas and the Gospel of James. The line of Christianity that the Qur'an connects to originates with the Jewish followers of Jesus, the group headed by Jesus' brother James and the apostle Peter.

Jesus appears in some 15 different chapters of the Qur'an, which emphatically declares that he is the Messiah. In the Qur'an, Moses, Jesus, Muhammad and all the other prophets are extraordinarily inspired reformers and lawgivers, but they are all human. None are supernatural, none the "son of God" in a literal sense, let alone God incarnate.

Both the Qur'an and the Torah are believed to have been revealed by God, and required to be recited by adherents. They both tell us about God, His creation of the world in seven days, His Laws and His prophets. Both Judaism and Islam stem from a time when social welfare fell under the charge of religion, so both have a strong tradition of religious law — Halakha in Judaism, Shariah in Islam. These laws cover the rules of personal observance (both call for male circumcision) and impose dietary rules prohibiting the consumption of animals considered not kosher (Jewish) or halal (Muslim); neither eats pork.

The pivotal difference between Judaism and Islam is that the Qur'an states that the Jewish people's long-awaited Messiah has already come and is Jesus of Nazareth. And the pivotal difference between Islam and Christianity is the Nicaean dogma: the doctrine of the Trinity, which holds that God is not one, but three coeternal, consubstantial persons or hypostases — the Father, the Son and the Holy Spirit — and that Jesus of Nazareth is that Son. The Qur'an strongly disagrees:

> People of the Book! Do not go to excess in your religion. Say nothing but the truth about God. The Messiah, Jesus son of Mary, was only the Messenger of God and His Word, which He cast into Mary, and a Spirit from Him. So have faith in God and His Messengers. Do not say, 'Three.' It is better that you stop. God is only One God. He is too Glorious to have a son. Everything in the heavens and in the earth belongs to Him. God suffices as a Guardian. The Messiah would never disdain to be a servant to God, nor would the angels near to Him. (Qur'an 4:171-172)

Neither Judaism nor Islam has a doctrine of the Trinity or anything like it; and neither religion accepts the doctrine of original sin or redemption. There is no mention of Saint Paul in the Qur'an, and the Christianity it relates to is certainly not Pauline. As we've discussed, Paul's focus was not on Jesus the Jewish Messiah, the man and his wisdom, a spiritual teacher whose teachings could revive, reform and liberate the somewhat decayed Jewish tradition of the time. It was centered on the death and resurrection of Jesus, the Christ, the deity. Paul was convinced that *"God presented Christ as a sacrifice of atonement, through the shedding of his blood"* (Romans 3:25 [NIV]), and insisted *"For what I received I passed on to you as of first importance: that Christ died for our sins according to the Scriptures"* (1 Corinthians 15:3 [NIV]).

In contrast, the Qur'an stipulates quite directly that *"no bearer of burdens will bear the burden of another"* (Qur'an 35:18 and 53:38), and that *"God requires not of anyone that which is beyond his capacity."* (Qur'an 2:287) As in the Qur'an, James, as leader of the early Jewish Christian community, strongly emphasizes that the works that one performs in life are the basis of one's validation in the sight of God: *"What doth it profit, my brethren, though a man say he hath faith, and have not works? Can faith save him?"* (Epistle of James 2:14 [KJV]). A similar idea, says Mary Boyce, began with Zoroaster: "According to him, salvation for the individual depended on the sum of his thoughts, words and deeds, and there could be no intervention, whether compassionate or capricious, by any divine Being to alter this."[44]

As far as we know, Jesus did not think of himself as forming a new religion. Neither did Muhammad, who never sought power nor took advantage of his situation or status: *"I am nothing but a warner and a herald of glad tidings unto people who will believe"* (Qur'an 7:188). Muhammad is referred to as the Messenger of God, *"But if they turn away from thee, O Prophet, remember that thy only duty is a clear delivery of the message entrusted to thee."* (Qur'an 16:82)

The original community centered around Muhammad sought the earlier, uncorrupted and pure form of monotheism, and they called themselves not Muslims but the "Believers" (*mu'minum*).[45] These Believers differentiated themselves from polytheism in all its forms: "*Those who say that God is the third of three, disbelieve; there is no god but the one God . . .*" (Qur'an 5:73). Christians, such as Arians or Nestorians, who had fled persecution for refusing to follow the Nicene doctrine were certainly welcome in the community of Believers, as were Jews who obeyed the laws of the Torah, and converts from paganism — anyone would be included who could truthfully declare the Shahada, the Muslim profession of faith, which states that "*There is no god but God. Muhammad is the messenger of God.*" In addition, Muhammad, like Jesus, and in common with many spiritual teachers, is generally understood to have had a special relationship with a small group of students whom he taught in private.

The Qur'an refers to Old Testament narratives and prophets such as Joseph, Jacob, Abraham and Moses, and New Testament figures such as Mary, Zachariah and Jesus. But as the historian and Islamic scholar Professor Fred Donner points out:

> They are told by the Qur'an not because they relate particular, unique episodes in the history of mankind or of a chosen people, but because they offer diverse examples illustrating the basic Qur'anic truths. . . . The lesson of every prophet is that there is an eternal moral choice — the choice between good and evil, belief and unbelief — faced by all people from Adam on in more or less the same form, and hence simply repeated generation after generation. . . . The apostles and prophets are not, in the Qur'anic presentation, successive links in a chain of historical evolution, each with a unique role in the story of the community's development, but merely repeated examples of an eternal truth, idealized models to be emulated.[46]

The sayings of Muhammad provide a picture of someone whose foremost concern, like that of Jesus, Hillel and other prophets, is to help humanity consciously evolve. It was time to develop a new perceptive capacity — which is only achievable when in a state of selflessness:

I order you to assist any oppressed person, whether he is a Moslem or not.

Do you think you love your Creator? Love your fellow-creature first.

Those who are crooked, and those who are stingy, and those who like to recount their favors upon others cannot enter Paradise.

By the One who holds my soul in His hand, a man does not believe until he loves for his neighbor or brother what he loves for himself.

You ask me to curse unbelievers. But I was not sent to curse.

Desire not the world, and God will love you. Desire not what others have, and they will love you.

Die before your death.

And, regarding the need to refresh spiritual tradition constantly:

The Prophet said: 'There will be a time when knowledge is absent.'

He was asked: 'How could knowledge become absent, when we repeat the Koran, and teach it to our children, and they will teach it to their children, until the day of requital?'

Muhammad replied: 'You amaze me . . . Do the Jews and the Christians not read the Torah and the Gospels without understanding anything of their real meaning?' [47]

The prophets of our major traditions had access to a stable higher consciousness which provided the insight and directed the action of their lives. Each understood his function included the need to reform, refresh and update his community's spiritual understanding and the religious practices which had ceased to serve an evolutionary purpose. With this common goal in mind, one could draw a straight line from Abraham, Moses and the other Jewish prophets to Jesus and his brother James and, finally, to Muhammad.

Idries Shah has observed:

It is this spirit and this claim to the essential unity of divine transmission which is what has been referred to as the 'secret doctrine.'

Unless this feeling about the Qur'an is conveyed correctly, the inevitable conclusions about the limited clash between church Christianity and formal Islam becomes the only frame of reference . . . [48]

La Convivencia – the Pursuit of Knowledge

"The practice of the Sufis is too sublime to have a formal beginning," says the Asrar el Qadim wa'l Qadim (*Secrets of the Past and Future*). But as long as one remembers that history is less important than the present and the future, there is a great deal to be learned from a review of the spread of the modern Sufi trend since it branched out from the areas which were Arabized nearly fourteen hundred years ago. By a glance at this period of development, the Sufis show how and why the message of self-perfection may be carried into every conceivable kind of society, irrespective of its nominal religious or social commitment.

Sufism is believed by its followers to be the inner, "secret" teaching that is concealed within every religion; and because its bases are in every human mind already, Sufic development must inevitably find its expression everywhere.

— IDRIES SHAH[49]

Within a hundred years after Muhammad's death in 632 CE, the Muslim Empire stretched from the Himalayas to the Pyrenees. As British physicist and author Jim Al-Khalili points out, it covered "an area larger in expanse than either the Roman Empire at its height or all the lands conquered and ruled by Alexander the Great."[50]

The Qur'an clearly states that there is "no compulsion in religion" (Qur'an 2:256) so — contrary to the views of some Christian historians — expanding the Muslim Empire did not mean that people who came under their jurisdiction were forced to convert to Islam. The Prophet had emphasized the importance of learning, insisting that: "The pursuit of knowledge is obligatory on every Muslim"[51] and that "the ink of the learned is holier than the blood of the martyr."[52] Islamic culture therefore favored learning and tolerance, resulting in a period of scientific and philosophical flourishing from the eighth to the 13th century known as the Islamic Golden Age. Although constantly beset with problems and political chaos, the period provided the freedom to search for truth, knowledge and understanding conducive to the visible activity of the Sufis.

In 750 CE the Abbasids overthrew the Umayyad Caliphate and moved the capital of the Empire from Damascus to Baghdad. During the reigns of the Abbasid caliphs Al-Mahdi and his son, the caliph Harun Al-Rashid — the same caliph who figures in *The Arabian Nights* — the city became a magnet for the greatest intellects of the time. Baghdad was home not only to Muslims but also to Christians, Jews, Hindus and Zoroastrians, attracting immigrants from the Middle East, Central Asia, Spain and beyond.

An academy called the House of Wisdom (*Bayt al-Hikmah*) was established by Harun Al-Rashid's son Abu Al-Abbas Abdallah ibn Harun al-Rashid, known by his regnal name, Al-Ma'mun. A great patron of science and scholarship, Al-Ma'mun went to considerable lengths to acquire Greek, Indian and Persian texts and set up a massive "Translation Movement" to have them translated into Arabic. By the seventh century, Muslims had already come into direct contact with the surviving Hellenistic cultures of the Near East, connecting, not only with Christian Syriac writers, scholars and scientists, but later with sources in the central and western Mediterranean. Most of the early Greek translations into Arabic were made by Christians from the many Greek texts that were already extant in Iraq in Syriac translations; additional texts were brought to Baghdad from Syria, Bactria, India, Persia and elsewhere. The Arabs were not passive caretakers who merely held Greek knowledge for later transmission to the West; rather, they took that knowledge and developed it further, in massive state-run enterprises that were carried out by some of the brightest minds in history.

From about the middle of the eighth century to the end of the 10th, almost all non-literary and non-historical secular Greek books that were available throughout the eastern Byzantine Empire and the Near East were translated into Arabic, which became the second classical language, after Greek. Among the works translated were many of the most important philosophical and scientific writings of the ancient world, including those by Galen, Hippocrates, Plato, Aristotle, Ptolemy, and Archimedes, as well as works in Sanskrit and Persian.[53] With the knowledge of papermaking recently arrived from China, translations could be made more easily and less expensively, and could be revised many times, each version correcting errors as the content became better understood.

The openminded approach to learning at that time was exemplified by Ishaq Al-Kindi of Basra. He applied philosophical thinking to Islam, emphasizing the importance of studying Aristotelian philosophy and not rejecting it, insisting that "we ought not to be embarrassed about appreciating the truth and obtaining it wherever it comes from, even if it comes from races distant and nations different from us. Nothing should be dearer to the seeker of truth than the truth itself, and there is no deterioration of the truth, nor belittling either of one who speaks it or conveys it."[54] Al-Kindi supervised the translation of numerous texts from Greek to Arabic. He was known as the "Philosopher of the Arabs," but he also wrote in other disciplines including mathematics, geography, music, medicine, astronomy and even cryptography.

When the Abbasids overthrew the Umayyad dynasty in 750, the deadly feud left the latter facing near extermination.

Luckily, one young Umayyad prince, Abd al-Rahman, escaped. With the help of those still loyal to the Umayyads he fled, eventually reaching Spain where he had Berber relatives on his mother's side. With loyal Umayyad help, he entered Cordoba (formerly Khordoba of the Visigoths) and became its ruler.

Having secured a power base, Abd al-Rahman I proclaimed himself the first Umayyad Emir of Andalusia and refused to recognize the Abbasid Caliphate in Baghdad. However, it was not until the early tenth century that his great-grandson established a center of learning to rival Baghdad.

Under Abd al-Rahman and his descendants, Cordoba became known as the "Ornament of the World," the capital of Al-Andalus – or Andalusia, as it is known today. For about a century beginning in 900, Al-Andalus was the most heavily populated area of Europe. Arabic philosophers, trained in the East, migrated there, and schools and libraries flourished. From 912 to 961, Caliph Abd al-Rahman III reigned as Emir of Cordoba and built a massive palace-library complex, the *Madinat al-Zahra*, near Cordoba, housing thousands of books. Hasdai Shaprut, the Jewish polymath, was not only a prominent advisor, physician and emissary of the caliph; he is also on record as traveling to Leon to treat the Christian king Sancho. Sephardic Jews engaged in explorations of philosophy and science, and created monumental legal codes and a revolution in poetry. One of the most prominent among them was Samuel ibn Nagrella (993–1056) a medieval Spanish Talmudic scholar, grammarian, philologist, soldier, merchant, politician and influential poet.

This *convivencia* (coming together) of cultures, religions, languages and brilliant minds in Muslim Spain changed the course of European history. As Steven Nightingale, author of *Granada: A Pomegranate in the Hand of God*, writes:

> It was a culture of preternatural brilliance, with its doctors and
> astronomers, poets and viziers, scholars, translators, poets, mystics,

and mathematicians. . . . By their work, these men shared the best of the science and philosophy present in one of the most advanced cultures in the history of the Mediterranean: a recent evaluation among historians places Al-Andalus at its zenith no fewer than four centuries ahead of Latin Europe. The texts they translated are a crucial part of the foundation of the Renaissance. It is impossible to imagine the rapid development of the West in science, culture, and commerce without just this gift of knowledge.[55]

In effect, the achievement of Arab civilization at its peak may be best described by the Arabic inscription on the wall of Abd al-Rahman's Great Mosque in Cordoba: "It embodied what came before. Illuminated what came after."

The Madinat al-Zahra library and palace complex was destroyed in 1009, when Cordoba was besieged by fundamentalist Berber troops. The Umayyad Caliphate ended in 1031, which led to the formation of multiple city-states, or *taifas*. The Christian ruler Alfonso VI of Leon and Castile conquered the Taifa of Toledo in 1085, an act that also provoked an invasion from the Berber Almoravids, which Alfonso would spend the remainder of his reign resisting. Alfonso allowed the Muslim inhabitants to practice their religion, though he exacted heavy financial tributes in return. For a short while religious tolerance in the region was such that even the synagogue (later church) of Santa Maria la Blanca was shared, with Jews using it on Saturdays, Christians on Sundays and Muslims on Fridays.

In the first quarter of the twelfth century, key locations of translation work included cities in Spain such as Barcelona, Tarazona, Segovia, and Pamplona. In Sicily, Roger II and his son William I preserved Arab and Greek culture. Translations from Greek and Arabic into Latin were made by such notable figures as Henry Aristippus, Admiral Eugenius, the monk Filagato Ceramide and Adelard of Bath. Beyond the Pyrenees were translation centers at Toulouse, Beziers, Narbonne, and Marseilles. Eminent translators include Plato of Tivoli, Robert of Chester and Herman of Carinthia with his pupil Rudolf of Bruges; Hugh of Santalla in Aragon, Robert of Ketton in Navarre and Robert of Chester in Segovia.

As the medieval scholar Maria Rosa Menocal points out, "It was by way of Toledo that the rest of Europe—Latin Christendom—finally had full access to the vast body of philosophical and scientific materials translated from Greek into Arabic in the Abbasid capital of Baghdad during the previous several hundred years."[56]

From 1126 to 1151, some three centuries after the Translation Movement in Baghdad, Archbishop Raymond of Toledo founded Toledo's School of Translators at the city's cathedral to promote the translation of philosophical and religious works from Arabic into Latin. In the thirteenth century, under Alfonso X, known as "the Learned" and "the wise," the work of Toledo's School of Translators translated works from Arabic into Castilian rather than into Latin, thus laying the foundations for the spread of the modern Spanish language. Alfonso sponsored the creation of the Alfonsine astronomical tables, updating the tables that had been generated in Baghdad and had been translated by Gerard of Cremona from the Arabic.

Mutamid, the last ruler of the Taifa of Seville, sought help from the fundamentalist Muslim Almoravids, and for the next 150 years, the taifas came under their control, followed by that of the Almohads, preventing the fall of Al-Andalus to the Iberian Christian kingdoms.

Eventually the Almohads were defeated by Ferdinand III of Castile, with Cordoba falling in 1236, Valencia in 1238 and Seville in 1248. The last Arabic ruler in Spanish territory was Abu abu Allah Muhammad XII (also known as Boabdil) of the Emirate of Granada, who formally gave up his sovereignty and territories to the Crown of Castile in 1492. Under Ferdinand II and Isabella I of Aragon and Castile, Muslims were pushed out of the Iberian Peninsula, and conversions to Christianity were forced on Jews and Muslims alike.

The luminaries who contributed to the work of the House of Wisdom and to the flourishing culture of Al-Andalus spoke multiple languages and were polymaths, with their knowledge and abilities spanning many different fields including science, medicine, mathematics, architecture, philosophy and poetry. They were geniuses, many still today recognized as major Sufi masters. The Persian Omar Khayyam, author of the famous "Rubaiyat" was not only a poet, but an astronomer, philosopher and a mathematician (he was the first to write the complete theory of cubic equations). El-Ghazali of Khurasan, known in the West as Algazel, is considered one of the most prominent and influential thinkers. His works influenced St. Francis of Assisi, Thomas Aquinas, Pascal and others. He pointed out that "those who are learned may be, and often are, stupid as well, and can be bigoted, obsessed. He affirms that, in addition to having information and being able to reproduce it, there is such a thing as knowledge, which happens to be a higher form of human thought. The habit of confusing opinion with knowledge, a habit which is to be met with every day at the current time, Ghazali regards as an epidemic disease."[57]

Amad ibn Rushd, known in the West as Averroes, wrote commentaries on all of Aristotle's works as well as on Plato's *Republic*, which he also translated. Averroes' many books were studied in Europe and initiated an intellectual revolution in philosophy, education and theology. One of the world's most important philosophers, he argued that religion and philosophy are not incompatible but, on the contrary, work together. "Truth does not contradict truth," he said.

As Idries Shah notes, "The pathways into Sufic thinking are, it is traditionally said, almost as varied as the number of Sufis in existence."[58] Throughout the vast Islamic world, Sufis adapted their approach to the needs of the particular communities in which they lived, teaching through architecture, music, dancing and works of literature. Among their number are Sufi teachers whose extraordinary poems, narratives and teaching stories continue to influence the world today — giants such as Jalaluddin Rumi, Saadi of Shiraz, Fariduddin Attar, Nizami, Hafiz, Jami, and Ibn el-Arabi, who, as you'll recall, intuitively understood the premise of *God 4.0* eight hundred years ago!

"It is from this background" says Shah, that "the Sufi mystics became known in the West, and they maintained a current of teaching which links people of intuition from the Far East to the farthest West."[59] He points out that the development of Islamic civilization in the Middle Ages enabled an expanded contact between "indwelling otherworldliness streams of all peoples"[60] — beyond the small, exclusive groups of the ancient world.

FOR FURTHER READING

After the New Testament: 100-300 C.E.: A Reader in Early Christianity, 2nd Ed., Bart D. Ehrman, Oxford Univ. Press, 2015.

The Authentic Gospel of Jesus, Geza Vermes, Penguin, 2004.

Beyond Belief: The Secret Gospel of Thomas, Elaine Pagels, Random House, 2003.

Bible Myths, and Their Parallels in Other Religions, Thomas Doane, Amazon & Cosimos Classic Reprints, 2007.

Caravan of Dreams, Idries Shah, Octagon Press, 1967 (original edition).

The Case for God, Karen Armstrong, Random House, 2010.

The Evolution of God, Robert Wright, Little, Brown & Co., 2009.

The Gnostic Gospels, Elaine Pagels, Vintage Books, 1979.

Granada: A Pomegranate in the Hand of God, Steven Nightingale, Counterpoint Press, 2015.

The Great Transformation: The Beginning of Our Religious Traditions, Karen Armstrong, Anchor Books, 2007.

The First Christmas: What the Gospels Really Teach About Jesus's Birth, Marcus Borg & John Domini Crossan, Harper Collins Publishers, Inc., 2009.

The History of God: The 4000-Year Quest of Judaism, Christianity and Islam, Karen Armstrong, Random House, 1993.

The House of Wisdom: How Arabic Science Saved Ancient Knowledge and Gave Us the Renaissance, Jim Al-Khalili, The Penguin Press, 2011.

How Jesus Became God: The Exaltation of a Jewish Preacher from Galilee, Bart D. Ehrman, Harper One, 2014.

The Islamic Jesus: How the King of the Jews Became a Prophet of the Muslims, Mustafa Akyol, St. Martin's Press, 2017.

Jesus: Nativity – Passion – Resurrection, Geza Vermes, Penguin, 2008.

Jesus and the Zealots, S.G.F. Brandon, Charles Scribner's Sons, 1967.

Muhammad: A Prophet of our Time, Karen Armstrong, Harper One, 2007.

Muhammad and the Believers: At the Origins of Islam, Fred McGraw Donner, Harvard Univ. Press, 2010.

No God But God: The Origins, Evolution, and Future of Islam, Reza Aslan, Random House, 2005.

The Prophet Muhammad: A Biography, Barnaby Rogerson, Abacus, 2003.

The Rise of Christianity: How the Obscure, Marginal Jesus Movement Became the Dominant Religious Force in the Western World in a Few Centuries, Rodney Stark, Harper, 1997.

The Sins of Scripture, John Shelby Spong, HarperOne, reprint edition, 2009.

The Sufis, Idries Shah, Anchor Books, 1971.

The Triumph of Christianity: How a Forbidden Religion Swept the World, Bart D. Ehrman, Simon & Schuster, 2018.

Zoroastrians: Their Religious Beliefs and Practices, Mary Boyce, Routledge (Taylor & Francis), 2001.

SECTION THREE:

Understanding Conscious Evolution

5

The Psychological Foundations Of Spiritual Experience

Our normal waking consciousness, rational consciousness as we call it, is but one special type of
consciousness, whilst all about it, parted from it by
the filmiest of screens, there lie potential forms of
consciousness entirely different. We may go through
life without suspecting their existence; but apply the
requisite stimulus, and at a touch they are there in all
their completeness, definite types of mentality which
probably somewhere have their field of application
and adaptation.

— WILLIAM JAMES[1]

So far, this book has been a review of the history of
humanity's search for a transcendental experience, its
special function in all societies and its higher manifestation
in the major prophets of the three major monotheistic religions
and the spiritual teachers who followed them.

So what actually goes on inside our minds when we experience altered states of consciousness? Why is that experience so similar in all peoples, in all societies and all over the world? What new evidence do we have of the neuropsychology of "higher experience"?

The Neurophysiology of Everyday – Is Our Reality Really Real?

Everyone has essentially the same basic brain structure. The reason we all experience the world in the specific ways that we do is because our bodies, genes and nervous systems are built the way they are, and because of the way we evolved.

Based on what we now know about the mind's workings, we can safely say that our everyday experience is *not*, in fact, "reality." Rather, our ordinary awareness is a "virtual reality" — a personal construction, something computed within our minds, not a full or accurate registration of what is outside.

In fact, human sensory systems serve mainly for data *reduction*. From the limited, tiny fraction of information and energy that passes through our senses, we are continuously making up a virtual reality inside our brain.

While our eyes can transmit to the brain a vast display of colors, shapes and movements, it's nothing compared with what is going on outside of us. Only a miniscule amount — as little as one-trillionth — of the outside ambient energy that strikes the eye gets passed through to the brain. The cells in the retina and in the occipital cortex translate this small sample as the experience of light, and they code its different wavelengths as colors. Sensing may be carried out with the help of our senses, but it actually takes place in the brain.

One interesting way to observe this in action is with a "Benham's disk" — a small circular diagram or spinning top that contains swaths of black and white. When you spin it, you see colors — usually red and green. There is no color in the disk itself, so what has happened? The black and white segments, at certain speeds, produce the same neural code that the eye sends to the brain for information about color. (You can find video demonstrations of this spinning disk online.) We don't — can't — see color or the world directly. In the same manner, only a tiny fragment of the vibrations in the air that reach the ear are selected, coded and sent to the brain to finally become the experience of sound. The brain makes it all up and calls it "reality." Although this may seem very, very strange, "strange" is actually the norm.

Since our reality evolved to ensure our survival, it of course has to have some correspondence with the external world, even on a miniscule basis. We are, after all, successful in being able to hold a coffee pot and pour coffee into a cup rather than over our hand, or to hear and respond to the cries of a hungry infant.

Each organism has evolved a sensory system and a nervous system to select what it needs to get through the day in its neighborhood. If you are a plant, you don't need to know much, really; if you are a frog, a few items reach your senses; a cat, more items; a bonobo, much more; and we humans, more still. All of these "small worlds," though different, are not arbitrary; they are virtual adaptations of external reality that evolved for the survival needs of each organism.

The "reality" each organism lives inside — whether it is our own or that of ants, cows and, for all we know, grass — is a virtual one.

Experiments on frogs first showed that no matter how enormous the variety of visual stimuli presented to the frog, its eyes process only four types of visual activity, each one relevant to its survival needs. Similar, if more sophisticated, versions of this kind of limited processing have been found in cats and monkeys.

More complicated organisms have a greater capacity to "retune" their sensory systems and adapt to changed circumstances. A person who puts on optical lenses that make the world appear upside-down can reorient quite quickly and, within just a few weeks, can even negotiate traffic on a bike while wearing the lenses. Many kids in very poor schools share books, and some easily adapt to reading upside-down.

The human nervous system is optimized to create a set of a few selections and connections from the many to allow us to live a safe and ordered life in the mundane, safe, "small world" that our brains limit for us. Living, or at least surviving, maintains this belief in a small world.

Because our brains are all organized in this way, we all perceive aspects of this world in the same way: We all see the sky, the moon, the ground and the sun, and many beliefs and myths are common to all of us. The three-tiered cosmos is an example we've already discussed: a Heaven above us, life on the ground, and the dangerous and hellish stuff below.

Think of the mind, then, not as reflecting a complete reality, but operating as a device that selects a few parts of the outside reality that are important for our survival and safety, making contact with the world like an elaborate set of cat's whiskers, physical antennae that touch parts of the world so that the cat can navigate.

There's no real reason to consider these neuropsychological complexities and limitations when we're all involved in the comings and goings of everyday life. That's the point of the automatic filtering and highlighting: it keeps us unaware of all the work going on behind the scenes. We blink our eyes about nine or 10 times each minute, all day, every day. This goes on constantly, except when we're asleep. Last week, you blinked about 50,000 times; last year, several million times. And each time your vision is blocked, it goes completely black for a moment. But you're not normally aware of this. What happens to those black moments — all of the millions of them during a lifetime? And think about your nose: If you look ahead carefully, you'll see it's that thing at the bottom of your field of vision — but why didn't you see it before? And in a few moments, your nose will fade from view once again.

At the end of the retina, there are cells that transmit signals to the brain's visual cortex. All the axons from the eye's ganglion cells leave the eye at the same point, where they are bundled together to form the optic nerve. But these cells, like the terminus of wires in a wall, take up some space. This tiny spot where the ganglion cells exit the eye on the way to the brain has no photoreceptor cells, so it doesn't respond to light. We are not normally aware of this "blind spot" because, paradoxically we always never miss it! The blind spots and the thicket of blood vessels in our eyes ultimately don't interfere with our perception of the outside world. Because they are always present, we never "mind" them.

If we did not filter out all this extraneous information, we would be flooded by it and be so overwhelmed that we would be unable to attend to critical input that might determine our safety and survival. So this "ignorance" is continuous and adaptive.

Sometimes referred to as an "illusion," our limited world and its continuous ignorance are what many esoteric or religious traditions say we need to shun or transcend in order to approach a higher wisdom.

The Imaginal World

Our construction of reality using this miniscule amount of information from the outside world is further modified by the mix of our memories and imagination. We live in an Imaginal World, a virtual "Imaginarium" that's rich with the stories provided by our culture and the stories we tell ourselves. Some people hold the struggles and the image of the Ascension of Jesus as the central elements in their lives. Shia Muslims celebrate the death of Hussein ibn Ali, a grandson of Muhammad, in an annual ritual of self-flagellation known as Ashura, memorializing the martyrdom of their venerated saint with the tearing of garments and cutting of flesh. Even though it is now one and a half thousand years later, some remnants of that event still fills the imagination of between 154 and 200 million people today and shapes their view of the world and themselves.

Others of us live with passed-down memories of more recent events: the holocaust; the "Middle Passage" of slave ships; the conquest of India or America; the success of an ancestor's company, invention, or courageous endeavor. All of it, everything in our mind, along with our sense of our family, our childhood, our past and future struggles, and all of our beliefs — religious or otherwise — inhabits our Imaginarium, defining how we understand and feel about the world.

The "World" at "Sunset"

Most of us love watching the sunset. On vacations in Hawaii, we (RO and SMO) often would go out to Ke'e Beach in Kauai to watch the sunset at, as we would say, "the end of western civilization." It's spectacular to see the red globe descend and disappear into the water. One evening, we sat near a family whose three-year-old asked, "Where did the Sun go? Is it drown-ded? Will it come back?"

In reality, this little girl expressed humankind's historically widespread view about the Sun's "movements." About 50 years earlier, when a freight ship on which I (RO) was working had docked in Lisbon, Portugal, I travelled out of the city to what, a millennium ago, was thought to be the end of (Western) civilization: Cabo da Roca, the Cape Point. There, one could see the blood-red Sun drown in the limitless Atlantic Ocean, just as it does in the Pacific Ocean in Kauai. The Romans called this point *Promontorium Sacrum* ("Holy Promontory"), the "Edge of the World" — a mystical whirlpool where the setting Sun sank down in the immense ocean.

The Sun disappears daily everywhere, not always into the deep green or blue water. For more than five centuries, we've known that the Sun isn't "setting," just as we know that it's not being quenched by water. It's the Earth, revolving on its axis at a speed close to 1,000 miles per hour that is the reality we "see" as the movement of the Sun. Yet we still call it a sun*set*.*

So why transcend the "obvious reality" of sunrises and sunsets? Our imaginal beliefs and explanations have consequences, based as they are on our very limited perception and understanding of "reality." We believe they are real and act accordingly. However, not knowing what is really going on has been the cause of conflict, wars and cultural divides, and now may even threaten humanity's survival. This is all due to our failure to appreciate the limits of our senses, the selective nature of our everyday consciousness, and our potential for developing a higher, more comprehensive, more connected form of perception and consciousness.

So, it's not a real world we experience but, a set of signals, carefully evolved and curated from much of what's outside. As T.S. Eliot said in *Four Quartets*, "You are the music while the music lasts." This "illusion" or "small world" that we live inside is controlled and is limited by the mind's barriers and filters, which evolved to ensure our survival. We can't have just any old illusion of what's happening or we'd walk into buses and tigers would have eaten our ancestors. But the experience we do have

---

*See Addendum: Chapter 5, Note #1

of life is more like connecting the dots in a constellation to form an image of a bird, an ancestor, a dipper (large or small) or even a god, than it is a comprehensive map.

It is this limited world, this "illusion," that, as many spiritual spiritual teachers have counseled, interferes with a more complete perception.

As the philosopher Aldous Huxley noted, "To make biological survival possible, Mind at Large has to be funneled through the reducing valve of the brain and nervous system. What comes out at the other end is a measly trickle of the kind of consciousness which will help us to stay alive on the surface of this particular planet."[2]

Simplicity in Understanding Our Minds and the World

The other night I (RO) had a long conversation with my father. It was a pretty dull one; we were — interminably, it seemed — going over house-renovation details and comparing the memories we each had of car trips to Canada that we took when I was a child, and he was describing his recent fishing trip to Minnesota with Vladimir Putin. When I woke up, it was considerably more interesting, because my father died in 1989. We all experience these kinds of extraordinary visions in our dreams. But because dreams happen nightly, by day we mostly disregard them, they're ordinary.

The achievement of the human mind is to have stability in a world where there is constant change. As adults, we experience our "world" as stable. We arise aware that we are in the room where we slept in the dark last night; that the streets outside are the same as they were, the town is the same, and we speak the same language. But it isn't always so in a person's life; the "world" of the young child is not so stable, nor is that of the teenager. Stability is something that we develop as we age.

There's a lot of work behind the scenes to make this happen, and it comes at great cost: We have to simplify, overgeneralize, ignore and make assumptions. It's a constant that much of our experience is edited out scene by scene, moment by moment, feature by feature. Remember: You haven't seen your nose lately, nor are you aware of what happens, thousands of times per day, when you blink and the world doesn't disappear into a black nothingness.

Our mental state actually changes radically during the day, each day — for example, when we dream or daydream, or in the hypnagogic state between sleep and wakefulness. The experience is so common that the resulting revisions and "program changes" are unremarked.

But some individuals have more extreme experiences: Some might see auras around other people while having a migraine; others can be blinded by an internally generated experience of bright light, as can happen in a seizure. Without a modern, scientific understanding of the causes, it would be easy to conclude there was something spooky or "mystical" going on.

God on High: Why Is It High, Anyway?

With the same brain structure as our ancestors, we modern human beings have the same responses to soaring structures, cataclysms, meteors, earthquakes, deaths and dreams — all of which affect our mental life and, especially, our sense of organization and meaning in the world. For instance, we experience objects and events when they are "high" in space as more positive and more meaningful. "Heaven" refers both to the stars way above us in the sky, and to a paradise that's high up there and attained — some devoutly hope — after death. Why is this?

There is considerable evidence to indicate that human beings, more than other animals, have evolved the ability to see well beyond the self and, in the process, to take a longer view and connect at a deeper level with others. It's likely that these changes were precipitated by our shift from moving around on all fours to standing and walking on two feet. We could then routinely look outward or upward, rather than just straight ahead at a low level or downward, and this enabled a huge change in perspective. It formed a basis, in due course, for a more encompassing awareness that extended beyond the immediate locale.

Fred Previc, a researcher in sensory and physiological psychology and cognitive neuroscience at the United States Air Force Research Laboratory, offers important information that sheds light on this. He finds that the connection between the physical ability to look outward and upward, and the more abstract ability to envisage other realms beyond ours — taking the "long view," in both senses of the term — is enabled by high levels of the brain neurotransmitter dopamine.

Dopamine — which is found in almost all creatures, going right back to lizards and reptiles that lived tens of millions of years ago — appears to play a leading role in processing what is going on at a distance. For instance, dopamine stimulates a whole host of upward-directed movements — rearing up, climbing, jumping, and making upward head and eye movements. But in humans, upward-directedness has also fostered the development of abstract thought and the ability to reason and plan, which give us the ability, literally and metaphorically, to raise our sights.

Drugs (such as cocaine) that increase dopamine transmission may produce euphoric effects and increase arousal. In humans, excess dopamine is often associated with delusions and hallucinations, and its raised levels may explain the upward eye movements that occur during dreaming, meditation, hypnosis and even seizures.

Try to recall a breathtaking view from high above, and the literal insight it presents to your surroundings. Sitting atop a mountain or on a high hill and looking down, you can see events and objects that on ground level appear as separate, but that from your high vantage point appear connected, forming whole patterns of activity that aren't perceptible lower down. Getting vertical distance from events makes them organized and unified — as, nowadays, a satellite view can give us information on rain that might arrive in an hour, even though nothing down on the ground indicates it.

Religious experiences represent the extension of this ordinary sense of distant space and time into abstract and cosmic realms. Both the ordinary and extended experiences are underpinned by the same brain pathways and mechanisms that oversee our movement in 3-D space.[3]

Another way to say this is that "higher states of consciousness" are a neuropsychological phenomenon scaffolded upon our awareness of distant space (and time) and the brain systems that mediate it. As we've seen, in most societies, there is a conception of a "three-tiered" cosmos consisting of a life below us, our mundane realm in the middle and an aspirational one "above" — Hell, Earth and Heaven. Temples such as those of the Maya are built on this concept, as are churches and mosques to this day. Why? It's because of our brain structure. Unsurprisingly, then, the earliest worship systems seem to have been related to the cosmos; the Lascaux caves, the oracular sites of ancient Greece, and the temples of the Neolithic period all suggest this.

God is known as the "Most High" or is considered to reside in the "High Heavens." People actually gaze upward to indicate Heaven's location. The "nurture" we receive — our family, education and cultural training — encourages a belief in a Heaven above and a Hell below, and prompts the way our temples are built "on high" so we imagine that they "elevate" us. Pairing God with a high vertical location is common and long-standing throughout Christian history. For example, since the sixth century, the Catholic Mass has often included the singing or reading of a hymn entitled "Glory to God in the Highest," while it is understood that the devil resides deep down below the Earth. In religious myths, humanity is thought to have descended from a previous high point, and the aim is to return to this elevated place.

Psalms 113:4 (New King James Version [NKJV]) tells us that *"The Lord is high above all nations, and his glory above the heavens."* Recall that the "Sorcerer" in the "Sanctuary" at the cave of Les Trois Frères, which was visited by the paleontologist Herbert Kühn, was drawn by someone very, very far above the ground—higher than it seems possible for anyone at that time to have reached.

Jesus' Ascension is an essential tenet of Christianity. Others went Up There, too. The prophet Elijah *"went up by a whirlwind into heaven"* (II Kings 2:11 [KJV]); Enoch was *"taken up so that he would not see death"* (Hebrews 11:5 [KJV]); Moses had to go way up and then come way down from Mount Nebo on the top of Pisgah to present the Ten Commandments. The Greek gods lived and cavorted high on Mount Olympus; the Nordic gods are usually found hanging out in the heights of Valhalla.

The Development of "Higher" Authority

Our personal understanding of "up" and "down" includes complicated associations that all develop from infancy. We grow "up" in a world where the sky above is limitless and is often filled with light, but the ground below is close, sometimes dirty, and can contain threats. People of authority are always higher than we are as children, and we literally and metaphorically "look up" to them.

Psychologist Jon Tolaas points out that, as babies, we are lying down and our orientation is the "above" — upward and up. Light, from windows or artificial sources, typically comes down from above. We learn that the source of light is "up." Those who deliver warmth, food and caresses are up there, above our view, in the light. A baby is often lifted up and learns that wellbeing and happiness are up.[4] Once babies can stand, they see things from a "higher" perspective.

This common early experience primes us to judge things that are higher as being more developed, more authoritative and better: highborn, high caste, high status, high income, your highness, and "higher" consciousnesses.

When we become erect and grow to adulthood, says Tolaas, "we continue our upward journey in a kind of magnified value perspective modeled on the experiences of the early child–parent relationship. We see this most clearly in religious metaphors." He points out that the word "religion" is derived from the Latin for "tied to." "We are tied to something or someone higher than us, transcending our everyday existence. . . . We are in the sway of the Almighty and Superior, who looks down at us from where light begins and ends — Heaven."[5]

The Holy Ghost is often depicted as a dove and angels as winged, shining beings of light. The ability to see upward and beyond ourselves has become connected in all cultures with what is positive and good. Good things get a thumbs-up, while bad things get a thumbs-down. We talk approvingly of people being farsighted, upwardly mobile, upstanding, high-minded and uplifted. We climb up the ladder, aim high, hit the top spot, ascend the organizational chart and rise to the pinnacle of success.

When we are babies, we are literally down, and everything is above us; later on in life, being down becomes associated with dependence, inferiority (low in status), helplessness. We even say "I'm down today" when feeling sad. Just as "up" is about control, "down" is about being controlled, subjected, subdued. As a baby learns to stand, falling down is about failure. Metaphorically, we refer to problems in contractual negotiations as "stumbling blocks," refer to shaky governments as "tottering," and so on.

What is down is grubby, and lowering ourselves is part of our common metaphor. We sink under burdens, drop our standards, become downcast and downtrodden, receive low blows, hit below the belt, reach rock-bottom, and plumb the depths of despair. And when we are depressed, we are not only down but turned inward.

Many important religious events involve ascension and/or elevation. A significant event in Christian theology is the Transfiguration when Jesus speaks to the spirits of Elijah and Moses on a mountaintop; in the highly significant Night Journey, Muhammad is lifted into the sky on a mythical winged horse to visit Jerusalem and then Heaven. Jesus is depicted high on the cross when he's crucified on a hill outside Jerusalem's city walls; angels seem to inhabit upper space, whence they may fly down to Earth for particular purposes. Thought of as the world's first astronomers, the Aboriginal people of Australia believed that the sky was the repository of all moral stories.

The Egyptians revered astronomer-priests; and their pyramids, pointing high into the sky, had both astronomical and religious significance; Mesopotamia's massive ziggurats connected heaven and earth, each providing a temporal dwelling for the city's patron god. Buildings across all religions, including major mosques, temples and cathedrals, extend into the sky; and monasteries tend to be built on mountainsides and hilltops rather than in valleys. Even famous mountains throughout the world, such as Fuji, Kilimanjaro, Olympus, Sinai and Shasta, have been imbued with sacred properties; and military pilots and astronauts sometimes claim to sense or experience God when flying.[6]

Conversely, negative concepts in religion — most notably Hell, Hades and so forth — have "downward" connotations. When we are prone or supine, we are helpless, worthless. Snakes, wriggling along on the ground, are often associated with evil in the Bible and are viewed as harmful in real life.

Shadowy creatures that inhabit the darkness, such as bats, have a negative image. Even darkness itself (more prevalent in lower space) is usually represented negatively, as a cover for thieves and ne'er-do-wells.

Psychologists have shown that these sorts of connections aren't just metaphorical, but are grounded in the mechanics of how we perceive and interact with our world. When we refer to our own person, the expression "below the belt" is often used to describe not only unfair experiences, but also things that are hurtful, naughty, dirty, or even dangerous. Below the belt is where there's not only the unclean waste that we need to get clear of, but also the sexual impulses that can lead to conflict and disease as well as fun and family. So growing up, seeing the sky above, the Earth below and the dangers below that — including insects and snakes — leads to a "higher is better" sensibility. In religion, "down" easily becomes associated with Hell, the Inferno or Hades.

We even think things are more important and significant, and "better," if they are displayed higher rather than lower. This is not only true in churches but, surprisingly, also on computer screens. People more quickly identify a word as positive if it is presented in a high position on a screen, while the reverse is true for words identified as negative.[7] Seeing things generally as more positive, more desirable and better when presented to us higher up is part of the way our brains are constructed. We automatically associate "high" with good — and, of course, "good" with "God."

The connection between looking down and despairing is not metaphorical, either. The more neurotic or depressed people were found to be, the quicker they were at detecting targets presented in the lower part of a computer screen.[8]

Since "up" is related to perception of power, it would seem to make sense that there would be an upward bias in societies with dominant religions involving an Almighty. Brian Meier of Gettysburg College in Pennsylvania, and his team, set out to discover whether the common linking of "high" with God and "low" with the devil merely represent metaphors that aid communication or are indicative of something deeper: the way our brain categorizes and stores information (the latter being their hunch).

They devised experiments to find out. First, they determined whether people implicitly associated "up" with God and "down" with the Devil. They found that people with a stronger personal belief in God showed a stronger tendency toward this association. Participants were faster at recognizing the words when God-related words were presented higher on the computer screen and Devil-related words lower. They also remembered the God-images as being presented higher on the screen and the Devil-images being lower on the screen than they actually were, with neutral images showing no such bias.

Further studies explored whether people thought strangers, whose images randomly flashed up at the top or bottom of a screen, believed in God or not. The higher up on the screen the faces were presented, the more likely their owners were deemed to be strong believers.

Meier and colleagues concluded, "...we obtained results that are consistent ... with the ... idea that representation of the divine versus profane 'borrows' from the vertical domain of perception."[9]

Awe, Some (and Belief)

Awe is the beginning of wisdom. — RABBI HESCHEL[10]

... if you believe in the awe and the wonder, and the mystery, then that is what God is. ... It's not the bearded guy in the sky. — OPRAH WINFREY[11]

... there are elements, which seem to mock at all human control: the earth, which quakes and is torn apart and buries all human life and its works; water, which deluges and drowns everything in a turmoil; storms, which blow everything before them. . . . With these forces nature rises up against us, majestic, cruel and inexorable; she brings to our mind once more our weakness and helplessness. — SIGMUND FREUD[12]

Have you ever gawked at the amazing show of the Northern Lights; or sat outside on a dark night looking at the stars, far from civilization, and perhaps saw a meteor shooting by; or been caught in a lightning storm?

An archaic meaning of "awful" is "inspiring reverential wonder or fear." Imagine being almost alone at night in the vast, dense darkness; or in the day, living under a limitless sky that sometimes drops objects to earth. We began in an awe-some world, indeed. Five thousand years ago, meteor strikes were much more common than they are today[13] — so much so that 2,700 years before iron smelting appeared in Egypt, Egyptian royalty wore iron beads and trinkets, which were harvested from fallen meteorites and known as the "metal of Heaven."[14] The sky was alive to people back then and was part of every moment of waking life, day and night.*

Awe is a feeling of wonder we experience when faced with something unfathomably vast or incomprehensively marvelous — such as panoramic vistas, the incredibleness of nature, childbirth, and great works of art.

Awe involves a sense of perceptual vastness and a jump outside our usual frame of reference. Psychologists Dacher Keltner and Jonathan Haidt propose that we feel awe in the presence of vastness in nature — mountains, vistas, storms: ". . . nature-produced awe involves a diminished self, the giving way of previous conceptual distinctions (e.g., between master and servant) and the sensed presence of a higher power . . . Natural objects that are vast in relation to the self . . . are more likely to produce awe."[15]

---

*See Addendum: Chapter 5: Note #2

The experience of awe engages a sense of timelessness, as during peak athletic performances and spiritual or mystical experiences.[16] Even people accustomed to looking at the wonders of nature report this sense of awe. In 2012, an interviewer asked David Attenborough, perhaps the most prominent TV director and presenter of the natural world, "You do exhibit awe, the type of emotion perhaps someone might display entering a very grand Florentine cathedral, for example. But it's not a religious awe that you are showing, is it?" "Isn't it?" Attenborough replied.[17]

Awe — from the caves of the Paleolithic Era to today's churches and mosques, from lightning to waterfalls to the vastness of the sky — always seems to raise us up, the higher the better. And what could be more awe-some than experiencing the vastness of outer space? Russian cosmonauts have noted the rush of an unusual, positive energy, "a sense of the soul's freedom as never before, also an exceptional awareness of their second 'Ego,' a connection to all peoples and a feeling of love for mankind in general. It is remarkable that, in space, people recall the past, and realize that inner freedom is life's essence."[18]

Experiencing awe slows our personal sense of time and, as a result, increases our perception of how much time is available, a step in the direction of believing in eternity. It can result in a diminishment of the individual self and its concerns, and an increase in prosocial behaviors such as generosity and compassion.[19] It also reduces impatience, which can lead to more prosocial and other positive behaviors, such as the willingness to volunteer our time.[20] The opposite — feeling pressed for time — has a negative impact on people's willingness to stop to help others in need. Experiencing awe causes a change in brain function to release a more selfless, transcendental consciousness.

Whether strongly positive or threatening (as in a huge storm), experiences of awe decrease our tolerance for uncertainty.[21] This blend of fear and wonder increases our tendency and motivation to look for patterns, to make sense of the world around us. It stimulates and increases the belief that there is a purpose in everything, which we may not understand or see.

Calamities and Disasters

Our belief in God changes in the face of calamities and disasters, whether natural or manmade. One reaction is to give up belief in any kind of higher power — as some have done, for instance, after terrorist attacks. People may think "God failed us" or "There can't be a God if He let something as terrible as this happen." But studies generally seem to support the conclusion that tragedy strengthens belief. For instance, researchers have discovered that religious faith becomes more appealing after reminders of tragic suffering and death.

One study that provides clear insight into whether people turn to, or away from, God after experiencing a natural calamity is The New Zealand Attitudes and Values Study. This 20-year-long national study began in 2009 with between 6,000 and 18,000 people responding to annual surveys of factors such as social attitudes, religious beliefs and health outcomes.

On February 22, 2011, during the second year of the study, a destructive earthquake measuring 6.3 on the Richter scale erupted near the city of Christchurch, causing massive damage and killing about 200 people. Church spires crashed down; the phone system, the power lines and the water and sewage systems were disrupted; and many emergency services were overtaxed — including hospitals, which lost power just when they began to be flooded with patients.

The fact that the earthquake occurred between the 2010 and 2011 survey points offered an unprecedented opportunity to examine how a natural disaster of that magnitude affected religious commitments. Psychologists were able to compare the beliefs of people in the Christchurch area before and after the quake, and to compare those beliefs with those of other New Zealanders, to determine whether people affected by the earthquake were more likely to believe in God.

Since 1996 a continual and steady drop in religious faith across New Zealand had been documented prior to this study. The first three surveys in 2009-2011 showed that this reduction continued for the country as a whole after the earthquake with a decline in believers of 0.9 percent per year over the 3-year period. But in 2011, people in the earthquake area went in the opposite direction: Their faith increased.

The authors of the study write: "This result shows that the steady erosion of religious faith observed throughout New Zealand for the last forty years was dramatically reversed among those most directly impacted by the Christchurch earthquakes."[22]

The Bible had this down correctly:

> *After the wind there was an earthquake, but the Lord was not in the earthquake. After the earthquake came a fire, but the Lord was not in the fire. And after the fire came a gentle whisper.... Then a voice said to him, "What are you doing here, Elijah?"* (1 Kings 19:11–13, [NIV])

FOR FURTHER READING

Civilizations: Ten Thousand Years of Ancient History, Jane McIntosh and Clint Twist, BBC Book Pub., 2003.

MindReal: How the Mind Creates its Own Virtual Reality, Robert Ornstein, Malor Books, 2008.

Multimind: a New Way of Looking at Human Behavior, Robert Ornstein, Malor Books, 2014.

The Dopaminergic Mind in Human Evolution and History, Fred Previc. New York, NY: Cambridge University Press (2009).

6

The Secreted Second System Of Cognition And Insight

A person can attain pure freedom only by being set
free from being a person.

— Naoki Higashida*

Trouble in Mind, and in Discovering Activity Inside the Brain

The brain is difficult to study. It is extremely complex, and it is protected like nothing else in the body — both by external factors such as our thick skull, and by internal factors like the blood-brain barrier, which filters out threats to the brain's workings. This makes it complicated to get the correct and precise measure of brain states.

First of all, brains are individual; not everything in the brain is in the exact same place in everybody. We said earlier that all human beings have the same brain structure, but there are differences — just as there are differences in arm length

---

*Mr. Higashida writes about his autism in *Time* magazine, July 13, 2017.

— that distinguish people from one another. Perhaps the best analogy is the human face: We can recognize anyone we know immediately, and one could say all human beings have the same general facial configuration, in the sense that everybody has a forehead above the brow, two eyes below the brow, a nose below that, and downwards to a mouth and a chin. But such a description would not help you recognize your blind date.

I (RO) was lucky enough, when I was a post-doctoral fellow at the Langley-Porter Neuropsychiatric Institute, to work with neurosurgeon Bert Feinstein at the University of California Medical Center in San Francisco on a project in which he was implanting electrodes in patients who were to undergo brain surgery to check cognitive functions in the brain areas where he was going to operate. As part of the project, I had to examine about a dozen brains from donors' cadavers, to ensure that our placement of electrodes was as accurate as possible. These brains were all arranged on a table in a cold room, and each time I entered, their shapes became more familiar, as do faces. I asked one of the interns to show me a few of them when they were unidentified, and I found I got them all correct, as did she. The bulges, promontories and sulci (grooves or furrows on the brain's surface) were all different enough, as are our facial eccentricities. So in studying the brain, we never really have "the" brain, we only have "a" brain, which can make some interpretations jumbled.

In looking for evidence on our topic, it's best to focus the analysis on one kind of brain cell, one area, and to only focus on results from specific localized brain damage, brain stimulation and brain deactivation. Activation of one area of the brain may increase or decrease activation in other areas. For instance, the frontal lobe is involved in concentration and attention, and is connected with the thalamus, posterior superior parietal lobe and limbic system (mainly the amygdala and hippocampus). The limbic system is where feelings, emotions, and states such as ecstasy are processed. Measures of cerebral blood flow reveal that the deeper people go in meditation or prayer, the more active the frontal lobe and the limbic system become. And when the frontal lobe is activated during meditation, the parietal lobe, which is responsible for temporal-spatial orientation, becomes *less* activated.[1]

One early tool used for study was the electroencephalogram (EEG), which measures the tiny electrical voltage that reaches the scalp from different areas of the brain. In the 1970s, my colleagues and I, using a very early version of the EEG, were able to demonstrate that in ordinary people, the two halves of the brain operate differently in different situations — such as reading and writing versus spatial tasks like arranging blocks to match a pattern.

But the EEG provides a gross measure. And even the much more elaborate systems used today record only the tiny electrical voltages that emanate from the brain and reach the scalp. In neurological space, the scalp is very far away from the brain underneath — not to mention the fact that there's a thick skull and other layers of defense between the two. Interpreting these faint recordings is tricky — it's a bit like trying to determine a city's activity from a satellite recording of noise generated in different parts of town.

Other brain activation measures have been developed in the last 40 years, such as the colorful positron emission tomography (PET) scans and magnetic resonance imaging (MRI), but they have been criticized for purporting to show more than is justified, and the results are often not repeatable and sometimes contradictory.

The reason PET and MRI scans are not as useful as they could be for our purposes is that these studies don't present a situation that is in any way representative of normal circumstances, since the person has to lie down inside a closed, whirring scanner and, perhaps, be shown pictures of events while in there. It is a weird situation, and there's no way to know whether the brain patterns in these scanners would resemble the patterns in ordinary life, nor what the person inside the machine is really thinking about and experiencing. This is very different from using a PET scan to, say, search for the location of a lesion or a stroke, both of which are defined and don't depend on the momentarily subjective state of the person in the scanner.

Since we are focusing on an alteration of consciousness beyond our normal limited "world" and outside time and space as we know it, most important for our story are the brain's parietal areas, especially the area in the right hemisphere. The parietal lobes, one in each hemisphere, sit in the cerebral cortex, behind the frontal lobes (which are mainly concerned with cognitive functions) and above the temporal lobes (concerned with auditory processing) and the occipital lobes (primarily responsible for vision). Our parietal lobes deal with sensory information, enabling us to identify where we are being touched, for instance, and to tell the difference between sensations such as heat, cold and pain. They also have a role in visuospatial attention, cognition and recognition, spatial orientation, coordination of movement, visual perception, speech, reading, writing, working memory and mathematical calculation.[2]

Indeed, pioneering behavioral neurologist Norman Geschwind dubbed the parietal lobes "the association area of association areas," because they manage information from so many sense modalities. The parietal lobes are thought to differ in function from the brain's left side to its right side more than do any of the other lobes, which is highly relevant for our story.[3]

Connecting Time and Space

Once upon a time, long, long ago, in a place . . .

. . .

. . .

. . . right next to us . . .

Why is it so surprising that the place mentioned as being "long, long" ago in the lines above is "right next" to us? It could have been anywhere, but we automatically reckon that something "long, long ago" has to be, somehow, "far, far away."

Why couldn't something that happened long ago just as well be near us? Or right here? Or anywhere at all? By any ordinary logic, there would seem to be no reason for time and space to always be linked in this way. Of course, the reason is not logical, but biological: The brain's processing of information not only about space and time, but also about the presence and number of objects, all takes place in one part of the right hemisphere.

In everyday life, we think and talk about time, space, things and quantity in isolation. Neuroscientists mostly do the same; they study temporal perception, spatial and object perception, and mathematical cognition separately and individually. But this doesn't mean that the four are actually separate in the brain. That's not the way the brain works, nor would it be an efficient system if it were. Instead of having separate mechanisms, there is a general system in the brain to deal with information on time, space, number and other parameters such as speed — because all these data need to be coordinated so that we can take the correct action (such as grasping a moving object).

A main function of the parietal cortex — especially in the right hemisphere, is to receive information and to code and synchronize "how far, how fast, what and how much, how long and how many" for the myriad things that are going on in the world, in order to prepare for possible action.

Knowing where we are in space, location and time is vital for our sense of self and for successful action in life. It seems reasonable that these functions would have evolved to be close to each other inside the brain so that they could quickly coordinate together. It is the parietal lobe area of the brain's right hemisphere that is extensively involved with these processes, for space, location, time and quantity to be used in concert. It correlates our movement, body position in the world and location of the body's components (we never have to think "where is my right arm?" when picking up a fork).

Here's a description by two neuroscientists of the real-life situation that the brain has to handle:

> There is no such thing as getting to the right place at the wrong time — shaking hands, kissing, catching, throwing, playing an instrument, gathering kindling or paying by cash all require spatio-temporal coordination. Behaviour may be spatial or temporal in a laboratory, but in the real world they originate in the same coordinate system applied to all magnitudes.[4]

We sometimes use space and time interchangeably; for example, the phrase "he needs some space now," when referring to a relationship, can mean that he's going to be taking time off from it. The brain treats these two dimensions together.

People get disoriented when there is interference to the right parietal area. The intrusion breaks off one's normal and necessary ability to orient in space, to know where one is, where and how one is moving, where one's limbs are. Such brain interference can cause strange experiences. For instance, in one study, perceived "out-of-body experiences" were linked to faults in the normal integration of the sensory information that this area provides.[5]

Time, space, quantity and other magnitudes, such as size and brightness, activate overlapping regions in the brain's right parietal lobe (RPL). Several studies using transcranial magnetic stimulation (TMS) have shown that stimulation of the parietal lobes in humans interferes with our perception of space and also disrupts our connectedness to society and our ability to understand others.[6]

This same area of the brain is also important in time perception, so that time and space experiences may coincide. One study involving a patient who had difficulty when seeing objects in the left side of space (controlled by the right hemisphere) also found evidence of confusion and mix-ups judging time.[7]

The parietal cortex — again, largely but not exclusively the lobe in the right hemisphere — also handles judgments such as "more than/less than," "higher than/lower than" and "faster than/slower than." So a young child learns how space, time, speed, size and quantity of events and objects are highly correlated — which is important to know when negotiating the environment. Number tasks may activate both parietal lobes: The RPL is concerned with the kinds of number tasks that involve estimation or comparison rather than exact calculation, for which language is needed.[8]

Scores of studies confirm that spatial, temporal and social distance all have a common nexus of connection, one that is accessed automatically by the mind, even when one mode or the other (say, space or time) is not relevant to the task at hand. We refer to a close friendship, a distant relative, the near future and the distant past, because "The degree to which information is removed from our current experience in time, space, or the extent to which it refers to someone else carries a common meaning with important implications for the perceiver: proximity for action and, thus, how concretely or abstractly it should be construed."[9]

When people are shown photos of a landscape containing an arrow pointing to a point close to the viewer or far away along with a word such as "tomorrow," "we," "year" or "maybe," and are then asked to indicate whether the arrow pointed to a far or near location, they are quicker to respond correctly when there is distance congruence—the spatially distant arrow contained a spatially distant word and vice versa.

"Far, far, away" jumps up the brain's queue when "long, long" ago is mentioned.

Again, from the two neuroscientists:

> The parietal cortex is already equipped with an analogue system for action that computes 'more than–less than,' 'faster–slower,' 'nearer–farther,' 'bigger–smaller,' and it is on these abilities that discrete numerical abilities [which come later] hitched an evolutionary ride.[10]

Both children and adults confuse magnitudes at times. Children often judge a bigger train to be running faster than a smaller train, even when told that the trains are travelling at the same speed. And, when asked to estimate the length of time that two lights were presented to them, children thought the bigger or brighter of the two lights was shown longer. Adults make similar misjudgments: In one study, when the numeral 5 was presented with another numeral alongside it, the adult subjects thought that the lesser numeral was presented for a shorter time than the 5, and that the greater one was there longer. And — back to our story — we are likely to imagine that something "far away" happened long ago.*

The Parietal Lobes and Transcending the Self, Objects, Time and Space

The parietal lobes are concerned with sense of self, placing oneself in relation to all the different kinds of information — sights, sounds, time and objects — that we experience. Since these are all connected (the sound of a train and its movement in space; the sight of a ball we need to catch, its speed and the timing of its movements; and thousands of other things), then it makes sense that damage or other means of "disabling" the lobes—especially to the right side—might cause us to lose track of the sense of self.

---

*See Addendum: Chapter 6

The right parietal lobe (RPL) is associated with defining or perceiving the self, including distinguishing it from not-self. Disabling it can lead to a connection with things "beyond the self," which is often experienced as a mystical state.[11] When people with brain damage in their RPL are studied, they report more transcendental experiences and develop beliefs to explain them. When this brain area is inactivated with electrical stimulation, the same thing occurs.

So *decreased* RPL functioning due to either traumatic brain injury or selective suppression can lead to an experience of transcendence. Neuroscientist Brick Johnstone and his colleagues studied 26 patients with severe traumatic brain injury and found that those with weaker RPL functioning experienced greater spiritual transcendence.[12] In a follow-up study, the researchers write:

> If individuals focus less on time, space, and relationships, the concept of the self becomes less salient. If one has diminished awareness of the self in terms of time, space, and/or relationships, the question arises as to what one is aware of? We propose that this selflessness, which can be learned and achieved through meditative and prayerful practices or experienced after brain injury or surgery to the RPL, allows individuals to focus on and emotionally connect with things beyond the self which is the very definition of self-transcendence.[13]

Why then does RPL-based selflessness sometimes show up as spirituality rather than, as in some people, obvious pathology? Of course, this most importantly depends upon the severity and placement of the brain damage, but if that damage isn't complete or devastating, then the person's interpretation of the experience has partly to do with perspective — personal relationships, religious/spiritual orientation and so on. Additionally the sense of transcendence experienced will likely reflect religious and cultural beliefs and practices — connection with the Void (Buddhists), or with Jesus (Christians) or with the Virgin Mary (Catholics). This happens in the same way as we develop language, learning to speak the one that is prevalent in our culture.

Johnstone and his colleagues note that:

> This continuum ranges on one end as a sense of connection with the beauty of nature/art/music (losing a sense of self while listening to a favorite piece of music), to romantic love with others, becoming one with your soul mate, to an ultimate transcendence that has been described as a trance state that involves the complete breakdown between a sense of the self and a complete connection with God/the universe.[14]

Another study investigated self-transcendence (ST), defined by the researchers as "the enduring tendency . . . to identify the self as an integral part of the universe as a whole."[15] The study compared ST scores before and after brain surgery, so as to observe possible changes in ST induced by specific brain lesions. It was found that damage to parietal areas may induce unusually fast changes toward a sense of transcendence of one's self. The researchers concluded, "Thus, dysfunctional parietal neural activity may underpin altered spiritual and religious attitudes and behaviors."[16]

Schizophrenia and autism are at extreme ends of a single spectrum[17] and both involve abnormalities in parietal lobe functioning.[18] People with schizophrenia have an inflated or all-encompassing sense of self, while people with autism have a diminished sense of self. Psychiatrist Karl Jaspers quotes comments from schizophrenics, such as "Every single thing 'means' something. . . . There is a connection to everything that happens — no coincidences."[19] Jaspers cites a key characteristic of schizophrenia: "The self is identified with the All. [The patient's] own life is experienced as the life of the whole world."[20]

Daniel Paul Schreber, a schizophrenic man who wrote an account of his own psychosis, believed he "became in a way for

God the only human being, or simply the human being around whom everything turns, to whom everything that happens must be related and who, therefore, from his own point of view must also relate all things to himself."[21] Others have reported feeling unable to distinguish themselves from others. Theirs is an exaggerated self-consciousness, the opposite of the diminished one of people with autism.

People with schizophrenia often find it difficult to integrate incoming information into a coherent pattern. One patient said that he saw the strap, face and hands of his watch but struggled to put them together to make one whole. Or there may be a loosening of associations, a feeling that everything is related to everybody or connected to ancestors. Or there may be a blunting of sensation — most marked in the experience of pain, in which the parietal is uniquely involved. Body awareness distortions — including "out-of-body experiences," as we noted — are the province of the parietal lobes and are very common in schizophrenia.

Very young autistic children often mix up the pronouns "you" and "I," using them indiscriminately, and may talk of themselves in the third person. In her autobiography, one autistic woman described an instance from her childhood when she was beaten up; coming home with her face crisscrossed with bloody scratches and looking at it with fascination in the mirror, as if it were nothing much to do with her.

Another autistic person said, "Autism makes me feel sometimes that I have no self at all, and I feel so overwhelmed by the presence of other people that I cannot find myself."[22] Autistics are unselfconscious, too, in the sense that they are disarmingly straightforward, with no dissembling. They can observe, from the outside, the "falseness" in others that comes from playing the social game and having personal agendas.

In *Autism and the Edges of the Known World*,[23] Olga Bogdashina notes that people with autism very often cannot filter sensory input and are made dizzy by the overload of information. This sensory flooding may lead to self-imposed sensory deprivation as a form of protection. Autistics who have written about their experiences often speak of a "knowing" — a sense of clairvoyance or telepathy or precognition, or even a sense of God, or a sense of themselves "being God." Quite a number of studies have found parietal lobe abnormalities to be central to autism. In one study, magnetic resonance imaging (MRI) showed abnormality in the parietal lobes in 43 percent of 21 healthy autistic people between the ages of six and 32. Other MRI studies in autism have demonstrated abnormalities in the parietal lobes and in the posterior sub-regions of the corpus callosum, where the fibers that connect the left and right parietal cortical lobes are concentrated.[24] One study involved MRI imaging of 51 autistic patients, aged from three to 42. It found a reduced size of the corpus callosum in the regions where parietal lobe fibers are known to project, indicating reduced function in the parietal area.[25]

The parietal lobes usually sort and integrate all arriving sensory information, but when they are not functioning, the individual may be flooded with stimuli and have hallucinations. In short, many distorted sensations and beliefs about self are due to under- or over-activation of the parietal lobes, especially the right parietal. This sensory disruption may also make noises seem louder, colors brighter and touch sharper.

While we have learned much from studying brain damage and stimulation, as well as disorders such as schizophrenia and autism, it's important to emphasize — in considering the neurological bases of human experience — that changes in brain functioning don't necessarily yield delusions, and aren't a sidebar, but can be an adaptive bypass of ordinary consciousness. The organization and breakup of the normal right parietal functioning explains why some people describe a "spiritual" state as being "outside of space and time."

The recent body of research addressing the personality of people seeking spiritual experiences has found that such people do not pursue them for neurotic or emotional compensation. In a paper entitled "Unusual but Sound Minds," the authors conclude: "Overall, this study has shown that individuals engaged with modern spirituality, who are often regarded as odd or eccentric because of their unusual perceptions and ideas, are mentally healthy. There is no indication that they possess an insecure or avoidant attachment style, and they are content with their level of social support."[26]

The Idling Brain and the Self

> It is the brain's preferred state of being, one that it returns to literally the second it has a chance.
>
> — MATTHEW LIEBERMAN[27]

After a momentary look at the underlying neuropsychology, it's surprising to find that some of the most important brain networks involved in social cognition are *more* activated when we are doing nothing — a time when most of the other neural networks are idle! Termed "the default mode network" (DMN), this is an innate system that operates like a reflex, prompting us to think about ourselves and our social world.

Think of the DMN as the brain's "background state" or "resting state," or the brain's "idling system," giving the sense that the brain is just plopping itself down on a hammock after a tough day at the office. It's important to remember that whenever our brains get a moment off "work," they go all social to get ready for what comes next in our relations with others. Activation of the DMN stimulates us to "mind-wander," to self-reflect and think about other people's thoughts and objectives.[28]

The DMN was discovered in 2001 by Marcus Raichle[29], a neurologist at Washington University in St. Louis, and since then has become the focus of much interest, research and discussion in the field of neuroscience. Even two-day-old infants' brains show activation of the DMN; it is not seen in premature infants, which means it probably turns on when, or just after, we are born. Social connection ensures an infant's survival; his or her safety and physiological needs are dependent on it. The brains of human newborns are only one-quarter the size of adult brains, so most of our brain development happens after birth, when the child is immersed in its culture and environment.

Along with other brain structures, such as the thalamus, pons, and cerebellum, the DMN connects the cortex to the older brain structures, such as the limbic system and the hippocampus. It is the center of the imaginal part of our life: the home, so-to-speak, of our Imaginarium. It activates when no sensory information from the world demands our attention, and there are no mental tasks we need to perform. It is where the brain goes to wander, self-reflect, daydream, mentally time-travel, ruminate and explore "theory of mind" — the ability to understand the mental states of others — and as it matures in the young child, to realize that other people may have a different understanding and knowledge than he or she does.

Some investigators describe the DMN variously as the brain's "orchestra conductor" or "corporate executive" — in some ways, a physical component of the self. There is compelling evidence that areas of the DMN are involved in the maintenance of a sense of the self in space and time.

The higher levels of brain activity such as the DMN (not to be confused with "higher levels of consciousness") are all lumped together and are often called "executive functioning." Their activation normally inhibits the brain's lower-level functions, like those involved in emotion and memory and actually helps inhibit mystical experiences.

Conversely, using different imaging modalities, *decreased* activity in the DMN has been observed both after administration of hallucinogens and during the practice of meditation. It appears that, with the central controls of the "executive" out of commission, the barriers between self and world, between subject and object, begin to dissolve. This dissolution is part of transcendence. The experience of unity involves selflessness, a decrease in egocentric thought, via reduced or eliminated self-referential processing — in other words, there is a reduction or elimination of all the overlapping "executive" processes that, together, we experience as our "self."

Dissolving barriers is, of course, involved in shamanic trance. David Lewis-Williams and Jean Clottes described this third stage of altered consciousness as an absorptive state distinguished by dissociation from external surroundings — a state that is cultivated in many mystical and contemplative traditions. One study used functional magnetic resonance imaging (fMRI) to examine the brain networks associated with trance. Fifteen experienced shamanic practitioners listened to rhythmic drumming and either entered a trance state or remained in a non-trance state during eight-minute brain scans. The induction of trance deactivated the DMN and disengaged awareness of the outside world. The authors write: "This network reconfiguration may promote an extended internal train of thought wherein integration and insight can occur."[30]

As we've seen, extreme pain and suffering ("sacred pain"[31]) has been associated with shamanistic trance states. Unsurprisingly, an experiment that used fMRI to study acute pain found disruption in the DMN.[32]

Awe experiences also result in relatively less activity in the DMN and reduce the focus on self. Michiel van Elk of the University of Amsterdam, and his colleagues, used fMRI to scan the brains of 32 participants while they watched three different types of 30-second videos. The videos featured awe-inspiring natural phenomena (e.g., stunning vistas from the BBC's *Planet Earth* TV series), funny animals (e.g., playful elephants) and neutral landscapes (e.g., a small babbling brook). There was less activation of the DMN when participants watched awe videos than when they watched funny or neutral videos. Subjects also reported experiencing a reduced focus on the self when watching the awe videos, a feeling that life is part of a bigger whole, and a loss of sense of space and time.[33]

This research on the DMN has also led to a reinterpretation of how psychedelics (and, by extension, other methods of changing consciousness) work in the brain. Neuroscientists have always assumed that psychoactive drugs that produce spectacular hallucinations and scenarios work by stimulating brain activity — hence the vivid visions and powerful emotions that people report. However, researcher Robin Carhart-Harris of Imperial College London discovered that these drugs substantially reduce the brain's activity in the DMN. Blood flow and electrical activity in the DMN areas fall sharply under the influence of psychedelics, which may help to explain the reported loss of the sense of self, since the largest reductions correlate with personal reports of ego dissolution.[34]

If the DMN functions as the "conductor" of the everyday symphony of brain activity, we might expect its temporary disappearance from the stage to lead to the concert coming apart and, thus, to an increase in dissonance and mental incoherence. This does, in fact, appear to happen during psychedelic "trips" and in other extraordinary experiences brought about by different means. Carhart-Harris has found evidence in brain scans that, when the DMN shuts down, other brain regions "are let off the leash."[35]

Once again, what goes on inside the mind at such times is a surprise, as well as interesting and relevant. During meditation, or while under the influence of psychedelics or during other "selfless"-inducing experiences, the DMN shows a shift away from what neuroscientists call a "small-world" mode, a mode of relatively few connections. This is the mode we're usually in; the mundane world of school runs, meetings that run late, discussions, accords, utility payments, conflicts with others, and roasts burning. The shift is to what is termed a "random graph" mode in which there are many more possible interconnections. These extra connections can often underlie a more complete, holistic mode of processing and a sense that the "ordinary" world is gone, broken up, and we've broken through.

There are different possible responses to this radical shift: One may conclude that things aren't as they usually seem, that other "worlds" are possible, or in extremis, that one has gone crazy and must get back to the "real" (which is our daily, ordinary, "small world").

FOR FURTHER READING

Autism and the Edges of the Known World: Sensitivities, Language and Constructed Reality, Olga Bogdashina, Jessica Kingsley Publishers, 2010.

The Imprinted Brain: How Genes Set the Balance Between Autism and Psychosis, Christopher Badcock, Jessica Kingsley Publishers, 2009.

Social: Why Our Brains are Wired to Connect, Matthew D. Lieberman, Crown Pub. (Random House), 2013.

7

Breakthrough Or Breakdown?

W e've mentioned the many different techniques that break through the barriers that limit perception. But, sometimes, under extraordinary situations such as brain damage, epilepsy, unbearable life stresses or accidents, consciousness can shift out of the daily "small-world" mode to an expanded view without any of these deliberate practices.

What was once called a "nervous breakdown" — a collapse of normal thinking, memory and reasoning — is undeniably a debilitating blow to the person and often results in serious problems such as hallucinations, difficulty adjusting, even committing violent acts. Many need to be hospitalized. But if the disturbance isn't so great, a real change in consciousness in a beneficial direction can happen. The occurrence of trauma or a major physical debility may cause a breakup of the "clouds" engulfing the mind and allow a glimpse of a new and more connected vision.

Brain Damage

Jill Bolte Taylor, a neuroanatomist, awoke one morning with a severe, sharp pain behind her left eye. She soon felt what she described as "a powerful and unusual sense of dissociation roll over me."[1] She felt detached from her normal cognitive functions and experienced a strange kind of mind/body disconnect. It was as if she were observing her own motions.

She attempted to take a shower. The unusual loudness of the running water shocked her into the realization that something serious had happened and, at the same time, she became aware that the usually ceaseless chatter of her brain had stopped and had given way to fragments and intermittent silence.

Taylor had suffered a severe left-hemisphere stroke, caused by a congenital arteriovenous malformation (AVM) that had suddenly burst, and hemorrhaged — bled out — all over the left hemisphere of her brain.

Surprisingly, she then felt "enfolded by a blanket of tranquil euphoria. . . . As the language centers in my left hemisphere grew increasingly silent and I became detached from the memories of my life, I was comforted by an expanding sense of grace. In this void of higher cognition and details pertaining to my normal life, my consciousness soared into an all-knowingness, a 'being at one' with the universe, if you will. In a compelling sort of way, it felt like the good road home and I liked it."[2]

By this point, propped up against the wall of the shower, Taylor had started to lose the sense of her own physical boundaries, "where I began and where I ended. I sensed the composition of my being as that of a fluid rather than that of a solid. I no longer perceived myself as a whole object separate from everything. Instead, I now blended in with the space and flow around me."[3] Although she was still able to grasp the extreme danger of her situation, she continued to be seduced by the euphoria of her experience. She no longer had any sense of the linear — of experience that flowed from past to present to future — instead experiencing each moment as existing "in perfect isolation," where there was no relationship between A and B, and one was not relative to two.

As the hemorrhage continued to blot out her brain's left hemisphere, so that it no longer inhibited or competed with the right hemisphere, Taylor felt "swathed in an enfolding sense of liberation and transformation....I'm no authority, but I think the Buddhists would say I entered the mode of existence they call Nirvana." She gave herself up to entrancing feelings of "tranquility, safety, blessedness, euphoria and omniscience." [4] Later, she recalled, "In the absence of . . . normal functioning . . . my perception of my physical boundaries was no longer limited to where my skin met air. I felt like a genie liberated from its bottle." [5]

Taylor no longer knew anything about the neuroanatomist she had been until that moment and no longer felt bound to her "self-induced limitations." [6] She also did not have her old passions or anger or the emotional baggage that she had been carting through her life — instead she simply "was."

Although a part of her wanted to give herself up to that place and just rest, another part of her managed — after nearly an hour and with huge difficulty — to dial her office number and mumble unintelligibly into the phone what she thought was, "This is Jill, I need help." [7] Fortunately, her colleague recognized her voice, and she was rescued in time and taken to the emergency room.

In the hospital, Taylor became aware that she couldn't distinguish the three dimensions of space, nor colors nor sounds. In addition she recalled, "It was impossible for me to perceive either physical or emotional loss because I was not capable of experiencing separation or individuality." [8] Although she felt, in a strange way, safe, others could see a woman in a desperate state, who couldn't speak, understand language or written words, or even move her body properly.

As she lay in her hospital bed, she was highly aware of the empathic qualities of her brain's right hemisphere — of what other people, visitors, doctors or nurses, who came into the room were thinking and feeling and of what she then considered the "healing energy" that they brought with them (or took away).

It took eight long, hard years of relearning everything before Taylor finally recovered the functioning of her brain's left hemisphere. However, her experiences made her unwilling to let go of what she had learned was important in right-hemisphere terms. Although she wanted her sense of self and status back, she didn't want to return to the old world of "separateness," in which greed, power games, egotism and other negative emotions took precedence.

"My goal during this process of recovery has been not only to find a healthy balance between the functional abilities of my two hemispheres, but also to have more say about which character dominates my perspective at any given moment," Taylor writes, "I find this to be important because the most fundamental traits of my right hemisphere personality are deep inner peace and loving compassion. I believe the more time we spend running our inner peace/compassion circuitry, then the more peace/compassion we will project into the world, and ultimately the more peace/compassion we will have on the planet."[9]

In this case, the complete knockout of the brain's left hemisphere led to the dramatic breaking of the barriers of the left hemisphere's control over the right hemisphere's perceptual abilities — abilities that, like the stars existing behind the brilliance of the day, are often obscured.

Epilepsy, Psychosis and Creative Inspiration

In an epileptic seizure, normal thought breaks up, and if the seizure is not completely debilitating, or if it doesn't occasion a damaging fall, a vision can develop. This mental picture is often called a "Dostoyevsky seizure," after the Russian author's description of Myshkin in *The Idiot*. But most of these epileptic visions are not, alas, in any way helpful to the person who has them. As an example, here is one verbatim account from an individual in the midst of a seizure:

> In these moments I kiss God....I can see all the colours now, under your skin! Look at your hand. Do you doubt that you contain an infinity of shades? ...i would be a river if i could. i would bleed eternal/divine....when you see all the colours. all the colours, in any one colour. that is to taste the divine....God is spectrum, infinite spectrum. sound, colour touch all a spectrum.[10]

It's important to realize that there is, obviously, a fuzzy line between psychosis and inspiration, between a wild hallucination and an altered state of consciousness that produces an insight or results in a creative experience. Each of us sometimes hears a prompt inside with a new idea or insight, or telling us to do or not do something. Sometimes these voices are incoherent or wrong. But many of our greatest works of literature were created that way. Samuel Taylor Coleridge and William Wordsworth both specifically acknowledged this. Nobel laureate Bob Dylan, who had an extraordinary period of writing early in his career, said, "I don't know how I got to write those songs.... Those early songs are almost magically written" (such as the prophetic *With God on Our Side*). But Dylan no longer has the same songwriting ability. "You can't do something forever," he said. "I did it once, I can do other things now. But I can't do that."[11] A similar phenomenon occurs in science, especially in mathematics and physics, and to major religious figures, such as the Prophet Muhammad. *What matters is not that one hears voices; what matters is the content, understanding and relevance of what is heard.*

Extreme Life Events

Sometimes an event or a series of them can be so severely traumatizing as to leave a person's life metaphorically dismembered

— as happens with the Tungus and other shamans' imaginative perception of being cut apart and reassembled. This is a level of extreme trauma so devastating that, even if the person survives, it may take everything she or he has to overcome what happened and return to any form of normality.

Triumph over this kind of trauma doesn't happen often. But sometimes — even if rarely — unexpected and transcendent experiences can occur.

That's what happened to Glyn Hood. Her 21-year-old daughter had died suddenly. Her son-in-law had quit his job to look after their one-year-old child, so she had to support two families, but the stress was too much, so her business went bust. Enough? One of her young sons had just been diagnosed with Asperger's Syndrome, and she was up all night reading about it, while her other little boy had developed a phobia about dying and was up all night unable to sleep. Glyn felt that "all the structures were breaking down."

What happened then? Driving to the market one day, she had a strange experience:

> ... something started to happen. It was as though I had shutters around my brain and they were being pulled up one by one.... And suddenly I'm aware of everything there is....Everything is connected, inside and outside.... [my daughter] couldn't die because we're part of the same energy. You can't lose anybody because we're all one.[12]

As she put it, the barriers holding in her normal thought were broken by the extreme stresses.

Michael Hutchinson had a terrifying and life-changing experience that was comparable to the shamans' hallucinated one. One day, he slipped on some ice and broke his spine, which left him a quadriplegic. Despite many, many surgeries, Hutchinson has been in pain for more than a decade. The "cushions" in his spine have degenerated, which makes it painful even to sit up. And yet this real "dismemberment" has made his experience transcend the norm:

> I feel oneness all the time . . . it's there from the moment I wake up . . . The important thing is to let yourself be conscious and aware. No thought no ideas, no images, nothing. . . . And that's the bliss.[13]

For both these people, the destruction of their "normal" mode of perception led to that breakthrough, even though it is just the initial stage of a perception beyond the mundane — a sense that all is, in reality, connected.

Spontaneous Experiences – Sometimes It Just Happens

While traumatic accidents, brain damage, drugs and strenuous rituals can cause a shift to a more comprehensive consciousness, sometimes a change in consciousness emerges without an obvious precursor. Psychologist Charles Tart gathered the stories of such experiences from scientists, a group of people who would seem most unlikely to have them.

While working in Antarctica, neurophysiologist Red Hong, a scientist with "no inclination toward spiritual seeking," had to walk with colleagues to a cleanup site:

> I was separated from my companions by the time I reached the top and sat down to recover. My mind was totally blank. After a while I realized that I had expanded. I was no longer a small discrete consciousness located in my head — I encompassed the whole valley. I was HUGE. I was part of everything — or rather everything was part of me. I was ancient and unbelievably powerful. It was wonderful.[14]

Allan Smith, an anesthesia researcher, noted his own experience:

> [It]. . . occurred unexpectedly while I was alone one evening and was watching a particularly beautiful sunset. . . . the passage of time seemed to become slower and slower. The brightness, mood-

elevation, and time-slowing all progressed together. It is difficult to estimate the time period over which these changes occurred, since the sense of time was itself affected. . . . Eventually, the sense of time passing stopped entirely. It is difficult to describe this feeling, but perhaps it would be better to say that there was no time, or no sense of time. Only the present moment existed. My elation proceeded to an ecstatic state; the intensity of which I had never even imagined could be possible. . . .

At this point, I merged with the light and everything, including myself, became one unified whole. There was no separation between myself and the rest of the universe. In fact, to say that there was a universe, a self, or any 'thing' would be misleading — it would be an equally correct description to say that there was 'nothing' as to say that there was 'everything.' . . . All words or discursive thinking had stopped and there was no sense of an 'observer' to comment or to categorize what was 'happening.' In fact, there were no discrete events to 'happen' — just a timeless, unitary state of being.[15]

The poet T.S. Eliot describes a similar experience:

At the still point of the turning world. Neither flesh nor fleshless;
Neither from nor towards; at the still point, there the dance is,
But neither arrest nor movement. And do not call it fixity,
Where past and future are gathered. Neither movement from nor towards,
Neither ascent nor decline. Except for the point, the still point,
There would be no dance, and there is only the dance.
I can only say, there we have been: but I cannot say where.
And I cannot say, how long, for that is to place it in time.[16]

And a similar sense is evident in Jalaluddin Rumi's lines:

My place is placeless, my trace is traceless,
no body, no soul, I am from the soul of souls.
I have chased out duality, lived the two worlds as one.[17]

FOR FURTHER READING

My Stroke of Insight: A Brain Scientist's Personal Journey,
Jill Bolte Taylor, Viking (Penguin Group), 2008.

Out of the Darkness: From Turmoil to Transformation,
Steve Taylor, Hay House UK, 2011.

The Varieties of the Religious Experience, William James,
Penguin, 1985.

8

Dissolving Barriers

*. . . we should keep all things only as if they had been
merely lent and not given to us, without any sense of
possessiveness, whether it be our body or soul, our senses,
faculties, worldly goods or honour, friends, relations,
house or home or anything whatsoever.*

— Meister Eckhart, "Selected Writings"

Transcending the Ordinary

All over the world, and seemingly throughout our history, those people interested in transcending to a higher consciousness appear to do strange things. They may stay up all night next to a fire and dance to exhaustion. They may just jump up and down or spin until they collapse in a trance. Some practice scarification, cutting their face or body in a specific pattern; others sit quietly for half an hour, repeating a phrase that means nothing (or that, through repetition, comes to mean nothing). Some ponder weird questions, such as "Show me your face before your father and mother met;" others go on long fasts or sit inside a cave and appear to do nothing; and some even hang upside-down with sticks piercing their body.

"Spiritual" practice may involve long marches, sensory deprivation, isolation, chanting, ingesting psychedelic drugs or inhaling psychoactive gases. What do all these practices have in common? They all aim to disrupt the normal control on conscious perception.

These practices jiggle-jaggle the mind's barriers — the "clouds" of the mind that occlude a deeper perception — in order to bust them up. We have to realize that most of us, most of the time, go through life "automatically," unconsciously going through tedious routine after tedious routine, in behavior and in our thought processes.

The first step common to all attempts to transcend our ordinary consciousness, therefore, is a disorganization or disruption of these ordinary routine thoughts and ways of thinking, to dissolve the barriers.

> Think of yourself as nothing and totally forget yourself as you pray. Only remember that you are praying for the Divine Presence. You may then enter the Universe of Thought, a state of consciousness which is beyond time. Everything in this realm is the same — life and death, land and sea . . . but in order to enter this realm you must relinquish your ego and forget all your troubles.
>
> — Rabbi Eleazar, Hebrew mystic[1]

Concentrative and Mindfulness Meditations

> Deep in the sea are riches beyond compare.
> But if you seek safety, it is on the shore.
> — Saadi of Shiraz, *The Rose Garden*

All authentic exercises are part of a whole system and set of related practices, a comprehensive effort to attain higher consciousness. Exercises and activities are prescribed to students individually by a contemporary expert who has "made the journey and returned."

The most familiar of these techniques is meditation which is primarily an exercise in the deployment of attention. It has been described as a process of dissolving the usual barriers to perception, and has been likened to calming the ripples on a lake so that the bottom, usually invisible, can be seen. In another metaphor, meditation is likened to the night: stars cannot be seen during the day, when their faint points of light are overwhelmed by the brilliance of the sun. Meditation, then, is the process of "turning off" the overwhelming competing activity that is the light of the sun until, late at night, the stars can be seen quite clearly. To someone who has seen the sky only during the day, the idea that many faint distinct points of light exist up there and can be seen is obvious nonsense.

The two main forms are mindfulness and concentrative meditation.

Mindfulness (or "open monitoring") involves a deliberate attempt to "open up" one's awareness of the internal environment, allowing thoughts, feelings and sensations to arise without attending to or evaluating them. Concentrative meditation requires the restriction of awareness to a single, unchanging process, such as gazing at an object or repeating a word or phrase. The procedure here is to empty the mind of everything except the perception of the meditation's focus. A Buddhist meditation script states that ". . . [The practitioner] must seek to annihilate all vagrant thoughts and notions belonging to the externality of things, and all ideas of individuality and generality, of suffering and impermanence, and cultivate the noblest ideas of egolessness and emptiness and imagelessness. . ."[2]

With our common nervous system, it isn't surprising that people from all the different recorded cultures have discovered that the external world can be shut out if we concentrate long enough on repeating a certain action, word or phrase, or if we focus on our breath or on an object. One instruction has it: "...if you desire to discover your soul, withdraw your thoughts from outward and material things, forgetting if possible your own body and its five senses."[3]

To find our way through the world, we rely on what we have learned from experience and form our expectations and desires on that basis. We habituate, which is a physiological process in which the brain stops responding to constant stimuli — as we do to the sound of a clock ticking in our room. This process of habituation enables us to tune out the familiar, constant bits and pieces of our world, such as the whirr of a fan or the feel of a chair pressing against our skin. Note that when one is moving along familiar routes, one's attention returns to the task at hand only when something out of the ordinary happens — the step on the stairs isn't where we expected it to be, the clock suddenly makes a clanging noise, or somebody darts or swerves in front of the car we're driving.

It is this selective and restricted nature of awareness that the practice of meditation seeks to overcome, as it shuts off the internal noise and shuts out the external environment. As a result of this temporary "turning off" of our input-selection systems, the practitioner sees "with new eyes" for a while when he or she re-experiences sensory input after the practice.

The aim of meditation practice is for these "new eyes" to endure. One study compared the recorded EEGs of non-meditators, with those of Zen masters — while all of the subjects were listening to repetitive clicking sounds. The unpracticed "normals" tuned the clicks out quite quickly, but the Zen masters registered all of the clicks equally. This accords with an aim of Zen: that seeing something for the 500th time should be the same as seeing it for the first time, indexing a state in which one always remains fully conscious.

While there are many confirmed benefits from practicing meditation, it is not always a rosy tale. For instance, one major study of meditation retreats examined 27 people with different levels of meditation experience. Sixty-three percent had at least one negative effect, and seven percent suffered anxiety, panic, depression, increased negativity, pain, feelings of being spaced out, confused and disoriented.[4]

A more recent interview and survey study found that a wide range of meditation-related experiences were reported as challenging, difficult, distressing or functionally impairing.[5] Traditional Buddhist teaching enumerates scores of deceptive or illusory experiences that are associated with the practice of concentrative meditation — including warnings about pleasant experiences that lead the meditator into a false sense of spiritual progress, resulting in misguided thinking and a tendency to confuse blissful and euphoric states with genuine insights.

Meditation is traditionally part of a triad: meditation, concentration and contemplation. Sufis warn that "any one of these indulged in isolation (not as part of a three-fold operation) produces fixity of opinion and illusions of certainty."[6] A recent study of 93 yoga students and 162 meditators confirmed this. The researchers found that the practice of meditation actually inflated self-perceptions. Participants were asked to evaluate themselves based on statements such as "In comparison to the average participant of this study, I am free from envy." Study participants had higher self-enhancement and self-centrality in the hour following meditation than they did when they hadn't meditated in 24 hours. It seems that practicing any skill can breed an inflated sense of self-enhancement. The researchers concluded that ". . . neither yoga nor meditation fully quiet the ego; to the contrary, they boost self-enhancement."[7]

Psychologists Miguel Farias and Catherine Wikholm describe a study they conducted that involved prisoners who practiced meditation. They found that the practice improved mood, and inmates experienced less stress — but remained as aggressive as before meditation. The authors note that: "... for all its de-stressing and self-development potential, [meditation] can take you deeper into the darkest recesses of your own mind than you may have wished for."

Farias writes of a woman in her late fifties named Louise, who attended one of his courses on the psychology of spirituality. She was a calm meditator, but reported that her sense of self had changed during one meditation session. She welcomed this as "part of the dissolving experience" but couldn't help feeling anxious and frightened. "'Don't worry, just keep meditating and it will go away,' the meditation teacher told her. It didn't." Subsequently, Louise spent 15 years being treated for depression, part of that time hospitalized. It's difficult to know whether this would have happened anyway, but losing contact with the self can be traumatic as well as positive.[8]

It can be confusing, even dangerous to leave our stable, safe, predictable world, which is why all authentic traditions involve preparation and prescription. Farias and Wikholm express their concern that the science of meditation "promotes a skewed view: meditation wasn't developed so we could lead less stressful lives or improve our wellbeing. Its primary purpose was much more radical — to rupture your idea of who you are; to shake to the core your sense of self so that you realize there is 'nothing there.'"[9] Such an experience without adequate preparation is obviously detrimental.

Brain Rhythms

The brain is made up of billions of nerve cells called neurons. They transmit electrochemical signals — information — to each other. Brainwaves are rhythmic fluctuations of this electrical activity that reflect the brain's state. Brain rhythms, or waves, of different frequencies have been observed in humans and other animals. For example, beta rhythms dominate our normal waking state when attention is directed toward cognitive tasks and the outside world. Such rhythms have a frequency range of 12.5 to 35 Hz (cycles per second) and are the fastest of the four different brainwaves.

It's been found, through EEG studies, that alpha rhythms are associated with a decrease in awareness of the external world. They have a frequency range of 8 to 12 Hz. Experiments with ganzfields (similar to wearing halved ping-pong balls over the eyes) produce a completely patternless visual field. Participants report episodes of an absence of visual experience — not only do they not see anything, but they just don't have vision anymore — that corresponds with bursts of alpha rhythms. This state is similar to that of concentrative meditation.*

When he was developing biofeedback in the 1960s and '70s, my (RO) colleague and onetime boss, Joe Kamiya of the Langley-Porter Neuropsychiatric Institute in San Francisco, used a system that converted alpha rhythms into sound. This showed that ordinary people could learn quite quickly to alter their brain waves at will, in order to enhance or suppress their alpha rhythms. This could be achieved in as little as seven minutes, in many cases. The physiological feedback enabled the creation of a connection that did not exist before, amplifying faint signals that are present in the nervous system and bringing them into the person's awareness.

Another brain rhythm, theta, with a frequency of 4 to under 8 Hz, has been found to increase only in very experienced meditators. Theta activity in the frontal lobes is associated with attention-demanding tasks, and this brain rhythm is our gateway to learning, memory and intuition. In theta mode, our senses are withdrawn from the external world and focused on signals originating from within.

---

*Of course, the interpretation of any brain rhythm depends upon the area from which it emanates. Alpha rhythm in the occipital (visual) cortex may mean the absence of seeing, while the same rhythm in the midline of the brain may indicate absence of movement.

Long-term meditators show increased alpha and theta activity even during deep sleep. It has been suggested that this may reflect the development of a transcendental consciousness that persists through waking, dreaming and deep sleep. Philosopher and neuroscientist Francisco Varela has suggested that meditation could produce neurophysiologic changes during sleep that correspond to a progression along a continuum, from being totally unconscious to totally conscious during deep sleep.[10]

One difficulty in all of this is that the alpha and theta increases that have been found to take place during meditation are also found in drowsy and early-sleep states, which makes the differences difficult to study. Some researchers suggest that the increases in theta rhythm observed in some long-term meditators may be related to their learning to hold awareness at a level of physiological processing similar, but not identical, to Stage 1 sleep, the first of the four sleep stages.

fMRI, a scanning measurement of the brain's blood flow, indicates which area of the brain is "working," and provides evidence of whether meditation alters the structure and function of parts of the brain that may also lead to an increased expansion of perception or consciousness. A small but growing number of studies shows that it does, but there are also discrepancies in the findings, with studies of different meditation styles and individuals often yielding different results.

Puzzles, Koans and Paradoxes

If someone who is teaching you sets the homework assignment for next week as "show me your face before your father and mother met," you might just quit or, better, knit your brain into a knot trying to figure it out.

In a Zen school, the "answer" to a koan such as this cannot be addressed through scientific or logical analysis. The "answer" might be just as strange as the "question," and could well be to slap oneself or the teacher in the face and shut one's eyes. Our normal reaction to being asked these kinds of questions might well be "Huh!?" But these puzzles — and there are many of them — are meant to tie the regular processes of the mind into knots until the whole thing snaps, a way of breaking through the "clouds" that surround us. The desired answer is not verbal or logical; ideally, it should communicate a new level of awareness brought about by the process of concentrating on the koan.

In one such story, a boy walks by with a lit candle and a man asks, "Where did that light come from?" The boy blows it out and says, "I'll tell you, if you tell me where it went." Again, these unanswerable questions are different from most kinds of questioning. They require a shift away from normal reason and step-by-step, sequential thinking, to a different mode, one of expanded perception.

Paradoxes such as this are used in spiritual studies. We've already mentioned the injunction of Muhammad to "die before your death," but there are others from different traditions, such as "the way up is the way down," "no answer is an answer" and "here are the rules: ignore all rules." They are all designed to make one think and get a new answer; not to destroy thought itself, but to help occasion a breakup of normal consciousness.

As were Zeno's famous paradoxes. To update a familiar one: If Usain Bolt and a turtle were to race, and the turtle got a head start, Bolt could never catch him (because each time Bolt reached a point where the turtle had been, it would have already moved further ahead, in successively small increments, ad infinitum.) In another paradox, this one about millet, Zeno noted that if one drops a ton of millet on the ground, it makes a thud, but dropping one grain of millet doesn't make any sound. He asks: How could all of it make a noise if each of its parts doesn't?

Drug Experiences and Altered States of Consciousness

> In all the great traditions, . . .teachers have constantly
> proclaimed that far from being essential to the
> spiritual quest, visions, voices, and feelings of devotion
> could in fact be a distraction.
>
> — KAREN ARMSTRONG[11]

> The ecstatic experience is absolutely the lowest form
> of advanced knowledge.[12]
>
> — IDRIES SHAH*

For all of human history, people have sought out, refined, purified, sniffed, snorted, ingested and injected drugs for almost every purpose — for providing pain relief, for stimulation of all sorts, for getting "high" and, of course, in the case of "psychedelics," for reaching a temporary altered state of consciousness. While the latter category includes many drugs — from peyote, to ayahuasca, to soma, to LSD and marijuana — the most relevant research, and the clearest effects, have involved psilocybin.

Painted on rocks in the Sahara Desert 7,000 to 9,000 years ago are scenes of what would appear to be the harvest, adoration and offering of mushrooms, and include large, masked "gods" covered with hallucinogenic mushrooms.[13] Although we have no earlier records, it's a good bet that people were experimenting with these mushrooms even before this period.

These "magic" mushrooms are fungi that contain psilocybin, a naturally occurring psychedelic compound. There are more than 180 species of mushrooms that contain it. Psilocybin mushrooms have a long history of use in shamanic and other religious rituals in Mesoamerica, and are currently among the most popular psychedelics in the U.S. and Europe.

---

*See Addendum: Chapter 8 for discussion of mystical states

In the 1950s, psychedelics were used fairly successfully to treat a wide variety of conditions, including alcoholism and end-of-life anxiety. During the same period, the U.S. Army conducted many different LSD experiments on people, looking for a confessional or disorienting drug to use on the enemy.

Then, of course, LSD was banned from research due to overuse and hysteria, fueled by the "turn on, tune in and drop out" mantra of the psychologist and writer Timothy Leary. After that came the "war" on drugs, as a result of which any smidgen of interest in LSD was deemed unscientific or downright subversive.

Disclosure: Late in 1961, I (RO) got a call from a physician and pastor named Walter Pahnke, asking me to help him in Boston, where he was going to give psilocybin to a group of people as an experiment designed to investigate the potential of psychedelic drugs to facilitate mystical experience. This was to take place on Good Friday in 1962, so "Good Friday" became the name of the study. (I went up to Boston to see if I could help, but by then they had enough volunteers, and I went home.)

In the study, 20 divinity students each received a capsule of white powder right before the Good Friday service at Marsh Chapel, which was on the Boston University campus. Ten of those capsules contained psilocybin, and 10 contained an active placebo (nicotinic acid, which has no psychoactive effects but produces a transient feeling of warmth and general relaxation). Six months after the experiment all the divinity students interviewed who had ingested the drug reported "a profound effect especially in terms of religious feeling and thinking."[14]

Rick Doblin, founder of the Multidisciplinary Association of Psychedelic Studies (MAPS), studied the Good Friday participants roughly 25 years later. All of the psilocybin subjects interviewed reported an "enhanced appreciation of life and of nature, deepened sense of joy, deepened commitment to the Christian ministry or to whatever other vocations the subjects chose, enhanced appreciation of unusual experiences and emotions, increased tolerance to other religious systems, deepened equanimity in the face of difficult life crises, and greater solidarity and identification with foreign peoples, minorities, women and nature."[15]

The results of interviews from both the six-month follow up by Pahnke and Doblin's later follow-up supported Pahnke's hypothesis that when used in a religious setting by religiously inclined people, psychedelic drugs could facilitate experiences that are "either identical with, or indistinguishable from, those reported in the cross-cultural mystical literature." But Doblin found much more that was negative in the study: Several people had acute anxiety during their experience, and one was given a powerful antipsychotic medication after he was reported to have gone outside of the chapel, possibly intending to follow the exhortation of a preacher that all Christians should tell people that there was a man on the cross.[16]

There has recently been a reawakening of interest in psychedelics, and a new freedom for their investigation. Researcher Roland Griffiths updated the Good Friday study in 2006, but with considerably more scientific rigor than was used in 1961. He found that "psilocybin occasioned experiences similar to spontaneously occurring mystical experiences." Personalities changed — people became more accepting of life and their role in it.[17]

Today psilocybin is used to treat anxiety, especially in those facing death or a problematic surgery, and is also used to treat headaches, addiction and depression — and to study the neurobiology of psychedelic experiences. One recent study notes: "Whereas depression had felt like a mental prison, they reported feeling a sense of mental freedom after the treatment. This feeling of expanded mental 'space' was often exhilarating during the dose, and seemed to last for weeks to months after the treatment." One participant recounted that, after the dose, "It was like this great shroud had been lifted."[18]

Griffiths believes that the long-term psychological effects of psilocybin are due to its ability to occasion such a transformative experience. So what seems most important is breaking through the clouds. As one participant said, "Reality is only an illusion;" or, as someone wrote long, long ago, "There are more things in heaven and earth, Horatio, / Than are dreamt of in your philosophy." (*Hamlet*, 1.5.167-8)

These days, psychedelic drugs are used for emotional satisfaction, pleasure or entertainment. The experience tends to be very emotional and can be overvalued, its significance misunderstood. Taking a "trip" without any preparation can be confusing or useless, or even dramatically counterproductive. Not everybody who busts up the barriers that keep our consciousness on the straight and narrow ends up getting home safely and with a new appreciation of living. Many do not.

It turns out that with psychedelics, preparation (what was called in the early days of the LSD frenzy "set and setting," with "set" being the mindset or expectation one brings to the experience, and "setting" being the environment in which it takes place) is critical to avoid having a "bad trip." Compared with other drugs, psychedelics seldom affect people the same way twice, because they tend to magnify whatever is already going on, both inside and outside one's head.[19]

Suppose you're detained and taken to the airport for a surprise "good trip." You separate from your everyday life and land somewhere, in a strange place. You ask the first person you see, "Where am I?" She says, "Θέλετε να πείτε." And you're lost as you continue on. You don't know that you're in Athens, what the language you hear spoken is, where the metro is and where it goes. If it all somehow works out positively, finding oneself "tripped" into another reality can put one's daily stresses into perspective, but it doesn't show how to navigate that new world "beyond the clouds of unknowing."

Others have realized these limits, even after using psychedelics. Aldous Huxley commented, "I am not so foolish as to equate what happens under the influence of mescalin or of any other drug, prepared or in the future preparable, with the realization of the end and ultimate purpose of human life: Enlightenment, the Beatific Vision. All I am suggesting is that the mescalin experience is what Catholic theologians call 'a gratuitous grace.'"[20]

Teaching Stories

> Imagine yourself the rose, and you will become the rose;
> If you want the unstable nightingale, you become the nightingale.
> You are the particle; the truth lies in the Whole.
> And if one day you think the Whole, you too will become the Whole.
>
> — Nur ad-Dīn Abd ar-Rahmān Jami[21]

In the 12th century, the Jewish philosopher Moses Maimonides of Cordoba wrote: "We must not . . . take in a literal sense, what is written in the book on the Creation, nor form of it the same ideas which are participated by the generality of mankind. . . . When taken in its literal sense, the work gives the most absurd and most extravagant ideas of the Deity."[22] Rumi, in his famous poem *The Mathnavi*, states, "People say that these are stories which happened long ago. But naming 'Moses' serves as an external appearance. Moses and Pharaoh are two of your entities, good man."[23] And again, "Do not seek from within yourself, from your Moses, the needs of a Pharaoh."[24] Both Rumi and Maimonides refer here to the ability of some literature to stimulate the mind along unfamiliar pathways, leading to a higher state of consciousness. Certain narratives, legends, parables, myths and fables are intended to establish in the mind not a belief but a pattern, a blueprint that helps it to operate in "another" manner, without resorting to indoctrination, emotional stimulation, intellectual discussion or becoming magnetized around certain ideas.

These special stories exist in every culture, but as with other esoteric psychological techniques, if they are arbitrarily selected, simplified, or taken literally, they lose their instrumental function. As the collector and exponent of the current corpus of this literature, the Sufi Idries Shah explains "Some are 'illustrative biographies,' they contain material designed for study, to cause certain effects, much in the way in which myths can contain dramatized fact." But he warns "with the passage of time they outlive their usefulness, and are then taken as lies or records of literal truth."[25]

Stories like these have been given the name "teaching stories," because their effect is not only to provide pleasure or a useful parable, but also to connect "with a part of the individual which cannot be reached by any other convention, and establish in him or in her, a means of communication with a non-verbalized truth beyond the customary limitations of our familiar dimensions."[26]

How can these stories work on consciousness and communicate in this way? Why are they intended to be read and re-read constantly? To look at it loosely, consider that we recognize only the familiar. We can recognize our name even when it's said more quickly and at a lower volume than we'd be able to recognize most other words. And we can recognize an English word (that is, if we're English-speakers) more quickly than we can a random sequence of letters.

The aim, of course, in esoteric traditions is to become attuned to information that is unfamiliar. Teaching stories purposely contain certain specially chosen patterns of events.

The repeated reading and absorption of the stories allows these patterns to become strengthened in the mind of the person reading them. Since many of these events are improbable and unusual, this effort begins to create new constructs in the reader — new "organs of perception," so to speak.

The stories can also serve as reflection points. "Reflection" can mean both "to think about" and "to mirror." Often an action caught in a story forms a pattern that is also present on another level of consciousness, as when an electron-microscopic photograph contains a pattern that can be seen in a photograph of a river taken from an airplane, or in a picture of the Earth as seen from a satellite. This is one meaning of the esoteric saying "As above, so below."

Some stories can serve as templates for consciousness, patterns frozen so that we can observe ourselves. We spoke about this mirror effect when looking at stories in the Gospel of John in Chapter 4. In one such story from the current Sufi corpus, the wise-fool folk hero Nasrudin is interested in learning to play the lute. He searches out the lute master and asks, "How much do you charge for lessons?" The lute master replies, "Ten gold pieces for the first month, one gold piece for the succeeding months." "Excellent," says Nasrudin. "I shall begin with the second month."[27]

Idries Shah published more than 20 books of teaching stories, Nasrudin tales, poems and narratives, all selected by him to provide preparatory study material for the potential student wishing to develop a higher perception, to transcend this "small world."

We include examples of these extraordinary tales, and more about them, in the Afterword of this book.

FOR FURTHER READING

The Buddha Pill: Can Meditation Change You?, Miguel Farias and Catherine Wikholm, Watkins Pub., 2015.

How to Change Your Mind, Michael Pollan, Penguin Publishing Group, Kindle Edition, 2018.

Learning How to Learn, Idries Shah, The Octagon Press, © The Estate of Idries Shah, 1988.

Meditation and Modern Psychology, Robert Ornstein, Malor Books, 2008.

Out of the Darkness: From Turmoil to Transformation, Steve Taylor, Hay House, 2011.

The Teachers of Gurdjieff, Rafael Lefort, Malor Books, 2014.

The Way of the Sufi, Idries Shah, Jonathan Cape, 1966.

For the complete works of Idries Shah, visit: idriesshahfoundation.org

SECTION FOUR:

Belief In "God"

9

Why Religion?

Religion and its Discontents (and Contents)

The last 1,500 years have produced a world substantially different from the way it was at the time of the genesis of any of the three monotheistic religions we've discussed. Those religions — which developed at an earlier, less comprehensive period of civilization than we have today — served their members the way governments do now, often providing the people with work, their role in society, rules for marriage, and the care and control of most needs. The church was the center of life in preindustrial societies.

Fast-forward to the modern world: Researcher Gregory Paul measured "popular religiosity" for the developed nations and compared it to the elements of the Successful Societies Scale, which includes rates of homicides, infant mortality, sexually transmitted diseases, teenage births and abortions, corruption and income inequality. He found that the most religious societies have the highest rates on all of these! This means that those nations with the highest levels of belief in God and the greatest levels of religious observance are also the ones with the greatest societal dysfunction.[1] Interestingly, the U.S. comes out worse than any other Western developed nation on every indicator, and is also the most religious by a substantial margin. First-world nations, as well as U.S. states, that have the highest rates of belief in God and religious observance also have the most societal disorganization. For example, there is a very high correlation between popular religiosity and the rates of sexually transmitted diseases and teenage abortions. Overall, Paul found that the healthiest nations are also the least religious.*

Immigration and diversity do not explain these relationships, nor does a country's lawless history (such as the U.S., which went through a "Wild West" period). It seems that religion becomes more important in societies when they are under extreme stress. This "stress" has been reduced during the last few centuries, with the expansion of civil society, the establishment of the rule of law and the creation of government programs to help the needy. These have continued to replace religion's role in most developed countries.

In Scandinavian countries, the social structure provides almost all of the needs that were formerly filled by religion. One contemporary Danish bishop noted that "Danes don't need to go to church on Sundays because they can go to their Danishness every day of the week."[2]

Fifty-six percent of Americans, as compared to just 27 percent of Europeans, currently believe in God as He is described in the Bible.[3] Americans are unusually fluid in their thinking, making them creators, inventors and idealists — as well as easier marks for fraud and implausible schemes, ideas, and utopias.

---

*Religion can take many forms: concrete, abstract, metaphysical, prescriptive, relationship-oriented, inner-motivation-oriented and existential quest-oriented. But, as with many other vague terms, one knows religion when one sees it. In many surveys, religiosity is measured by weekly attendance at religious services and by respondents reporting that religion is important in their daily life.

It's estimated that 41 percent of Americans believe in what they call the "rapture" — a time when true believers, living and dead, will be taken up into the air to meet the Lord.[4] This is a new form of the "end of days" archetype; this time, "the end" is expected to come by 2050, and to include explosions and blown-up bodies, just like in a superhero film. The world has seen many such predictions, which are always expected to come true a few years from whenever the present happens to be.

To examine how the U.S. compares with the rest of the world in terms of belief and adherence to religion, psychologist Ed Diener of the University of Illinois along with his colleagues and the Gallup Organization, conducted a global survey of nearly a million people across the globe, including a state-by-state sample in the United States.[5] The researchers gathered data on how well the respondents' basic needs were met, such as their sense of personal safety and whether they had sufficient money for food and shelter.

It was found that income, education levels and other variables determined which respondents were living in "difficult circumstances." Two-thirds of those surveyed in the U.S. regarded religion as important in their lives. People from different states, however, varied in how important they felt religion to be; for example, 44 percent of those in Vermont rated religion as important, compared with 88 percent of those in Mississippi. In states where religion was considered very important, people were much more likely to be living in difficult circumstances.

While a 2018 Gallup survey showed that 72 percent of Americans still believed in the importance of religion in their daily lives, it also showed that only 51 percent believed religion to be *very important* — a decline of nearly 20 percent since 1965.[6] A surprising finding of Diener's earlier study showed that in U.S. states where religion was considered very important, inhabitants had *lower* scores of subjective happiness than those living in less-religious parts of the country. But didn't religion make them happier, as previous studies had shown? Yes, but they still felt worse-off than the contented non-religious residents of more-affluent states, where faith mattered less.

Diener and Gallup's world survey on religion included 154 countries, with an average sample of almost 3,000 people per country.[7] Overall, three out of four respondents reported that religion was important in their lives, but among countries, this varied by a factor of six — ranging from 16 percent in Sweden to 99 percent each in Bangladesh, Egypt, Sri Lanka and Somalia.

This global poll again showed that a difficult environment coincided with greater national religiosity but lower life satisfaction. If you live in a nation where daily existence is difficult, your life satisfaction is understandably lower than those who live in places where life is easier. In countries where life is hard, being more religious appears to confer an advantage in happiness that one's less-religious neighbors do not enjoy. If the living is easy, however, both nonreligious and religious people have a similar, relatively high, subjective sense of wellbeing. This is true for all of the religions represented in the sample: Buddhism, Christianity, Hinduism and Islam.

The researchers observe that "religion helps people cope with difficult circumstances and therefore is most beneficial when people's life context is difficult. Economically developed nations, on average, are superior in meeting basic needs, education, safety, and longevity. They also have better infrastructure that safeguards against natural disasters and epidemic diseases. Thus, in economically developed nations, we surmise that people are better able to achieve high subjective wellbeing without the help of organized religion. When people are frequently faced with hunger, illness, crime, and poor education—all of which are relatively more uncontrollable and more prevalent in poor societies — religion can perhaps make a greater contribution to wellbeing."[8] More importantly, whether a person was struggling or thriving was found to be not nearly as predictive of religiosity as were the society's conditions and norms. While individuals may have choice in what they believe, these choices are most often shaped by what people around them believe. If everyone around you is religious, you are very likely to be religious too.

In Scandinavia, for instance, the attitude is determinedly secular. Sarah, a 20-year-old grocery clerk from a village in Denmark, said: "Young people think that religion is kind of taboo. As a young person, you don't say, 'I'm a Christian, and I'm proud of it.' If you do that, you often get picked on."[9] Denmark and Sweden buck conventions in more ways than one. They have the lowest church attendance in the world. Ask people in those countries if they believe the basic tenets of Christian doctrine, and by and large they say they do not. Even many of the clergy don't believe in God. Yet most Danes and Swedes baptize their babies, get married in churches and pay a tax that supports the church.[10]

Founding a religion is possibly the world's second-oldest profession. It's difficult to keep accurate track of how many religions exist, but most estimates center on about 4,000 in operation today. But who really has any idea? How could anyone determine how many religions arise and then die out in places such as the remote hills of New Guinea, where about 850 languages are spoken? Researchers estimate that approximately 50 to 100 new religions are founded every month somewhere in the world and are constantly in chaos, flux and evolution — with most of them being short-lived.

For now, in the modern era, God is everywhere, all over the world. While polls do indicate a decline in religious affiliation, almost all Americans believe in God or a higher power, and about half of adult Americans believe that God determines what happens to them most or all of the time.[11] Even where there's no "God" that is part of the explicit belief system, individuals

— including atheists — are found to hold their own god-ish beliefs. When asked, individual Buddhists say they believe that unseen, higher forces are determining the course of their lives. Surprisingly, so do many, if not most, scientists and atheists; like believers in UFOs, they attribute at least some aspects of life to outside forces.

Societal norms — from what is permissible to eat; to how, when and whether to limit sexual behavior (i.e., whether it should only be for reproduction or might also be okay for fun and even profit); to the necessity for human or animal sacrifice; to specifications of how to dress — have nothing to do with an extension of consciousness, but are as much a part of a specific culture as whether one eats cereal or herring or crickets for breakfast.

But again, given the major role that religion played in the past, defining and including societal norms as part of a religion made sense, as there were no other institutions to do this. In his book *The Guide for the Perplexed*, Maimonides clearly presents two separate tracks. Without religious laws, he says, it would be impossible to build a righteous nation. But the individual can take steps beyond these laws, as he or she strives toward perfection: "Intuitive knowledge, which is like prophecy, is the ultimate goal after obeying the law."[12] John Haldane, Professor of Philosophy at the University of St. Andrews in Scotland, explains this further: "What Maimonides is doing all the time is emphasizing the transcendence of God as the ground of Being, the ground of Knowledge. God's Knowledge is the same as Reality. . . . What are we to do? How are we to perfect ourselves? We are made as images of God, we have intellect, we have will, we are to engage in this *imitatio Dei*, this imitation of the Divine, by becoming to the extent that we can godlike, by transforming the world that God has expressed out of His nature back into mind, through our knowledge of it. . . .

So the world is a creation out of mind and is a reception into mind....We come to perfection in understanding the reality that surrounds us."[13]

If God Is the Answer, What Was the Question?

The physicist Richard Feynman made a good point to contemplate. "God was always invented to explain mystery," he said. "God is always invented to explain those things that you do not understand. Now, when you finally discover how something works, you get some laws which you're taking away from God; you don't need him anymore. But you need him for the other mysteries. So therefore you leave him to create the universe because we haven't figured that out yet; you need him for understanding those things which you don't believe the laws will explain, such as consciousness, or why you only live to a certain length of time — life and death — stuff like that...."[14]

"Everything happens for a reason" is a common saying. While it is strictly true (everything happens for *different* reasons), the tendency is to have the simplest possible explanation for as many happenings as possible. This is what science does: It seeks increasingly simple and general explanations for phenomena.

But in a person's life, it's more problematic: seeing one's dead father alive in a dream, experiencing a violent storm or flood, losing one's house to a devastating fire, suffering the death of a child — all need reasons.

The simplest, most comprehensive and hardest to disprove explanation for absolutely everything that ever could happen anywhere, at any time, is, of course, "it was God's will."

Comfort of Knowing Why Bad Things Happen

To get on in the world all of us need to understand it as much as possible; and to get along with others, and to manage ourselves, we need do the same. It's simplest to think that our internal world's chaotic changes, and the external world's chaotic and cataclysmic events — meteors, earthquakes and the like — all come from one source: "God."

Having the sense of "God" helps in many kinds of understanding. How else but through "God" or the spirit world could our ancestors — lacking knowledge of weather systems or plate tectonics — have explained an earthquake, or a devastating storm, or floods that wiped out settlements and destroyed crops?

Even today, the world is full of the unexplained. It's important, when extreme events happen, to believe that one understands why. We say, "Why did God let this happen? What did I do that was wrong, and how did I deserve this? God must have planned this." To help us handle the loss of a loved one, we may say, "She's in a better place and is with God now."

A group of neuroscientists noted recently that "... religious conviction buffers against anxiety by providing relief from the experience of uncertainty and error, and in so doing, strengthening convictions and narrowing attention away from inconsistencies."[15]

A study of religious fundamentalism that measured the brain's response to uncertainty buttresses this idea. EEG measurements of neural reactivity showed that greater religious fundamentalism is associated with lower sensitivity to new and cognitively disturbing or upsetting information. This is evidence that religious fundamentalism, by providing a sense of coherency and control, may offer relief from distress and uncertainty.[16] And it has been well documented that religious passion and/or the simple belief in God prompts a person to have far less anxiety after making a mistake, and actually decreases the likelihood of their making one.

We seem to be born to believe that things are fated. A study of European and Asian Canadians suggests that culture affects the type of fate that people see in the world — God or an interconnected universe — but fate it is.[17] And this belief seems to begin early in life; most young children see a design in the objects and events in the world.

Beliefs, whether in God or something else, create meaning and reduce uncertainty. Interestingly, a higher percentage of atheists and agnostics believe in extraterrestrials and UFOs than those who self-identify as religious.[18]

We've all heard comments like these: After a devastating fire that destroyed her home someone might say "I guess it's just a sign that it's time for a change in my life. God said, 'You have too much stuff.'" A father, after his child was born with severe defects, might say "God made Pearl the way He wanted. She's perfect." Again, the simplest and most encompassing explanation for everything that happens is, of course, "God did it."

The Answer to an Ever-Changing, Surprising, Incoherent World

The traditional understanding of the relationship between humanity and that which is Above was well-stated by John Calvin in the 16th century. In his work *Institutes of the Christian Religion*, Calvin gives the following description of a specific mental faculty, the *sensus divinitatis* (divine sense):

> There is within the human mind, and indeed by natural instinct, an awareness of divinity. This we take to be beyond controversy. To prevent anyone from taking refuge in the pretense of ignorance, God himself has implanted in all men a certain understanding of his divine majesty. Ever renewing its memory, he repeatedly sheds fresh drops.[19]

To have any degree of success in life, it's vital to be able to make sense of what's going on inside of us and immediately around us, and to know how to act properly. Human society provides us with many ways to do this: laws, the advice of others, our common culture — all work to maintain order in life.

It is important to have rules, stability, coherence — the sense that things will proceed pretty much in an orderly way, and that we know what is and what will be. In fact, this is so important that, when disturbed it's a risk factor for disease.[20] Religious conviction and belief in God help form this sense of coherence; together, they can provide a cushion against anxiety about death, increasing our feelings of safety and security.

God's will can envelop everything from the sudden death of a young child, to the bully's cruelty toward the weak, to legal and moral injustices, to one's work and life struggles, to one's weird dreams — and even to hallucinations. This all-encompassing belief in God, and the religions that have formed around it, provide a ready-made explanation for how the universe began, what the purpose of life is, and how to understand injustice and death.

God is the quickest and easiest explanation for how the world is organized, for changes in the world, for changes in our consciousness, for madness, for loss. It is the all-embracing, universal reason.

A large review of all the relevant surveys conducted in the last 20 years found that a sense of coherence about the world — a concept first proposed by sociologist Aaron Antonovsky, that the world in general is explicable and generally predictable[21] — results in a loss of anxiety and allows people to be happier as well as healthier.[22] So when all other circumstances are equal, religious people — of any religion — are actually much happier than those who are not religious. The religion with the happiest people is a bit of a surprise to Westerners, given our current perspective on the world: it is Islam.[23]

A study headed by researchers at Northwestern University and the University of Texas at Austin asked people what patterns they could see in arrangements of dots or plotted points of stock market information. Before asking, the researchers made half the participants feel a lack of control, either by giving them negative feedback unrelated to their performance or by having them recall experiences where they had lost control of a situation. The results were striking: Those who sensed a loss of control were much more likely to see patterns where there were none. The authors write: "We were surprised that the phenomenon is as widespread as it is." So what's going on here? The study results suggest that when we feel a lack of control, we fall back on superstitious ways of thinking.[24]

God can explain all and everything. An earthquake might be explained as God's retribution for rampant adultery and other acts that are considered depraved, or as punishment for one's (or, most likely, others') theft or liberalism or homosexuality. The Southern Baptist televangelist Jerry Falwell famously claimed that "AIDS is not just God's punishment for homosexuals, it is God's punishment for the society that tolerates homosexuals."[25] At a time when the COVID-19 virus had already ended many thousands of lives in the U.S., a poll reported some 44 percent of Americans saying that the pandemic was a "wake-up call" from God and a "sign of coming judgment." A popular U.S. pastor, John Piper, appeared to endorse his fellow ministers who blamed the pandemic on "sinful cities and arrogant nations." He agreed that "God sometimes uses disease to bring particular judgements upon those who reject him and give themselves over to sin." Ralph Drollinger, a Christian minister and leader of a Bible study group for members of then-president Donald Trump's Cabinet, argued that the disease was "God's consequential wrath on our nation," warning that "whenever an individual or corporate group of individuals violate the inviolate precepts of God's Word, he, she, they or the institution will suffer the respective consequences." Robert Jeffress, another Christian minister in the U.S., echoed this idea by warning that "all natural disasters can ultimately be traced back to sin."[26]

The Psychological Evolution of Religion

Why do many religious-minded people endow conscious abilities to material objects, seek help from talismans and fear the anger of broken taboos? According to many evolutionary psychologists, this behavior is a natural result of religious belief itself, and is a consequence of how the brain evolved during early human history. One conception is that religion is an accidental, even "parasitic," byproduct of mental routines that evolved in response to needs that were completely unrelated to religious belief.

The late evolutionary biologist Stephen Jay Gould used the metaphor of an architectural "spandrel" for these inadvertent behaviors. A spandrel is the space that incidentally forms between two adjacent arches and the ceiling above them. In this view, religion is one such spandrel, since it is a byproduct, rather than an adaptation, of the activity of the specific mental routines of agent detection, causal reasoning and theory of mind. Gould held that endowing material objects with religious qualities is a natural result of this process.

When our senses detect something unexpected or only partially perceive something, an immediate reflex is to assign the cause to something living and potentially threatening. This process is called "agent detection" and likely evolved in response to the most immediate survival need our early ancestors faced: to avoid becoming a predator's next meal — better safe ("It was nothing, really") than sorry (no statement, as dead).

So, it would seem that individuals who experienced many false positives were much more likely to survive than those who too readily dismissed threats (false negatives). Our mental apparatus still includes agent detection, of course, and its hyperactive nature means that we quickly assume that an event of unknown origin is caused by some unseen agent. Today, we tend to over-respond continually to potential threats — such as random noises in the night — and often see a deliberate activity behind what are chance happenings.

Our normal restricted thought emphasizes "causal reasoning," which assigns a narrative of cause and effect to a sequence of events, no matter how randomly occurring they may be. Causal reasoning itself might be the outgrowth of another adaptation: the ability to manufacture complex tools. Toolmaking required picturing in detail how, where and when a tool would be used and, additionally, communicating that narrative to the group. This mental process — of picturing and verbally describing a procedure that does not as yet exist — activates the same areas in our brains that are also involved in imagining and detecting unexplained events.

Of course, a supernatural, all-encompassing being, able to do anything, anywhere, at any time, provides a compact and efficient explanation for the causes of a multiplicity of unexplained events — from sudden illness to weird dreams, to unusual weather — that is, to *everything*.

One result of possessing causal reasoning is that when it — like everything in our mind — gets extended, we can easily go from there to conceive of disembodied minds and assign consciousness to abstract entities. But the view that religion and the search for higher consciousness is just "misattribution" and an inappropriate extension of the common abilities of understanding causality wildly overstates the case. It obscures some of the real functions of religious groupings.

Religious traditions encourage their adherents to behave for the benefit of the group, and this cooperation provides the group with an advantage. This didn't happen by design; there isn't any "religion center" in the brain, any more than there is a "patriotism" center. Rather, religions are best thought of as a product of sociocultural evolution.

Ritual Connectedness

Many studies have found that rituals enhance social cooperation, among other things. One important recent study found that rituals, especially those involving synchrony, improved the participants' cooperation and enhanced group cohesion. The more closely actions were synchronized, the stronger was the group's solidarity.

This interesting and innovative study compared people performing at three different levels of synchrony. The first level, "Exact Synchrony," included people practicing yoga, Buddhist chanting and a form of Hindu devotional singing, with participants deliberately matching each other's movements and/or vocalizations for more than 30 minutes. The second level, "Complementary Synchrony," in which movements and/or vocalizations were not exactly matched in time but were close, included a group performing Capoeira (a Brazilian martial art), a Brazilian drumming group and a Christian choir. In the third level, "No Synchrony," participants did not perform movements or vocalizations at all.

The researchers found that synchrony increased perceptions of the merging of self with others. In all cases, "Exact Synchrony" was stronger than "Complementary Synchrony," which was stronger than "No Synchrony." Also, the stronger the synchrony, the greater the participants' contributions to the group later on. The researchers concluded that ritual has an effect on our connection with others: ". . . ritual synchrony increases perceptions of oneness with others, which increases sacred values to intensify prosocial behaviors."[27]

Strange Beliefs and Costly Signals

Until about 12,000 years ago, our hunter-gatherer ancestors formed tightly knit groups, whose members were genetically related or bound by kin selection. Within each group the members trusted each other and cooperated in hunting, foraging and childcare. This cooperation enabled them not only to survive but to out-compete other groups. As populations grew, larger groups formed around shared experiences and beliefs. Religion then is an evolutionary adaptation that unifies a large number of people who are otherwise unrelated, making its devotees interact in cooperative ways and more likely to survive and pass their genes on to the next generation.[28]

A shared religious belief is often communicated by unusual dress, rules and rituals; odd eating habits; or other "costly" signals. These behaviors may seem crazy to the outsider, especially since they often require sacrifice, but they actually enhance a member's belief and commitment to the group, and contribute to the interpersonal trust within it and to its social cohesion as a whole.

As already mentioned, to be accepted in the group can necessitate taking on many strange beliefs. Evangelical Christians believe in "the Rapture"; Mormons believe that their sacred book was translated from "reformed Egyptian" on golden plates discovered with the help of an angel by their religion's founder, Joseph Smith, on September 22, 1823. Mormons also believe that contraception is "in rebellion against God," and that those using it are "guilty of gross wickedness."

Some unusual or extreme acts also serve to establish closed boundaries for group membership and keep members in place. This is especially true in religious groups, although the same attention to clothing, body decoration and ritual are also found in companies and gangs and on sports teams.

This is why, for instance, "Moonies" (followers of the Unification movement founded by Korean religious leader Sun Myung Moon) shave their heads, and why Jain monks wear elaborate gear on their heads and feet (to avoid killing anything that may come near). It's why, in the Jerusalem summer, the ultraorthodox Jews still wear bulky, heavy, super-warm black clothing that's much more suitable for a winter blizzard in Ukraine. It may seem insane, but wearing heavy clothes in the hot Israeli sun communicates, on a basic level: "I'm a devout Jew, so you can trust me, because what other possible reason would I have to wear this heavy stuff?"

The use of unusual or inappropriate garb, or of adherence to specific rituals or dietary rules (such as not eating onions or pork), communicates to other group members that the person in question has membership in their restricted society and is therefore trustworthy — at least, to others similarly outfitted or food-deprived.

Such members are more likely to be charitable to others whose appearance shows that they belong to the same group. For instance, ultraorthodox Jews are more likely to lend money with no collateral to someone who has the same distinctive hairstyle and wears the same costume. So, while such costly signals may seem odd and unnecessary to an outsider, they do have a function.

Until recently, a young Masai man had to kill a lion by himself to become a full member of his tribe. In religion and other groups, being willing to do these sorts of things earns trust. Lion-killing is outlawed now, because lions have become endangered. A Masai man once told me (RO) "this [restriction] is going to be the death of us." It wasn't; the Masai are thriving, and that man was even doing banking transactions with a basic smartphone in the early 2000s, before the practice had spread to Silicon Valley.

Although it seems paradoxical, many religious ideas have become widespread precisely *because* they violate our standard worldview. A painted wooden statue that can talk, or a stone that listens to your problems and provides guidance shatters our normal assumptions — for instance, that "listening" is done only by living things. A man ascending to Heaven after death is a pretty vivid image. All of this makes the *super*natural more natural, dramatic and exciting — and, because it's so unusual, it's easy to remember.

These semi-magical, literal forms of beliefs could well have started as far back as in Paleolithic times, when our ancestors saw cave walls as permeable barriers to the spirit world, whose dramatic stories could be etched and painted, remembered and reiterated, developed and changed. Stories were later carved on giant megalithic structures, like the pillars of Göbekli Tepe and Nevali Cori, or represented in the looming bulls' heads protruding out of the domicile walls at Çatalhöyük — and carried on from there. Images were transported along with their stories and the beliefs they enshrined. Symbols such as spirals — thought to represent the trance state —travelled to Malta and to the passage tombs of Gavrinis in France, Newgrange in Ireland and beyond.

The major religions of today all contain violations of normal experience: A wafer and wine are the flesh and blood of Christ; fasting or cleansing one's body rids one of sins; a Virgin Mother gave birth to a Son of God. Moses descends a mountain with stone tablets written upon by God. Muhammad flies on a winged creature from Mecca to Jerusalem and on to Heaven, and returns before the water in a jug he knocked over in his ascent spills on the floor.

These very strange beliefs are surprisingly prevalent. Many people believe in stones that talk, and in oracles, or believe that soda wafers are the Body of Christ, or that God is Three-in-

One, or that the scrolls in Judaism are sacred, or that an Ojibwe dreamcatcher made of willow and twine protects babies.

Such striking, strange and certainly counterintuitive ideas are "catchier" than the ordinary features of life, and are recalled better and remembered longer than mundane, intuitively plausible statements.[29]

Of course, the idea that seems the strangest, in terms of our ordinary daily experiences, is the claim that there are invisible forces — such as God, spirits or other supernatural agents — that exist, regulate and even determine the physical world. But these conceptions and beliefs may well be functional if one seeks to stimulate a cognitive shift, first by freeing the group members from association with conventional life, and then by holding these unusual ideas in mind. This not only establishes the uniqueness of the group but also prepares or primes its members for a more comprehensive consciousness, one that is less bound by our "small world" of everyday life and the usual perceptions of time, space and ego.

Most likely, then, both biology and sociocultural advantages have contributed to the development of religion: Elements of religious belief could well have first arisen as a "byproduct" of the brain's natural evolution, but religions per se persisted and spread, permeating every human society, because they successfully promoted group survival and conscious evolution. To quote from Idries Shah's *The Sufis*:

> Formal religion is...merely a shell, though a genuine one, which fulfills a function. When the human consciousness has penetrated beyond this social framework, the Sufi understands the real meaning of religion....outer religion is only a prelude to special experience. Most ecstatics remain attached to a rapturous symbolization of some concept derived from their religion. The Sufi uses religion and psychology to pass beyond all this.[30]

Being Watched Over, or Being Watched

There's a famous competition demonstration, much-loved by psychologists, called the "dictator game" or "ultimatum game." The instructions are as follows: "You have been chosen as the giver in this economic decision-making task. You will find 10 one-dollar coins. Your role is to take and keep as many of these coins as you would like, knowing that however many you leave, if any, will be given to the receiver subject to keep." You have never met this other person and have no expectation of ever doing so.

Psychologists Azim Shariff and Ara Norenzayan found that of the 50 subjects who participated no one left as much as $5 to the other, the average amount left was $1.84, and 52 percent left $1 or less, confirming what has been found — most act selfishly in such games. However, half the group was subtly primed with God concepts, and of this group, the average amount left was $4.22, with 64 percent leaving $5 or more. The thought of God or spirits being around, watching them, presumably being aware of their individual actions, made those people act in a more generous and equitable way. And they point out that "although religions vary profoundly, central to all faiths is the idea of one or more omnipresent and omniscient moralizing agents who defy death, ignorance, and illusion; who demand costly sacrifice; and who arbitrate behavior in groups."[31]

In another study, Shariff and Norenzayan sought to replicate and expand on these findings. This time people played a different "ultimatum" game, in which they decided how to divide up a sum of money among anonymous strangers. They gave more money to the strangers after "God" concepts had been mentioned in an "unrelated" situation, than they did after neutral concepts or none at all had been mentioned. But they also found that "implicit activation of concepts related to secular moral institutions restrained selfishness as much as did religious suggestion."[32]

Reminders that "God is watching" are everywhere in our society and often go unnoticed. The watchful eye of God is often depicted in the stained-glass windows of churches. People in the U.S. have many reminders in their pockets or purses, as the phrase "In God we trust" is printed on U.S. paper currency, and some denominations also include that watchful eye looking right at the bearer — and floating atop a pyramid, no less (U.S. readers: If you doubt this, check your wallets).

An ever-watching god-figure might also have been instituted to deter people from cheating, which would have been an important adaptation as we formed societies that relied on cooperation. In one study, undergraduates were asked to complete a computerized spatial intelligence test, but were told that because there were still glitches in the system, occasionally the answer to a question they were asked might accidentally pop up on the screen (of course, the popups were deliberate). If that happened, the students were supposed to press the space bar immediately to clear it.

Before beginning the test, some of the undergraduates were told a ghost story about a student involved in the study who died suddenly and whose ghost had been recently seen in the testing room. The researchers found that these participants resisted the opportunity to cheat by pressing the space bar more quickly than those who merely saw, at the end of the instructions, that the test was dedicated to a student who died, or who were told nothing at all.[33]

All of these studies depend on theory of mind, which, as you may recall, is our tendency to suppose that others (even dead others) have minds and intentions. There doesn't even have to be a supernatural or ghostly element involved; the same effect can be triggered by an image of a pair of (watching) eyes. Professor Melissa Bateson and her colleagues carried out a now famous experiment in the psychology department lounge at England's Newcastle University. They displayed images of eyes or flowers next to the "honesty box" for coffee contributions. In all, 48 people were involved in the 10-week study.

The notice placed above the coffee/tea-making equipment gave the instructions for payment and prices, and included a banner at the top. On alternate weeks, the banner depicted either eyes or flowers, with the specific eyes and flowers also varying weekly. Because of the layout of the lounge, it was unlikely that anyone would notice if someone did or did not feed the honesty box. Yet the eye images had a large effect, with contributions almost three times as high during weeks when eyes were displayed than when flowers were displayed. Which eyes — blue, brown, hazel, round- or almond-shaped — and which flowers proved to be irrelevant.[34]

However, only a small group of people used these facilities every day, and everyone knew the person who ran the coffee fund. Would the "eye effect" be as strong when similar posters were used in more anonymous places with a higher volume of traffic? Also, even though the notices seemed to be prominently placed, was it possible that the eyes had drawn extra attention to them, thus accounting for the results?

To answer these questions, the researchers used a university cafeteria that served many hundreds of people a day, most of them not known to each other or to the cafeteria staff. There were four scenarios: eyes at the top of a poster asking people to put trays in the racks provided after finishing their meal, or at the top of a poster telling people they could eat only food or drink purchased on the premises; and these same two posters, but with flowers instead of eyes. The researchers found that more people cleared their tables when there were eyes present on a poster, regardless of the poster's message.[35]

The Value of Religion

For very many adherents religion is comforting; it provides coherence to life, mysteries are explained and action is prescribed. For others, religion is restricting, bizarre and stultifying; and for still others, it's just the family's crazy ideas to put up with occasionally when going with them to worship.

The situation is so complex that there can never be a simple, direct, yes/no answer to the question of the value of religion to humanity as a whole — nor even any possible metric. How does one measure the countless meals served, the housing and other forms of assistance provided to the poor; the role played, for example, by churches in ridding Sierra Leone of the Ebola virus? During the coronavirus pandemic, religious organizations mobilized their extended social networks in order to raise funds and recruit volunteers to provide food, healthcare, educational and job opportunities to those struggling from the effects of the pandemic and to ensure that frontline healthcare workers had meals and medical equipment.

There are many other examples of religious enterprises providing shelter and succor to those displaced by natural disasters. Places of worship, and enterprises that religious organizations run provide assistance to communities, and support to social groups. The Southern Baptists in the U.S. are legendary for the generosity and efficiency with which they provide food during hurricane crises. Countless homeless people have been fed or housed by churches, mosques and synagogues, and countless waifs have been taken in after being abandoned and families cared for after disasters.

But countless others have been deprived of a decent life by religious institutions, and many have been abused sexually. So along with religion's beneficial contents, there are the discontents. One has to take into account the cruelty of wars of conquest such as the Crusades; the depredations of the Spanish

Inquisition; the Catholic/Protestant-bred "troubles" in England and Ireland; conflicts between Islam, Christianity and Judaism (as well as those involving minor religious communities such as the Yazidis); and those devout Buddhists in Malaysia who rape, burn and murder Rohingya Muslims, whom they consider subhuman in the same way that soldiers dehumanize their war enemies.

The value of any religion or religious intervention depends on the state of society, the state of the religion and the particular people involved, and on who's doing the ministering and administering.

That said, "It was God's will" or "God's doing" surpasses every other possible explanation. While there are millions of small human groupings that people belong to such as companies, families, or teams, everyone can still believe in the same god. That sense of unity and connection beyond our individual selves, family, tribe or nation is the fundamental feature that has made humanity the most successful large animal on the planet; our ability for transcendent understanding was built upon it.

Morality: Down from God or Up from... Plants?

> The moral sense, or conscience, is as much a part of man as his leg or arm. It is given to all human beings in a stronger or weaker degree, as force of members is given them in a greater or less degree.
>
> — THOMAS JEFFERSON[36]

For years, the overwhelming consensus was that morality had its origin in religious thought, and that without belief and guidance from a higher source, human beings would revert to the immoral savages we used to be. But is that really the case?

Of course, different societies have different perspectives, but "Do unto others as you'd have them do to you" seems to be universal. It is repeated everywhere and is intended, for the most part, to help maintain local peace and harmony within society. This advice has obviously served humanity well, as have moral rules such as "Don't steal, kill, rape" and the like.

There are many issues about morality. Who gets the credit for the good and the blame for evil? How do people differ, and what makes an act (e.g., capital punishment) moral in one society and not in another? But our focus is more specifically on whether religion and the concept of God are responsible for our moral sense.

Forever, it seems, human beings in all societies have decided that morality "cometh to them from above." In many religions, a divine influence — the same influence that gave us the Ten Commandments, the Five Pillars of Islam and the Hindu *Purusarthas* — is believed to direct and organize humanity's moral principles. Follow God's rules, and you and yours will flourish.

This idea continues, as the titles of two recent articles demonstrate: "If There Is No God, All is Permitted"[37] and "Morality Requires a God, Whether You're Religious or Not."[38]

For many thinkers, the human being stands out as "the moral animal" — a phrase that's even the title of a popular book,[39] a thoughtful and well-reasoned account of human moral life. But taken alone, out of this context, that title reveals the same center-of-the-universe mentality as our pre-Copernicus predecessors had. There are lots of other "moral" animals throughout the animal kingdom; we are not "the" moral animal but, "a" moral animal.

Thankfully, recent studies in animal behavior, developmental psychology and neuroscience have transformed this notion of morality. Basic morality isn't even limited to animals, so perhaps a better way to think of us would be as a "moral life-form." Much recent research demonstrates that our moral behavior is innate; it evolved over millions of years to promote enhanced cooperation, support, and survival within the group.

Our moral rules — like our language and reasoning — are in fact built upon the biology of the animals that preceded us on the evolutionary tree, and are not holy writ that was dropped down from the sky. As the anthropologist Robert Ardrey once famously remarked, "…we are born of risen apes, not fallen angels." There is plenty of emerging evidence that our sense of the good, or of right action, does not derive from a higher being, one most usually identified as God, but, rather, is a bottom-up phenomenon whose basis is present from birth, and we build on it according to our capacity and culture.

Elementary moral behavior benefits one's relatives, group or tribe and not others, so each group has its own slightly different moral code, which provides a map for how individuals can live successfully within it. This is an important foundation of cooperative societies and is, in part, how the human race was able to evolve, adapt and expand as it has.

The evolutionary origins and advantages of recognizing, cooperating with and connecting to one's kin and kind have even been found in plants that compete for space and nutrients. For instance, a paper on "plant kin recognition" notes that plants allocate fewer of their own roots to gather nutrients when surrounded by other plants of the same kind, than they do when surrounded by "strangers."[40] In 2009, researchers showed that a beach weed called sea rocket senses whether it is growing among siblings or among unrelated plants of the same species. When it detects the presence of "strangers," it allocates more resources toward sprouting nutrient-grabbing roots than when it recognizes kin.[41]

Some plants, such as ragweed, develop larger common mycelial networks (systems through which plants and fungi trade nutrients) when growing among kin than they do when growing among non-kin, and are also better protected against pathogens. Interacting with kin plants also yields more seeds, compared with interacting with plants that are not kin — a process described as "a clear indication of mutual benefit and cooperation."[42]

We can't account for each and every step in morality's growth from the grasses to our own species. One way researchers try to determine the degree to which human morality is the product of natural evolution is by examining behavior in other species that is analogous to our own.

> Many non-human primates, for example, have similar methods to humans for resolving, managing, and preventing conflicts of interests within their groups. Such methods, which include reciprocity and food sharing, reconciliation, consolation, conflict intervention, and mediation, are the very building blocks of moral systems in that they are based on and facilitate cohesion among individuals and reflect a concerted effort by community members to find shared solutions to social conflict. Furthermore, these methods of resource distribution and conflict resolution often require or make use of capacities for empathy, sympathy, and sometimes even community concern.[43]

There are thousands of studies of "moral" and/or empathic awareness in animals. In one experiment, each rat learns to press a lever for food; then another rat is introduced into the next cage, and the lever's wiring is altered so that when the first rat presses the lever for food, the second rat gets an electric shock. Researchers found that the first rats stopped pressing the lever for a while, forfeiting their chance to get food. However, they eventually returned to pressing the lever, because otherwise they would have starved. But an empathic response to their fellow rats' distress dictated their initial responses.[44]

A similar experiment was carried out with rhesus monkeys. They learned to pull on a chain to get food delivered into their cage; then another monkey was put into the next cage, and the wiring was altered so that the second monkey got a shock when the first monkey pulled the chain for its food. The upshot was that the first monkeys desisted from pulling the chain and voluntarily starved themselves for between five and 12 days. They were more likely to do this if they were familiar with the second monkey than if the second monkey was a stranger, and were also more likely to do it if the second monkey was a rhesus rather than a member of another species. But regardless, they still did desist. So some of the core capacities underlying our own morality preceded us into the world and are present in nonhuman animals.[45] Like rats and monkeys, we're more likely to help those who are like us.

Connectedness to others involves both reciprocity and empathy — the two pillars upon which morality is built — and both are found in bonobos and other apes. We can see the beginnings of this when these primates soothe relations between others of their group, broker reconciliations (bring parties together after a fight) and break up fights in order to reinstate and maintain peace. This is because everybody in the group has a stake in a cooperative atmosphere.

Chimps console and comfort each other when things go awry, and have been seen to mourn the death of another chimp. Primatologist Frans de Waal tells of a mentally handicapped rhesus macaque that got away with breaking the rules of the group because the other members all seemed to realize she was inept and her actions were not deliberate.

Just as with humans, the ape mother-child bond has implications for the future behavior of the child; orphaned apes are likely to be less empathic than those raised by their mothers. Bonobos who have undergone a bad experience and recovered are much more likely to comfort another bonobo who is similarly afflicted. It seems, says de Waal, that, just like us, "It's almost as if one first needs to have one's own emotional house in order before one is ready to visit the emotional house of another. This is true for children, and apparently also for bonobos."

When a bonobo named Kuni saw a starling hit the glass of her enclosure at the Twycross Zoo in Great Britain, she went to comfort it. Picking up the stunned bird, Kuni gently set it on its feet. When it failed to move, she threw it a little, but the bird just fluttered. With the starling in hand, Kuni then climbed to the top of the tallest tree, wrapping her legs around the trunk so that she had both hands free to hold the bird. She carefully unfolded its wings and spread them wide, holding one wing between the fingers of each hand, before sending the bird like a little toy airplane out toward the barrier of her enclosure. But the bird fell short of freedom and landed on the bank of the moat. Kuni climbed down and stood watch over the starling for a long time, protecting it against a curious juvenile. By the end of the day, the recovered bird had flown off safely." [46]

Studies of chimpanzees have found clear-cut examples of caring behavior, carried out without expectation of personal benefit. Chimps may go out of their way to help another. In one experiment, chimps in one cage released a reward for chimps in a neighboring cage when the unrelated neighbors signaled (by pulling a chain) that they wanted it. [47] Chimps have even been found to help a different, but related, species: They have been seen to climb several meters to get an out-of-reach object for both a known and an unknown human.

All human beings come into the world primed with the basis of a moral foundation that helps us survive as individuals within a very small group. So our first priority is to know what group that is, and who's in it. Babies constantly have to distinguish between "Us" and "Them" and are primed to prefer "Us." Newborns make distinctions between familiar and strange people almost immediately.

Babies learn to use the rate at which they suck on a pacifier to indicate which voice they prefer to hear read them a story: their mother's or a stranger's. And at less than three days old, infants show a uniform preference for their mother's voice. As babies develop, they quite naturally base their preferences —

their adaptive biases — on the people around them, those of their own group.

It seems that we are born with the ability to judge who is "like me" and who isn't — not only in terms of appearance, but also in terms of mind. Babies as young as seven months prefer people who are like-minded — who might reflect their own tastes by preferring, for example, Cheerios to Graham Crackers — and dislike those whose opinions differ.

More than 80 percent of babies under the age of one year, and 100 percent of those slightly older than that, continue to prefer like-minded individuals even when those individuals appear to harm others who are not like them. It obviously had to be a priority for us to distinguish and prefer our own kind, our own group, from the start, and to be wary of outsiders.

Psychologist Karen Wynn's Baby Lab at Yale University has run repeated experiments with three- and five-month-old babies, and has established that the overwhelming majority of them — more than three-quarters of those tested — recognize and show preference for nice actions over nasty actions, leading the babies to prefer nice individuals over mean individuals. Just about all the six- and 10-month-old infants preferred the helpful individual to the hindering individual. In study after study after study, the results consistently show that babies feel positively toward helpful individuals and disapprove, dislike, maybe even condemn individuals who are antisocial toward others.[48]

In an experiment to assess whether babies have the ability to make a distinction between good and bad (as exemplified in this case by kindness versus cruelty), researchers created a situation where one puppet struggled to open a box, and another either helped the puppet open it or slammed it shut. Surprisingly, even five-month-olds preferred the good puppet to the naughty one. The researchers and their collaborators conclude that we naturally possess a moral sense.[49]

Babies have a rudimentary sense of connectedness to others and favor fair divisions of resources. At the age of 15 months, a child will look longer at an unfair division of goodies than at a fair division, suggesting that he/she found it surprising.* By the age of 16 months, babies prefer a puppet that is seen to act fairly (by its dividing resources equally between two other puppets) over a puppet that is seen as unfair; when two 19-month-old toddlers clean up a room, they expect equal reward, even if their efforts were unequal.

Something very similar was shown with 21-month-olds. In this case, two experimenters each held out a toy to the child. One experimenter then teased the child, withholding the toy, while the other "accidentally" dropped the toy while handing it over. In neither case did the child get the toy. But when the toddlers were then given a toy to give to one of the two experimenters, they tended to choose the latter person rather than the teaser.[50]

When deciding whether to help someone, three-year-olds take into account the intentions of third parties. In one study, an actor modelled two situations: He deliberately attempted to harm someone and failed, and he "accidentally" actually did hurt someone. Three-year-old children seeing both events were more likely to give something to the "victim" when the actor had bad intentions than when the outcome was accidental.[51]

So three-year-olds are more likely to help someone whom they have seen help others, and are less likely to help someone who has been unkind to another person. They really are motivated by genuine care, since they actually get involved in accomplishing the goals of the person they help, and they act with that person's interests, rather than their own, in mind. For example, if asked to pass a cup so that someone can pour water into

---

*A control study ruled out the possibility that they just look longer at asymmetric displays.

it, three-year-olds will make sure that the cup is not damaged, even though it was previously selected by the experimenter.

Babies prefer to hear the language that is most familiar to them, and by the time children are five years old they tend to prefer a playmate who speaks their own language — which makes sense, since communication is so much easier. There is also a bias not only toward the same language, but also toward the same accent. Race plays no part in young children's choices: A white child will tend to choose a black child with the same accent over a white child with a different accent.

All of this research supports a general picture of baby morality. Babies probably have no conscious access to moral notions — no idea why certain acts are good or bad. They respond on a gut level. Indeed, if you watch the older babies during the experiments, they don't act like impassive judges — they tend to smile and clap during good events and frown, shake their heads and look sad during the naughty events. Babies' experiences might be cognitively empty, but they're emotionally intense, replete with strong feelings and strong desires.

Human babies are also born with innate and indiscriminate tendencies to be cooperative and helpful. Even in the first year of life, babies show distress if they harm someone; and one- or two-year-olds — particularly girls — will try to sooth someone in pain and to comfort someone in distress. As early as the age of six months, children begin to help spontaneously, and the extent to which they do so increases in the following years — although this is mainly with friends and family, and rarely with total strangers before the age of four.

Interestingly, young children focus primarily on social comparison, so much so that they routinely choose to get less for themselves from the options offered, to avoid getting more than the other party. However, once children are seven or eight years old, about 80 percent of them will give candy to someone they don't know; and by age nine or 10 (by which time they have been acculturated, and to some degree, educated), they may deliberately give the other person more than they take for themselves.

Frans de Waal writes: "Would it be realistic, for example, to urge people to be considerate of others if we didn't already have a natural inclination to be so? Would it make sense to appeal to fairness and justice if we didn't have powerful reactions to their absence? Imagine the cognitive burden if every decision we took needed to be vetted against handed-down logic."[52] Psychologist Paul Bloom suggests that over time, altruism evolved because cooperative individuals were rewarded while those who were uncooperative were punished or avoided and so produced fewer offspring.

So we're connected deeply to the world by our biology; and this sense of connectedness to others, friend or foe, long predates our species. Morality is not somehow granted from somewhere On High to us "sinners." Rather, it comes to us from our nervous system and from the nervous systems of our ancestors — as do all the other characteristics of human experience that we've discussed. "Risen apes," if you like, or perhaps "extremely complex and evolved sprouted grasses" — but not "fallen angels," except in a metaphorical sense.

Marco Iacoboni, one of the foremost researchers on mirror neurons (the neurons that fire both when we act and when we observe the same action in another, literally "mirroring" the behavior as though it were our own), noted that while it has traditionally been thought that our biology is self-serving, and that we have to use social codes to rise above this and live together cooperatively, the roots of that behavior are in our biology:

> The research on mirror neurons, imitation and empathy, in contrast, tells us that our ability to empathize, a building block of

our sociality and morality, has been built 'bottom up' from relatively simple mechanisms of action production and perception."[53]

There is substantial research to support this view of morality, as there is for other "uniquely human" capabilities, all of which have been built from the bottom up on the evolved structures of earlier living things.

FOR FURTHER READING

The Belief Instinct: The Psychology of Souls, Destiny, and the Meaning of Life, Jesse Bering, W.W. Norton, 2011.

The Bonobo and the Atheist: In Search of Humanism Among the Primates, Frans de Waal, W.W. Norton, 2013.

Born Believers: The Science of Children's Religious Belief, Justin L. Barrett, Ph.D., Free Press (Simon & Schuster), 2012.

Conceiving God: The Cognitive Origin and Evolution of Religion, David Lewis-Williams, Thames & Hudson, 2010.

The Faith Instinct: How Religion Evolved and Why It Endures, Nicholas Wade, Penguin, 2009.

Genius: The Life and Science of Richard Feynman, James Gleick, Vintage (Random House), 1993.

Just Babies: The Origins of Good and Evil, Paul Bloom, Crown Pub. (Random House), 2013.

Maimonides: The Life and World of One of the Civilization's Greatest Minds, Doubleday, 2008.

Mirroring People: The Science of Empathy and How We Connect with Others, Marco Iacoboni, Picador, 2009.

The Moral Animal: Why We Are, the Way We Are: The New Science of Evolutionary Psychology, Robert Wright, Vintage (Random House), 1995.

Our Inner Ape: A Leading Primatologist Explains Why We Are Who We Are, Frans de Waal, Penguin, 2006.

10

Mind Wars: The Religious, The Spiritual And The Scientifically Minded

Science without religion is lame,
religion without science is blind.

— ALBERT EINSTEIN

A great part of the difficulty in understanding spirituality, religiousness and conceptions of God is the countless confusing terms in use to describe them. For instance, being "religious" is not at all the same as having an interest in "spirituality." And a significant reason for the contentiousness and perennial lack of a solution to it, is that different people have major and pretty unshakeable differences in viewing the world, ranging from a focus on the precise mechanics of life and how things work, to a focus on what and how people think and feel. It is not either-or, but a continuum — the way hair color ranges from very light blonde to very dark black. And like everything in our biology, different individuals vary widely in their place on this continuum from the intuitive artist to the engineer, or somewhere between the extremes of disorder from schizophrenia to obsessive-compulsive disorder (OCD). A very large study of people in dozens of countries found that there is a continuum of severity of such responses, just as there is a continuum of people's height.[1] It's important to realize, too, that people vary on the frequency of individual psychological symptoms such as psychoticism or autistic-type episodes or hallucinations; some have them occasionally, some very often.

These differences are at the root of many of the conflicts about spirituality as well as political and cultural attitudes. Sadly, the gaps between the differences usually aren't negotiable or subject to discussion or compromise. Just as some people don't "get" jazz, or opera, or baseball, some people just don't "get" spirituality. But this is very often a matter of differences in individual cognitive style, genetics, brain organization, life experience and temperament, not truth.

Barriers in the Mind — Through Thick and Thin

What is the determining psychological factor in the differences in disposition? Since there have been many attempts to analyze important personality differences, psychologists have developed different terms for them, but if we examine all these together, we find a central tendency. One major personality dimension that's been described, on the basis of many years of research and supported by hundreds of studies, is "openness to experience" which is one of what are called the "big five" dimensions of personality.* Another concept is "barriers" in the mind, which distinguishes between people who have "thick" barriers, who compartmentalize their different experiences, from those

---

*The big five are: openness, conscientiousness, extraversion, agreeableness, and neuroticism.

with "thin" ones, whose experiences merge together. Many investigators use the term "boundaries," but we think "barriers," which can be porous, is a better descriptor.

There is a distinction between people who keep dissonant thoughts and ideas apart and those that allow them to influence each other. Similar distinctions might be convergent thinkers (linear, logical and systematic) versus divergent thinkers (flexible, creative, and explorative); or tough- versus tender-minded people. People also differ in "absorption" — the ability to become fully involved in an idea or mental image (often assessed by the ease with which one is hypnotized); and in "transliminality," the degree to which information, thoughts and ideas, move in and out of consciousness.

Most of us fall somewhere mid-way, but a look at the extremes on the barrier continuum makes this concept easier to follow. Having thin "barriers" seems to make people more open to experiences and more likely to be "spiritually inclined." Those with thick barriers tend to be detached, they tend not to have close personal relationships and experience little connection between their waking and dreaming state.

Interestingly, although the underlying reasons are subject to a lot of different interpretations (both cultural training and something inherent in female biology have been proposed), females have been consistently found to have thinner barriers than males. This is positively linked to their ability to make connections and is a disposition that most often stays stable across the course of life.

Anyone whose barriers are at the extremes is likely to encounter considerable difficulty. Those with exceptionally porous or thin barriers may struggle to separate their personal sense of self from their environment, making them quite highly variable and emotional. People at the extreme end of this thin barrier spectrum may have a lot of sensory experiences all at once — including synesthesia, where different senses are coupled so that sounds, perhaps, are perceived as colored or having different shapes. Such people are easily hypnotized; see themselves as having aspects of the opposite sex; have less clear personal space boundaries than other people; may blend past, present and future; think in shades of gray, as opposed to black and white; and experience themselves as belonging to, and identified with, different groups at different times. Of course, if they can control these extreme tendencies, they are also more able to transcend the "small world," everyday way of thinking.

Thin-barriered people are more intuitive and emotional, and have more unusual experiences; they show interpersonal dependency, social introversion and egocentricity. They are more insecurely attached, more easily reactive and more easily alienated than are thick-barriered people, who are more defensive. Thin-barriered people are more connected to spirituality than are thick-barriered people, who are more connected to religiousness.[2] Those with especially thick barriers tend to be very detached, both from other people and from their own experiences, and are often thought of as cold and calculating.

Thick-barriered and thin-barriered types also show differences in sleep patterns. Thins spend more time in hypnopompic or hypnagogic (half-awake or half-asleep) states as they awaken or fall asleep. In their article *Boundaries in the Mind: Past Research and Future Directions*, researchers Ernest Hartmann, Robert Harrison and Michael Zborowski make some telling points about barriers and dreaming. Examining the all-night sleep records of people with either very thick or very thin barriers, they say, "we were struck by the fact that people with thick boundaries appeared to have more clear-cut states of waking, NREM* sleep, and REM sleep, whereas the records of those with thin boundaries showed more in-between states, or diffi-

---

*In REM (rapid eye movement) sleep, we tend to have dreams that are vivid and have a lot of imagery. In NREM (non-rapid eye movement) sleep, dreaming appears to be rarer, more thought-like and less vivid.

cult-to-define states." They also note that "people with thinner boundaries in a psychological sense, also had thinner boundaries between REM and NREM sleep: the brain activity characteristic of REM sleep often 'escaped' into NREM sleep. More work along these lines is definitely needed."[3]

Anthropologist Tanya Luhrmann notes that "... the intriguing question is whether different sleep cultures encourage different patterns of spiritual and supernatural experience. That half-aware, drowsy state is a time when dreams commingle with awareness. People are more likely to have experiences of the impossible then. They hear their mother, many miles distant, speaking their name, or they see angels standing by the window, and then they look again and they are gone."[4]

Individuals with autism spectrum disorder — in whom the barriers are extremely thick — are usually non-believers (atheists and agnostics). Analysis of online discussion posts by autistic people compared to non-autistic "neurotypicals" tend to show more rationality, less imagination, more social discomfort and disinterest, less involvement in organized religion, more atheism, and more "own construction" of belief. People with autism lack both theory of mind and the ability to mentalize — that is, they have difficulty understanding or even thinking about the mental states of others. These deficits also reduce belief in a personal God Being. The less mentalizing there is — and males typically do less compared with females — the less tendency there is to believe.

Luhrmann and her colleagues made an important similar observation, noting that people who enjoy being absorbed in imaginative internal worlds — people who in our terms have thin barriers — are more likely to have unusual spiritual experiences.[5] She studied a group of evangelical Christians who expected to experience God directly, immediately and concretely, and who were taught that their direct experience was the result of prayer.[6] Luhrmann observed that the prayer "experts" spoke as if they had learned to take their inner sensory world more seriously than other people do, and to perceive their thoughts, images and sensations as more meaningful, blurring the line between internally and externally based experience.

This was the point. The aim of the group members was to experience the external presence of God through internal phenomena. Luhrmann found that the more people attended to their inner sensory world, the more vivid these sensations became — with some sensations being experienced as if in the external world, when in fact they were not (i.e., what they saw, smelled or heard was not actually caused by external material stimulus).

She conducted in depth interviews with 28 congregants, measuring their readiness to be caught up in imaginative experience, such as music and a dramatic scene in nature. Their comments were revealing and included such statements as "I can be deeply moved by a sunset;" "Sometimes I can change noise into music by the way I listen to it;" "The sound of a voice can be so fascinating to me that I can just go on listening to it;" "Sometimes I feel and experience things as I did as a child;" and "I find that different odors have different colors."[7]

Luhrmann found that those subjects who scored high on "absorption" in imaginative internal worlds, those with thin barriers, showed significantly high focus (i.e., deep concentration on prayer that took them away from the here and now to a different place in their minds). Their internal sensory experiences had significantly more emphasis, vividness, and hallucination-like phenomena.[8] One subject who was considered a prayer expert checked off 33 of the 34 items on the absorption scale and said, "The man who created this scale lived inside my head."[9]

Interestingly, although the absorption scale didn't ask about hallucinations, those who answered 18 or more of its questions were far more likely to report hallucinatory experiences than the other subjects. There is also growing evidence that such experiences are much more common in the general population than was once thought.

People at either extreme of the brain barrier make what statisticians call "Type 1" and "Type 2" errors. A Type 1 error involves concluding that something exists when it doesn't, or when there's not really enough evidence. Thin-barrier people are prone to make such over-conclusions. Type 2 errors involve denying that something exists even when the evidence is pretty good; those making these kinds of errors stick to what they already know and keep their barriers solid. These two types of errors are the cause of much misunderstanding in life — in marriage, at work, in politics and certainly in the study of higher consciousness and "God."

Again, neither extreme is ideal. What's needed is a balance between the two.

These different cognitive predispositions — thin barriers versus thick, open versus closed — are better correlated with spirituality than is adherence to a church-, synagogue-, or mosque-based religion. And these predispositions may be in our genes.

Religion, Spirituality, Social Outlook and Genes

There's no doubt that one's religious involvement and preference are influenced by one's social environment, upbringing and culture. Catholic families are more likely to raise Catholic children; Jews, to raise Jews; and Native Americans, to raise children with traditional Native American beliefs. Furthermore, as we've already noted, numerous studies associate religious participation with improved wellbeing, stronger social connection and prosocial behavior. But it would be incomplete to conclude that the social and cultural environment alone determines our religiosity. Families share not only traditions and practices, they also share genes.

One important study on the genetics of religiosity analyzed data on twins, taken from the MIDUS (Midlife in the United States) database, 1995-1996. It included answers to questions about religious life, for instance: How religious are you? How important is religion in your life? How important is it for you — or would it be if you had children now — to send your children for religious or spiritual services for instruction? Spirituality was gauged with questions such as: How spiritual are you? and How important is spirituality in your life?

The findings included the obvious conclusion that both nature and nurture are involved in determining one's religious life. But the most sizable (in the range of 40 to 44 per cent) genetic effects were found for "daily guidance and coping," "favoring conservative religious ideologies" and for "religious or spiritual transformations."

Daily guidance and coping involved two questions: When you have decisions to make in your daily life, how often do you ask yourself what your religious or spiritual beliefs suggest you should do? How often do you seek comfort through religious or spiritual means such as praying, meditating, attending a religious or spiritual service, or talking to a religious or spiritual advisor?

Conservative ideologies were gauged with two measures: Biblical literalism and exclusivist beliefs. Biblical literalism was measured with the question: How much do you agree or disagree with the following statement: The Bible is the actual Word of God and is to be taken literally, word for word? Exclusivist beliefs were measured with the question: Do you believe that one should stick to one's faith?

And finally, religious and spiritual transformations and their subsequent commitments were measured with the following question: Have you been "born-again," that is, had a turning-point in your life when you committed yourself to Jesus Christ? The researchers write:

> One useful way to . . . interpret the findings reported here is to frame them in terms of individual desires versus social constraint. . . . Genetic influences . . . likely represent . . . gene-based, innate predispositions, needs, wants, desires, or motivations, while . . . environmental influences broadly tap family-level social influences and wider social contexts respectively.[10]

One puzzling question is: Why are those who are strongly religious often more socially conservative than the norm, while those who are "spiritually-minded" are less so? Surprisingly, the differences stem from genetic inheritance. Genetic factors that foster "traditionalism" are responsible for adherence to both religious and social principles and practices that have been handed down from the past. "Degree of traditionalism" (perhaps best understood colloquially as "how far one falls from the tree") is the extent to which one follows the ways of the culture into which one was born — in terms of everything from religion, to profession, to political belief, to food, cultural and sexual preferences, to marriage partners.

How and why did such adherence to the past become functional?

We've seen that as our early human ancestors began living in larger groups, one of the useful adaptations — evident from at least the Neolithic era — was obedience to authority. Geneticist and psychologist Thomas Bouchard and his colleagues have described the evolution and workings of this adaptation. They note that authoritarianism determined how families should be organized, conservatism determined how societies should be organized, and these both led on to religiousness to make sense of who controls society and life.[11] Traditionalism, which is associated with thick barriers, is influenced significantly by the same genes that significantly influence religiousness. So this study shows that it is the genetic influences on religiousness, spirituality and meaning in life that are primarily responsible for people's sense of comprehension and purposefulness.[12]

One comprehensive personality test was used to tease out differences between tradition-oriented religiousness and personal spirituality. The researchers concluded that "there are important personality and cognitive differences between traditional religious and modern spiritual individuals."[13] Traditionals, as you'd expect, have high confidence in their received doctrine — the sources of authority that mandate rituals and specify rules for controlling social and sexual behavior (including what's sometimes referred to as "family values"). Accordingly, they're highly authoritarian, with low "openness to experience." In contrast, "modern spirituals" are concerned with attaining a personal insight into the nature of reality and, as a personal trait, have porous barriers. They can get easily absorbed in relevant — or sometimes irrelevant — phenomena, and are sometimes fantasy-prone, given their high openness to experience.[14] However, as we noted in Chapter 6, they are not disordered.[15]

Individuals who identify themselves as conservative are most often strong on obedience to rules and authority, and concerned with "ego defense" — safety, security, cleanliness and concern about outsiders or intrusion. They are less concerned with equality, freedom, love and pleasure, and they devalue open-mindedness as well as intellectual and imaginative thought.[16]

This all fits with the three major dimensions of attitudes and beliefs studied by psychologists that relate to the thickness of one's barriers: Authoritarianism, Religiousness and Conservatism (or "ARC," to use the jargon). So there is now a large body of evidence demonstrating considerable genetic influence on all three, with each one underpinned by the same genetically inherited propensity for traditionalism.[17]

The degree of traditional thinking in any individual seems to remain consistent over time, at least from adolescence through adulthood. Whether one has thick or thin barriers, even in adolescence, predicts whether one will likely join a conventional, formal religion or seek an extended, personal, "spiritual" consciousness in later life. In one study that tracked this, "religiousness" was found to be related to a tendency to rigidly follow orders (called "conscientiousness" in the jargon of personality testing), whereas "spiritual seeking" related to openness to experience.[18]

Surprisingly, conscientiousness (i.e., following set routines) during adolescence is an even more important predictor of whether a person later becomes religious than whether that person was religious during adolescence. Similarly, those who are open to experience in adolescence are likely to become spiritual seekers in later adulthood.[19]

Of course, as we saw in Chapter 9 with Ed Diener's research,[20] societal forces play a large part in determining which religion one adopts: If you're French, Italian or Spanish, you're probably Catholic; whereas if you're from the Andaman Islands, you probably believe Paluga to be the God of All. But how much you adhere to your familial religion, and whether you break away and reject it or even seek a more direct approach to transcendence, is in some part due to your genes.

The Right Hemisphere – Connections and the Paranormal

Belief in paranormal phenomena is the source of much disagreement and debate. Paranormal behavior refers to behavior beyond the range of normal experience or scientific explanation; examples include telepathy (mind-reading), extrasensory perception (ESP) and telekinesis (the ability to move objects at a distance by nonphysical means).

Peter Brugger, head of the neuropsychology department at University Hospital Zurich in Switzerland, and a variety of colleagues, have been conducting research into belief in paranormal phenomena for more than 15 years. The researchers have shown that both people considered "schizotypal" (healthy people who have hallucination-like experiences as well as beliefs in the paranormal that some might view as delusional) and people who don't fit into that category but score high on "magical ideation" (magical thinking), are more likely than others to believe in "luck," superstitions and the significances of coincidences, and see associations where others might not see them. These looser associations appear to be caused by two things: the reduced participation of the brain's left hemisphere in tasks where it is normally active, and the increased involvement of the right hemisphere.

One study conducted by Brugger and others involved 24 female undergraduates, half of whom were strong believers in paranormal-type events, and the other half not. In a word-association task they were shown 240 pairs of nouns, each with three to seven letters; the second of which was directly, indirectly, or not at all related to the first or else was a pronounceable non-word. The "believers" made much looser connections between the words in each pair than did the "non-believers." This suggests that belief in the paranormal could be a consequence of the tendency (shared with poets, painters and other creative people) to see connections between things that, to others, are only remotely connected. In the case of belief in the paranormal, this tendency may give rise to an attribution of meaning to what are really just coincidences. They write: "A relative preference for distant over close associations may reflect an overreliance on semantic processing characteristics of the right hemisphere." [21]

Psychologist Christine Mohr collaborated with Brugger in a study where 20 men and 16 women were blindfolded and asked to walk along a straight black line that bisected a six-foot wide, 60-foot long hall. As they each walked the line, their wobbles to the left or right were recorded. The more strongly the participants believed in extrasensory experiences and paranormal phenomena such as telepathy, clairvoyance and psychokinesis, the more likely they were to drift slightly to the left! In addition, on word-association tests, they were apt to make more connections more quickly than skeptics were, had many more notions about what a murky ink blot might resemble, and were faster at identifying meaningful shapes among randomly generated patterns.[22]

So what's the connection here? It is a person's habitual right-hemisphere activation that controls both the extra leftward drift when walking and the greater creativity that these participants demonstrated. The tendency to see meaning in random patterns influences one's worldview and, taken to an extreme, characterizes people with schizophrenia, who also show leftward-veering proclivities.

Along the spectrum from rigid obsessive compulsiveness on one end to schizophrenia on the other, believers in psychic phenomena fall somewhere in the middle and have increased creativity within the bounds of normalcy and above-average involvement of the brain's right hemisphere. The right hemisphere is involved in language, especially in understanding metaphor and interpreting inflection and vocal stress. We've seen how patients who have suffered damage to the right hemisphere can often form associations only within narrow limits, and how irony and metaphor typically escape them. In comparison, those with a penchant for extrasensory phenomena draw quick metaphorical links, and schizophrenics make associations that soar well beyond normal perceptions.

Healthy people with schizotypal tendencies have been shown to think of more numerous and more creative uses for things, such as an eraser. It's been found that the more magical someone's thinking, as determined by the relevant assessment scales, the more the areas on the right side of the brain's prefrontal cortex are involved in the task being tested.[23]

As with every human characteristic, each person falls somewhere on a continuum with regard to the mind's barriers, but people at one end of the barrier spectrum often view as pathological those at the opposite end. Those who go strictly "by the book" and are "what's right" people see nothing but semi-deranged behavior, sloppiness, weird thinking and perhaps a touch of mental disorder in thin barrier types. The latter, on the other hand, see rigidity, intractable resistance to change, fear of the unknown (as we see in the world's ongoing refugee crises) and lack of a spiritual sense in those with more rigid barriers. Neither perspective is completely incorrect, of course, but these habitual, stereotypical thinking patterns limit a broader understanding. One need look no further than politics to find ample illustrations of this.

The Fundamental Problem with Fundamentalism

The crowning achievement of Isaac Newton was to show that universal gravitational principles underlie everything from the fall of an apple to the way the planets move. This step-by-step deterministic thinking ushered in an amazing new era in mechanistic science, including the Industrial Revolution, the steam engine and much more. So many thought the "clockwork universe" would be the answer to all questions. But, like everything in science, it didn't explain it all.

Part of the problem of exclusive reliance on an allegedly "scientific," strict, sequential thinking is that it inflates, conflates and confuses a single successful determination. For example, just because you see that a ball each time it's dropped from the same place takes as long to land, and hits the ground at the same spot, or just because you know that a portion of the cheeseburger you eat becomes part of your body and the rest becomes waste material, doesn't mean you can accurately conclude that everything else in the world — not to mention the whole universe — is just as strictly determined.

In her Cambridge University inaugural lecture entitled *Causality and Determination*, philosopher Elizabeth (usually referred to as G.E.M.) Anscombe, a student and later associate of the philosopher Ludwig Wittgenstein, made this clear, citing Newton's balls-in-space clockwork universe as an example:

> The high success of Newton's astronomy was in one way an intellectual disaster: it produced an illusion from which we tend still to suffer. This illusion was created by the circumstance that Newton's mechanics had a good model in the solar system. For this gave the impression that we had here an ideal of scientific explanation; whereas the truth was, it was mere obligingness on the part of the solar system, by having had so peaceful a history in recorded time, to provide such a model.[24]

And, well, there was just one problem with Newton's precisely determined solar system, and it threatened to derail everything: the planet Mercury. Every planet moves in an ellipse around the Sun. Mercury had been observed with precision since the 1500s, but the "clockwork universe" was out of adjustment, it seemed, by a tiny bit — by 43" (arcseconds) per century, to be precise — which had no explanation in Newton's framework. But Einstein's new theory of relativity, in which gravitation was not a fixed mechanism but was influenced by matter and energy that curved space, predicted exactly this miniscule but precisely observed effect.

Later, a dramatic, difficult photographic expedition by the renowned British astrophysicist Arthur Eddington determined that light passing around the Sun bends the apparent position of the stars — and by an amount consistent with Einstein's theory — again a radical change to the "balls in motion" view.

The *New York Times* even ran this headline on November 10, 1919:

LIGHTS ALL ASKEW IN THE HEAVENS
EINSTEIN THEORY TRIUMPHS

Stars Not Where They Seemed, Or Were Calculated to be,
but Nobody Need Worry

Views stemming from personal thought styles still dominate the arguments about God and higher knowledge. In one corner is the challenger, the "New Atheists," and in the other corner is the long-time world champion, "Fundamentalist Religious Believers." They're like the extreme left and right of politics: lots of heat but little light. Far too often, both sides show evidence of extreme reductionist thinking and ignorant hyperbole.

This is the classic drama: science and reason on the one hand, religion and faith on the other — with scientism asserting that once we get rid of all ancient religions, we will get rid of evil. And religious fundamentalism asserting that to banish evil we only need rid the world of different beliefs. So the fundamentalist scientistic proselytizers externalize evil and the fundamentalist religious proselytizers do the same, pointing to where evil appears in religions other than their own, in liberal religions or (God forbid!) in secularism.

It should not be surprising that both scientists and religionists — these two "pillars" of our world — suffer greatly from the same characteristics of thickness. Religious fundamentalism is an intensely thick-barriered worldview, one in which humanity and our actions are neatly and completely divided into "good" and "evil." Traditionalism and obedience to authority hold sway. The churches proclaim their knowledge about the creation of the Earth, the origin of the universe, the nature of the planets and the nature of the relationship between the Earth and Sun. In the past, the Catholic Church persecuted, prosecuted and even executed those who had actually studied these phenomena, and today it still declaims on what kind of research is permitted.*

On the other side, an equally thick-barriered worldview is expressed by science fundamentalists, who arrogate ridiculous positions regarding the search for transcendence. Some, throwing the baby out with the bathwater, make withering attacks on religion, dismissing this major preoccupation of humanity as merely a delusion and ignoring its evolutionary functions as well as its role in creating our civilizations.

When one has no idea, one can have any idea. A few years ago I (RO) ran into a neighbor of Native American descent. I told him that I had just seen a coyote waddling blithely down the street, and over coffee he mentioned that his grandparents held strong traditional beliefs, among them that Coyote created the world. This Ohlone myth was not the only one he was familiar with — he told me that the Pomo people hold that the world was created when a god rolled his armpit wax into a ball, while the Maidu people believe the world was made from mud scraped from under a turtle's nails. I smiled smugly, but my Native American neighbor asked me whether all this was any weirder than believing that an incorporeal entity created the world in six days a few thousand years ago.

At the extreme end of the thick-barrier group are individuals who are black-and-white, us-versus-them thinkers — who separate thoughts from feelings; focus on one thing and ignore all else; see themselves as all male or all female; are very aware of their own personal space; are either awake or asleep; and separate past, present and future. Social conservatives and religious traditionalists share these characteristics, as do those scientists who are particularly reductionist. Mechanism — a

---

*For example, the Catholic Church supports some adult stem-cell research but does not support research that uses human embryos.

preference for orderliness and set, sequential action: knowing how gears mesh, how plants work, how genes cause growth or disorder, how the planets revolve — is what science is about.

But an exclusive focus on mechanism is just as odd as believing that Coyote created the world. The mechanistic individual is like someone who, listening to a concert, thinks only of the way the notes are written in the score, which reduces the fullness and depth of the experience. He or she often proclaims that this is "rational" thought, but it is actually just reductive, focusing on something amenable to explanation — and sometimes missing the point. The self-styled "New Atheism" is a good example of this; the texts of its adherents are far too often merely pretexts for scorn and denunciation.

Adherence to a single extreme way of understanding gives comfort to the "believers" in both extremes but is the cause of much incompatibility, and one way or the other, both miss the truth. The arguments just pass each other by; it's like listening to a flat-earther debate with an alien-from-outer-space adherent.

The New Atheist's assertion is that belief in God is "delusion" rather than an often-useful metaphor for many people, and one that has been central to humanity's success. Yet their attacks on religious fundamentalism are, all too often, justified. Some of the ideas of divine creation and intervention, and the Old White-Bearded Male deserve no better treatment than the disdain which Richard Dawkins heaps, merrily, on them. You might not know that the Creationist Museum in Kentucky has a replica of Adam and Eve inside their Garden of Eden and, among other fascinating works, presents dinosaurs as existing contemporaneously with early humanity.

Certainly, Dawkins and company make many good arguments about the other extreme point of view, and they are not all wrong, of course. We would certainly make no real argument when they counter the idea that God created humanity and the world, literally, in only one week just a few thousand years ago

— and the belief that He (usually a male figure) intervenes in every aspect of our lives. But one doesn't need a hand grenade to swat away a mosquito. Instead of having imaginary friends, Dawkins, in particular, seems to have imaginary enemies. He goes far beyond a clearheaded critique, and lumps everyone who "believes" into one category, imagining them all as 19th-century dolts.

Of course, it must be acknowledged that the doctrines of all of the Abrahamic religions — Judaism, Christianity and Islam — hold that there was one Creation, in which God "created" everything. But these dicta were produced a millennium or more before the last 600 years of science and have not been revised. They were never intended to be taken literally.

And in fact, today's self-styled "Young Earth" creationists are actually expounding the ideas of James Ussher, who was the 17th-century Church of Ireland Archbishop of Armagh and the Primate of All Ireland. Ussher tried hard to produce a coherent view of how organisms came about, and he accordingly came up with a calculation that the Earth is approximately 6,000 years old and underwent (literally) six 24-hour days of creation — a magic week that saw the miraculous creation of all life forms, including *Homo sapiens*. Although so many people, especially Americans, believe this, it is obvious folly; there's so much evidence now of the age of the Earth and early life.

Creationists (in this narrow sense) enthusiastically embrace something known as "Intelligent Design." The 19th-century clergyman William Paley gave the most striking and well-worked-out early example of this concept. Suppose, he wrote, that while walking in the woods, you found a watch on the forest floor; could you then possibly believe that the watch itself, with its intricate mechanisms and stylish design, had appeared there just by chance? If not, then there must have been a Designer and Creator — someone must have been the Watchmaker.

Paley extended his argument to human development, and specifically to the human eye, a much more precise instrument than a watch, and one with amazingly intricate workings — such a brilliant piece of biological machinery must also have been created, he maintained. It is too complex to have arisen by chance.

Dawkins, to his credit, demolished Paley's argument brilliantly, showing how the eye evolved from a primitive light-/dark-sensing mechanism to today's complex human color-vision system. The reason it could evolve is that the process took scores of millions of years. It is the timescale of evolution that changes the argument. It could never have been completed by biological evolution or any other process in a mere six thousand years, let alone in six days.

Another positive aspect of the New Atheists is their desire to keep religious ideas separate from politics. Of course, in America it isn't actually forbidden to keep religion away from influencing politics, the original intent having simply been not to have a *controlling* State religion, such as the 18th-century Church of England, which was well worth fleeing.*

Reading the New Atheist books, fun, funny and well-written as they are, shows a blatant intolerance of religion in general and its people. Richard Dawkins himself is shockingly strident about normal people who are religious, urging his supporters to "show contempt" for them.[25] His analogy of religion as a virus adds to the impression that religious believers suffer from some kind of a serious communicable condition and must somehow be

---

*The First Amendment's Establishment Clause prohibits the government from making any law "respecting an establishment of religion." This clause forbids the government from setting up an official religion, and prohibits the government from favoring one religion over another. To paraphrase Barack Obama's famous 2004 speech, "We aren't a Christian state, or a Jewish state or a Hindu state, or an Islamic (State) or a Sikh state or a Buddhist...but the United States."

removed from the populace. The critic John Cornwell cautions Dawkins: "Should you ever acquire political influence or actual power, your policies would inevitably follow from your vision of faith as a disease."[26] A scary thought.

Dawkins first became famous for his very clever book *The Selfish Gene*, which, like Desmond Morris' earlier work *The Naked Ape*, presented to the lay public the idea of the hidden biological determinants of human behavior. The contribution of Dawkins' book is the notion that one's genes may have different priorities than does our conscious intent. It's a bracing and different perspective on life.

The idea followed from a statement of the biologist J.B.S. Haldane who, it is said, had been calculating on the back of an envelope for some minutes before he finally announced that he was prepared to lay down his life for eight cousins or two brothers. That quip probably stimulated the later work of biologists Robert Trivers and William Hamilton, which showed that altruism and sacrifice may be best understood as helping one's relatives (those who share genes with us) survive. Dawkins, though, wildly overemphasizes this effect. Given how little we actually know about the world and ourselves right now, Dawkins' beliefs could feature in a book called "The Scientist's Delusion." We're living in an age when science, although it hasn't even scratched the surface of reality, has provided us with no end of benefits. But hyping science to the point where it represents the only way to knowledge is a mistake.

Science's step-by-step approach has changed the world that Western society, at least, lives within. Modern life has been transformed and even created by many of the early scientific discoveries. Surgery was greatly advanced by the discovery of anesthesia in 1846, and survival from disease was transformed by antisepsis in about 1865.

Many more of the scientific and transformative technologies were developed during a period that ended about 100 years ago.

All of us alive now in Western countries have never known anything else. From 1870 to 1920, sewage and running water systems were installed, antisepsis and vaccination developed and distributed, the generation of power, and its delivery to homes and factories achieved; and the radio, telephone, telegraph, automobile and airplane all came into being.

Those were amazing discoveries, but even today there are many people throughout the world who haven't benefited from them. Billions of people still don't have running water, reliable power or decent medical care.

Despite the advances of the past century and a half, modern science has achieved nothing close to a genuinely comprehensive knowledge of either the external or our internal world. Even in such fields as infectious disease, where tremendous progress has been made, we are all too often confronted by novel challenges and have to admit, "We just don't know." Look no further than the early baffled response to the coronavirus and COVID-19 pandemic. The most informed scientists often referred to how little was known about this novel disease. When it comes to our overall understanding, we are at a point somewhat comparable to Columbus' understanding of world geography a week or two after he made landfall on San Salvador Island in the Caribbean. It was clear that he had discovered something previously unknown to European civilization and revolutionary in its implications for understanding the world — an unidentified land with new people, animals and flora. But he had not yet reached the Americas. (He made it to the eastern coast of Venezuela on his third trip, but he never did reach North America).

Although scientific research, at its best, is a fantastically valuable enterprise, it is not the only way to understand the world, and it is important — although not easy — to shift our viewpoint so that we realize what we still don't know. As the vast American continents lay beyond a tiny island in the Caribbean

— beyond our current island of scientific knowledge lies a huge unexplored territory.

Reading about discovery after discovery, we miss how incomplete our scientific knowledge really is. The function of almost all of our DNA (our genome) has still to be well understood, although breakthroughs made in identifying mutated genes in many diseases, such as cancer and Parkinson's disease, have led to understanding and treating them. Until quite recently most of our DNA was thought to be "filler" or junk, just as the brain's vital glial cells were once thought to exist only to support neurons.*

Geneticist Siddhartha Mukherjee pointed out that ". . . of the several million chemical reactions in the human body, one estimate suggests that only 250 — a fraction of a percent — are currently targeted by our pharmacopoeia (this number changes every year, of course). The rest of our physiology is still impenetrable — invisible to pharmacology, like dark matter."[27] And about 90 percent of the material in the universe is such "dark matter," and we don't understand what it is.[28]

Astronomers have discovered trillions of unknown galaxies, each one containing hundreds of millions of stars. So forget Ptolemy. (One recent news headline, among the usual traffic accidents and political news, stated "Hubble Reveals Observable Universe Contains 10 Times More Galaxies Than Previously Thought.")[29] And just recently, light has been recorded from stars that are 20 billion light-years away. If science shows us anything, it is that human beings obviously have to give up any sense of being central to anything beyond ourselves.

---

*Glial cells (derived from the Greek word for "glue") are non-neuronal cells that provide support and nutrition to neurons, maintain homeostasis, form myelin and participate in signal transmission in the nervous system. Glia are estimated to outnumber neurons by about 10 to one in the human brain, and are essential agents in the nervous system.

Overreaching claims are inevitable when the basis is shaky, and scientific research is not as far along as many of its adherents believe (notwithstanding the fact that some of its discoveries form the basis of this book). Although it's natural to believe that what's already been discovered is important — and much of it is — there are social and career factors that create scientific distortion. For example, getting a study or an experiment to "come out" (i.e., to produce a good result) is, unfortunately, tied to the scientist's academic or institutional success. Thus, researchers often run a study over and over until it finally does "come out," at which point they stop doing the study and seize on the result, since, if repeated, it might not happen again. This has led to scandal: Many studies in psychology and other disciplines have been found to be unrepeatable. One recent investigation attempted to repeat studies published in *Science* and *Nature*, both highly prestigious journals: of the 21 studies, only 13 could be repeated with the same results.[30]

Without any doubt, there has been unprecedented, massive progress in science and technology over the past 600 years, accelerated greatly after the Second World War. And by connecting the bits and pieces we have from archeology, paleontology and modern brain research, we can, for the first time, get a glimpse of what it might mean to transcend normal consciousness and gain a "higher" understanding — how this comes about and how/why we need not be bound by the religious formulations of millennia ago.

Although we have a long way to go, we know enough now to stop rejecting completely the idea that spirituality and religion are just snares and delusions to be trashed. Our ideas of spirituality and the search for meaning can be updated on a firmer basis — one that involves knowing who we are, where we came from and how consciousness evolved.

FOR FURTHER READING

Darwin's Angel: An Angelic Riposte to 'The God Delusion,' John Cornwell, Profile Books, 2009.

The Dawkins Delusion: Atheist Fundamentalism and the Denial of the Divine, Alister McGrath and Joanna Collicutt McGrath, InterVarsity Press, 2007.

The Naked Ape: A Zoologist's Study of the Human Animal, Desmond Morris, Rand (Dell), 1967.

The Selfish Gene, Richard Dawkins, Oxford Univ. Press, 2016.

When God Talks Back: Understanding the American Evangelical Relationship with God, Tanya M. Luhrmann, Vintage (Alfred A. Knopf), 2012.

The God Gene: How Faith is Hardwired into Our Genes, Dean Hamer, Doubleday, 2004.

11

It's Not What You Believe ...

Words cannot be used for referring to religious
truth except as analogy.

— HAKIM SANAI, THE WALLED GARDEN OF TRUTH

Even though prophets and teachers such as Moses, Jesus, Muhammad, Ibn el-Arabi, Rumi and Maimonides have made it clear that spiritual understanding is something that people need to "see" (it's about perception not intellection or emotionalism), most of us are brought up learning a dreary, cumbersome and rigid set of beliefs about our Founder's Famous Feats and the often self-serving and even screwball ideas of the bureaucrats who followed.

In *The Passover Plot*, biblical scholar Hugh Schonfield wrote: "The Kingdom of God was right beside them, under their noses, ready to appear whenever they were willing to comply with the conditions which would inaugurate it. Be alive, be alert, Jesus insisted. The goal will not be reached by a sleeping partnership with God."[1]

Moses came down from Mount Sinai with a tablet, and since then, there have been more revelatory inscriptions found, and more divine visitations and recitals reported, in many different cultures. But very rarely do people get instructed in person by the original prophet in how to develop the ability to "see" beyond. Instead, we get the bureaucrats — Warren Buffett's "Imitators" and "Idiots" — who follow the "Innovators" years, centuries, even millennia, later, bringing with them only misunderstood fragments of the original insights, along with their own books of rules, restrictions and regulations.

"Acts of God" and Acts of Humanity

Things, as they say, happen. In 1348, the Bishop of Edmonton in England, decreed that the cause of the contemporary outbreak of the plague was due to licentious sexuality. He proposed that, in order to mount a defense against the disease, people should go to market each Thursday and say the Lord's Prayer. This seems, and is, "medieval," but we are still doing the same thing in the 21st century. The expression we use for major natural events such as deluges, mudslides, earthquakes, volcanic eruptions and tornadoes is "Acts of God," and it's still a standard phrase in insurance policies.

There is an unfortunate and never-ending confusion between the real world and the world of metaphor and imaginings that can become an obstacle to a genuine understanding of the world and of life. Unexpected events can sometimes stimulate religious belief, as we saw with the Christchurch earthquake. When a meteor struck the town of Chelyabinsk in Russia in 2013, many of its citizens believed that this cataclysm was a divine admonition; one local Christian minister preached that it was "a message to humanity from God."

A 2011 poll by the PRRI (Public Religion Research Inst.) found that 38 percent of Americans believed natural disasters to be signs from God. Ironically, the report of the study implied that the researchers were surprised at how few people did so!

It was found that even fewer (29 percent) believed that God sometimes punished a nation for the sins of some of its citizens. The exception to this pattern were white Evangelical Protestants, almost 60 percent of whom believed that natural disasters were a sign from God, compared to only about a third of Catholics and white mainstream Protestants. A majority (53 percent) of white Evangelicals believed that God punished nations for the sins of their citizens — a view held by just one in five white mainline Protestants and Catholics.[2]

When Hurricane Katrina hit the southern U.S. in 2005, the Mayor of New Orleans said that it was a warning about the citizenry's wayward and dissolute behavior. A Christian minister noted that it was a specific punishment for lasciviousness, homosexuality and other depredations.

It's not only professional religionists who make this mistake. It's rumored that at the beginning of the 20th century, when England's King Edward VII saw a hissing eyesore approaching he said, "What the devil is that? Good God, it *is* the Devil!" It was an early automobile.

When it was first proposed to build Boston's subway, just before the beginning of the 20th century, many religious groups tried to block it, believing that those who travelled underground would be too close to the dangers lurking deep in the netherworld, and hence would be dangerously near to the Devil — in "God's eyes" this would be taking too much of a risk.

Combating and Canceling Literalism

Though the number of literal believers is decreasing, the legacy of antiquated religious beliefs hangs on today. For example, a recent Pew poll found that 72 percent of Americans believe in Heaven, and 58 percent believe there is a Hell.[3] A Harris poll conducted as late as 2013[4] found that 57 percent of U.S. adults believed in the virgin birth of Jesus, 72 percent believed in miracles, 68 percent believed in Heaven, 68 percent believed Jesus to be God or the Son of God, and 65 percent believed in the Resurrection. A 2009 Rasmussen poll indicated that 82 percent of Americans believed that Jesus was the son of God who came to Earth and died for our sins, and 79 percent believed the central claim of the Christian faith — that Jesus literally rose from the dead and ascended to Heaven. It's repeated, over and over again, all over the world, every Sunday.

As we saw, Pauline Christianity is actually an outlier in the main line of the Abrahamic monotheistic insight, and is considered by many historians to have succeeded in the Roman world of two millennia ago because it presented people with a "better offer" than the other options of the time. Over the subsequent two millennia the inflation of Christianity's promise, combined with the need to compete with what modern societies can provide, has increased this "offer" to absurd lengths. A sign from the contemporary Creationist Museum and website upped the "deal," informing and assuring its Christian adherents that:

"Jesus Paid the Full Price of Our Sin Debt."

Becoming bodily disassembled and reassembled anew, walking on water, instantaneously flying to Jerusalem and beyond, communing with ancestors and, of course, the resurrection from the dead and ascension to Heaven — if taken metaphorically as originally intended, these descriptions could function to uplift our conceptions of who we are. As Idries Shah wrote: "You must conceive of possibilities beyond your present state if you are to be able to find the capacity to reach toward them."[5] These metaphors of "impossible possibilities" are meant to raise the bar and help dissolve the barriers to the "elevation" of our consciousness.

Faux Past — "Based on a True Story"

> It is midnight, at the first moment of December 25th. The temples are lit up. Priests in white robes stand at the altar. There's incense. The congregation celebrates the birth of their Lord God. His worshippers believed he had come from Heaven to be born as a man in order to redeem men from their sins.
>
> He was born of a virgin on this day of December 25th. Shepherds were the first to learn of his birth. At sunrise, the priests would announce: 'The god is born.'"[6]

This story, about a remarkable birth and the ceremony celebrating it, is that of the Sun god Mithras. Recall that at the time Christianity was introduced, Mithraism was a leading religion in ancient Rome.

The origin story — the "back-story" of emperors and kings, prophets and teachers — has always been created, or at least revised and embellished, posthumously. Its authors might draw from ancient and traditional tales that were already in circulation at the time. Again, it was not a question of strict accuracy or factual information, but of "metaphorical truth." There are terms, phrases, titles, structures and plot dynamics that appear in these stories again and again. Some of these, such as virgin birth, portentous signs at birth, unusual abilities in childhood, were well-known devices used to alert the audience to the fact that the protagonist was exceptional, important, highly esteemed and worthy of close attention.

We're accustomed to stories on TV and in the cinema that are said to be "based on a true story," but we don't realize that many of our major cultural and religious myths are equivalent, being tales that stemmed from natural occurrences or events that happened. As the Sufi sage, Sayed Imam Ali Shah commented, "It is not necessary for [a] story to be untrue for it to be significant for teaching illustration."[7]

Recall that "high" mountains were often associated with the sacred. The ancient Greeks called Mount Etna the "mountain of God;" the Romans, Indonesians, Japanese, Icelanders, Hawaiians and Kenyans have all, at one time or another, called their volcanic mountains "mountains of God" and incorporated them into their stories. Attributing celestial origins to unusual but natural phenomena can be seen throughout our human history.*

In the tradition of the Old Testament, Moses visits Mount Bedr, or Sinai, "the mountain of God," where an "isolated volcanic cone is displayed atop the massive natural plinth of one of the largest table mountains in the world."[8] "Bedr" actually refers to the full moon, and Mount Bedr was already a sacred place that, before the Israelites arrived, was dedicated to the Moon-god of the Midianites.**

As we said, events are retold, embellished and changed to suit the audience of a given time, place and circumstance. In much the same way as Greek Homeric tales developed, the Jewish oral tradition in its earliest times included stories absorbed and adapted from the whole region. As early as 725 BCE, the northern Kingdom of Israel was conquered by Shalmaneser of Assyria. Many Jews were taken into exile in Assyria, while foreigners from Babylon, Persia and surrounding areas were brought to Israel to replace them. The first of the three writers of the Pentateuch (the "five books" of the Old Testament: Genesis, Exodus, Leviticus, Numbers and Deuteronomy) began at about this time to weave oral tales with legends from Babylon, the Persian Empire and other places into biblical accounts of the Creation and the Deluge.

Presentism, which involves applying contemporary values, concepts and meaning when attempting to understand the

---

*See Addendum: Chapter 11 for other examples
**See Addendum: Chapter 11

peoples of the past, results in serious misunderstandings. The designation "Son of God" as a title given to people of great accomplishment, was in wide use in the world of two millennia ago — much as we now use the term "star" metaphorically for someone famous. We know "star" is fanciful in such cases, since the lead actor in a film is not a real star that's high above us in the sky, millions of light-years away. However, one could imagine — going full literal now — the attribution of "star" leading to a cult a few hundred years from now, perhaps centered around a "star" that (like the well-known movie actress Angelina Jolie) had a name like "Beautiful Angel" who helped poor refugees (as she does).

Plato was said to be born of the union of a virgin and the god Apollo; Alexander the Great was said to be the son of his mother Olympias and Apollo; after Julius Caesar was posthumously made a god in 43 BCE, his adopted son Augustus, born Octavius, became Son of God, and the first Emperor of Rome. From that time people in much of the Roman Empire worshipped their Emperors as gods, right up to the time of Constantine's conversion and beyond. Recall that the Akkadian king Naram-Sin declared himself divine; the Ancient Egyptians believed their Pharaohs became divine after death; the Emperor Qianlong of China was the "Son of Heaven." Still today, the Indian guru Sathya Sai Baba, who died in 2011, is believed by millions to be the Son of God.

For millennia, people have been captivated by stories, myths and legends in which characters fly to distant lands, find buried or hidden treasure, descend from on high to save someone or find a jewel, conquer dragons or demons. Similar themes play out in superhero movies today.

Myths become fixed, hardening into things people really believe and take literally — even though, for example, the two versions of Genesis and the three versions of the Synoptic Gospels often contradict each other. And these stories are encased in our canon.

Because it's so central to Western culture, we've mentioned several times how the early story of Jesus' life changed over the decades of the first century CE and continued to change all the way into the fourth century. Ideas such as the virgin birth and the ascension and eternal life of Jesus, the Savior who died for our sins, were initially intended to be understood metaphorically and to place Jesus in the Jewish tradition ("... *and the Lord has laid on him the iniquity of us all*" [Isaiah 53:6]). Sadly, it is the literal interpretation of these stories that has become the bedrock of the beliefs of many Christians.

This confusing of the mythical with the real happens in many areas of life, not only in religion and spirituality. Some people believe that Elvis Presley has begun a "mini-ascension" along the lines of the one Christians believe Jesus experienced; Elvis is said to be still alive and hiding in a remote country. Others believe that their computer's data stored in the "cloud" will be interfered with if it rains.

Fortunately, there are still sane voices to be heard from those who have a better understanding. The Rev. John Shelby Spong writes of the Gospel of John:

> The good news of the gospel, as John understands it, is not that you — a wretched, miserable, fallen sinner — have been rescued from your fate and saved from your deserved punishment by the invasive power of a supernatural, heroic God who came to your aid. Nowhere does John give credibility to the dreadful, guilt-producing and guilt-filled mantra that 'Jesus died for my sins.' There is rather an incredible new insight into the meaning of life. We are not fallen; we are simply incomplete.[9]

"You gotta believe!" is a better motto, really, for a sports team than it is for a religion. Transcendence of ordinary consciousness is not a belief; it's a discovery and a development inside our minds of a different kind of knowledge. It is not intellectual or emotional, either, but the development of conscious insight.

"You gotta perceive."

FOR FURTHER READING

The Fourth Gospel: Tales of a Jewish Mystic, John Shelby Spong, HarperOne, 2013.

The Miracles of Exodus: A Scientist's Discovery of the Extraordinary Natural Causes of the Biblical Stories, Colin Humphreys, Harper Collins, 2004.

The Passover Plot: New Light on the History of Jesus, 40th Anniv. Ed., Hugh J. Schonfield, Disinformation Company Ltd., 2005.

SECTION FIVE:

God 4.0

12

It's What You Perceive

You did not see the pattern as you entered; and when
you entered — you saw another pattern. When you
saw this apparent pattern, you were prevented from
seeing the threads of the coming pattern. Until you
see both, you will be without contentment.

— Hashim the Sidqi, on Rumi[1]

The Second System of Cognition and Connection

There's a way of accessing a reality that is always present
but is not always perceived. To return again to the
metaphor we used at the beginning of this book,
perhaps there are "clouds" obscuring the stars above them.
Maybe we're focused on a routine task, or worrying about
overdue bills, the neighbors, or whether we'll get somewhere on
time. As we saw, almost every culture and tradition has a sense
of a perception of something "beyond" the mundane, and has
sought ways to transcend the obstacles to perceiving it.

The import of *God 4.0* is that, until recently, there has not been a means to understand this "second system" in modern terms, because we didn't have the necessary knowledge of psychology and neuroscience; hence all the old metaphors, which were the best our ancestors could do. But we are now better equipped to understand what this faculty is and how it works — or rather, how we might make it work for us.

The activation of this "second system" of perception happens in those moments when things change, and we "see" and understand things differently. This can occur in multiple situations: when one goes from being stuck on a problem, large or small, and suddenly has an insight into how to solve it. It's activated in the process of creating art, music and writing; it's reflected in experiences, some of which we've described, that can offer a sense of peace, or a change in understanding and in the direction of one's life.

The second system is an innate network of connections in the brain that when developed can access an awareness of a parallel reality, one that provides insights and understandings that are more objective — "outside the self." There is a continuum of this activation, from our experiences of creativity and insight in daily life, to the ecstatic experiences of saints and shaman, to the transcendent experiences of prophets and spiritual teachers — many of whom described their experiences in metaphorical terms such as "seeing God."

When Called Upon, the Brain Stops for a Second to Yield to an Insight

> Nasrudin returned to the village from the imperial capital, and the citizens gathered around him to hear what he had to say.
>
> 'I shall be brief,' said Nasrudin, 'and confine my remarks on this occasion simply to the statement that my greatest moment was when the King spoke to me.'

Overcome with wonder and staggered by the reflected glory, most of the people fell back, and went on their way to discuss this wonderful happening.

The least sophisticated peasant of all hung back, and asked: 'What did His Majesty say?'

'I was standing outside the palace when he came out, and he said to me, quite clearly, for anyone to hear: "Get out of my way!"'

The simpleton was satisfied. He had now, with his own ears, heard words which had actually been used by a King.[2]

As this story illustrates, for our second system to be activated, the everyday operations of the brain, the social network that the "default mode" (DMN) is usually dealing with, has to "get out of our way." Our "small world" — the close set of associations (friends, plans, daily life, burnt toast) that need only a limited set of a few brain connections — shifts to a mode in which large numbers of links are possible, and a wider set of connections can take place.

Just before getting an insight, and just before or after sleeping, are times when we move out of daily, event-driven consciousness and step back to get a more fluid view "from on high" of our concern — whether that concern be a musical composition, the workings of a machine, a scientific problem or the nature of life and death.

Clearly, most people have not undergone the rigorous preparation, nor are anywhere near as exceptional as Jesus or Muhammad. But it is important to realize that when any of us face a problem and suddenly have a "breakthrough" insight — when we go from being stuck to suddenly "seeing" the solution — we are partially activating the same second network of cognition accessed by the great prophets and spiritual teachers in forming their transformative insights. As we've said, it is an innate faculty and it can be developed.

The French artist Paul Gauguin famously once said, "I shut my eyes in order to see," meaning that he closed out the rest of the world and let his brain stop working on mundane stuff, in order to free it so that it could come up with great visual thoughts.

Archimedes shouted "Eureka!" ("I have found it!") when he suddenly discovered that water displacement could be used to calculate density. This kind of experience comes from, and can lead to, a loss of ordinary awareness. According to the legend, Archimedes ran home from the baths shouting "Eureka!" but was so focused on his insight and so unaware of everything else that he forgot to put his clothes back on first (he was, of course, in the bath when the water-displacement insight came to him).

The 18th-century English poet Samuel Taylor Coleridge, in an opium reverie, suddenly saw the lines of his poem "Kubla Khan," which is now considered one of his greatest works. He awakened and was in the process of writing it down when he was unfortunately interrupted by the now-famous "man from Porlock" — which is why, alas, "Kubla Khan" remains unfinished.

We've all found that new ideas and new understandings appear in our mind after sleep, or after a distraction, intense physical activity, losing oneself in the surf or flying down a mountain on skis — even looking at a sunset can do it. I (RO) find cooking a delicious meal and entertaining friends often works. While thinking of physics solutions Albert Einstein took time off to play his violin. Insights — the mundane ones as well as the divine — are frequently the result of the reorganization or restructuring of the elements of a situation. But how does this work in the mind and brain? What happens inside the brain during a cognitive breakthrough to a new realization?

Of course, getting the right neurophysiology recorded and analyzed at the exact moment of a mystical experience would itself be miraculous. However, researchers have observed a set of brain reactions that seem to throw light on what happens at the moment of insight.

What happens is this: When you have that "eureka experience," it seems to appear out of nowhere. But in fact, the left hemisphere of your brain has actually been working continuously behind your "scenes," in an intense, moment-to-moment, bit-by-bit mental search for relevant information — until it finally gets stymied and, at that point, goes offline. The brain switches over to its right hemisphere, to explore unpredicted ideas and associations. The specific actions of the brain that come next are surprising. Milliseconds before an epiphany, the activity in the right hemisphere's posterior (back) area basically shuts down. This is what provides the "bypass" of the barrier between normal thinking and a new understanding. The clouds part in the moment right before the solution hits you. Neuroscientists John Kounios and Mark Beeman use the term "brain blink" to describe this moment when your brain turns off the competing activity, just before the "aha!"[3]

The insights we get at such times are specifically associated with a burst of high-frequency (40-Hertz gamma-band) EEG activity, as measured by electrodes located in an area adjacent to the brain's right parietal lobe (in the temporal area). Immediately prior to that EEG burst, there is a flareup of alpha waves over the right side of the back of the head, which indicates idling of brain activity. Depending upon the type of creative task, these findings suggest that a possible solution to a problem is present in the right temporal lobe, so the brain carries out a temporary reduction in interfering activity that allows the solution to pop into awareness.

Again, it's reasonable to surmise that this innate brain reaction takes place each time we achieve a new understanding of a problem, a text, or a life situation — and along with other brain processes, it forms the foundation behind "higher" perceptions.

It works this way because, as with other brain proclivities, a similar pattern holds — in this case, from breaking through the barriers that constrain small daily insights, to achieving breakthroughs in artistic and scientific creativity, and onward to a transcendent understanding.

What's Left and What's Right

There is a different and independent line of research that confirms how our brains open up to enhanced connections to the world. It uses directed and localized electrical stimulation to shut down the left hemisphere and/or directly stimulate the right hemisphere. This technique, called transcranial direct current stimulation (tDCS), applies current directly to specific areas of the brain.

A very small electrode with a small current is placed atop the skull, and depending on the polarity, either stimulates or inhibits neuronal activity in a given area. This lets us determine, almost at will, how a living brain's function is enhanced or depressed. Although it doesn't hurt, the procedure is, in fact, invasive, since it does invade the naturally occurring workings of the brain.

One tDCS study showed that activating brain areas near the right parietal lobe and deactivating the corresponding left side enhances novel thought and insight. I (RO) write "near," because tDCS cannot pinpoint the precise brain area. It's not clear whether the changes in cognition are due to inhibiting the left side or to stimulating the right, or both, but the activation itself gives an effective insight into the brain's workings: Altering the balance by reducing left frontal activity and enhancing right frontal activity reduces cognitive control, thus allowing for more creativity.[4] Again, as the King in the story said: "Get out of my way!"

As we saw in Chapter 6, the brain's right hemisphere will tend to shift focus toward wider and larger relationships by *deactivating* the right parietal lobe and the DMN, whereas the left hemisphere will tend to focus on components. As with tool-making, when doing almost anything with an object, you have to focus on it one part at a time, which activates the left hemisphere; but this hemisphere is not engaged in the initial creative inspiration and is unaware of the whole.

One study observed the two sides of the brain in people with brain damage, to determine which kind of lesion affects originality. The researchers studied patients with right-hemisphere lesions, patients with left-hemisphere lesions, and patients with lesions in both hemispheres (bilateral lesions). It was found that patients with right-hemisphere or bilateral lesions experience impaired creativity.

These brain-damage studies support the idea that creative cognition involves a right-hemisphere network that generates ideas, and that the sequential processing (which is necessary for syntax and other basic language abilities) of the left-sided network may compete with the function of the right hemisphere and diminish insight and creativity.[5] A common feature, as the neuroanatomist Jill Bolte Taylor noted in writing about the stroke she suffered, is the diminution of interference, suppression and competition from the left hemisphere, which seems to dissolve a barrier or two — sometimes too many.

You may recall that the neurotransmitter dopamine stimulates upward-directed movements, including our ability for abstract thought and to reason and plan. Creativity relies on the ability to combine remote concepts into novel and useful ideas, an ability that depends on making remote associations. It has been found that the brain's right parietal lobe is critical in this "associative processing," which is also modulated by dopamine, and that the differences in amounts of dopamine between hemispheres may influence creativity.

In one study, it was found that *lower levels* of dopamine in the right hemisphere released the brain's restriction on remote associations — and, importantly, *increased* people's creativity.

"Our findings offer unprecedented empirical support for a crucial and specific contribution of the right hemisphere to creativity," the researchers write.[6] This shift in the brain happens because of the different ways the two hemispheres handle information. With languages, for instance, several left hemisphere areas engage in precise semantic coding, strongly focusing on a few words closely related to the word that's currently being heard, read or considered. This is very effective for most straightforward daily language and conversation, where we have to keep the dialogue relevant and not stray from the topic, and have to know and remember what the other person is saying and what we ourselves have said. But when subjects were asked to make up creative stories from a set of unrelated words (e.g., from "flea," "sing" and "sword"), it was found that areas of the brain's right hemisphere were more involved.[7] As we previously noted when we discussed "believers" and "nonbelievers" in the paranormal, the right hemisphere's processing of language encompasses many concepts, even those that are only distantly related to the words and context being considered. This is useful when drawing together parts of a story, or perhaps various scientific findings, that seem only distantly related.

This interplay between the hemispheres is reflected in the drawings that are done by patients with brain damage. When asked to copy a picture of a house, those whose right hemispheres were out of action depicted houses whose front doors floated in space and whose roofs were upside-down. However, these patients carefully sketched the house's specifics — devoting lots of effort to capturing the shape of the bricks in the chimney, and of the window curtains, for example. In contrast, patients who were forced to rely on the right hemisphere tended to focus on the overall shape of the structure, and their pictures lacked details. And different people, of course, use the sides of the brain differently, which is a fundamental basis for personality differences.

Many of our acts of insight involve the brain's right hemisphere, an idea that I (RO) proposed half a century ago in *The Psychology of Consciousness*, and that stirred controversy. The research since then has filled in the gaps and made our understanding of the process more specific: Not only do different parts of the right side of the brain have different roles, but different cultures use the brain differently.

For example, where one falls on the selflessness/selfishness continuum is affected by whether one comes from a Western culture (where the emphasis is on individualism) or an Eastern culture (where the emphasis is on collectivism). One recent study showed that people in Eastern cultures are more likely to use their right hemispheres than are those in the West — confirming something that some people have understood but others have thought to be merely a stereotype. Cultural links have also been found in spatial-verbal and holistic-analytic differences between people,[8] with East Asians and South Asians emphasizing right hemisphere functions more than do Europeans and Americans. So it seems that the dominance of the brain's right or left hemisphere may, to some extent, "map" on to East-West cultural differences.

A Biological Adaptation – or a Workaround?

As we've said, the second system isn't a specific physical organ, like the eye or ear. It is second system of cognition, an innate quiescent faculty within all of us and one that can be developed. All the techniques we've mentioned, have been found to bypass or transcend our "normal" perception (which evolved to ensure our survival in the world) and to break through to a "higher" perception. This second system allows what Aldous Huxley called "Mind at Large" to be perceived. (We are usually stuck inside what might be termed "Mind at Small," which is our daily world of the narrowed connections of the DMN and the active place-keeping of the parietal lobes.)

In technology terms, this second system might be called a "workaround." But it's a workaround that is discovered independently, one we can learn how to use to defeat, or slide right around, our normal, workaday awareness. We've done this for millennia, and almost every society on Earth has discovered and activated this second system. It is part of the brain that connects us to humanity and the world as a whole — the network that has founded civilization.

"I am he and you are me and we are all together" was a fine statement as sung by the Beatles, and derived from the pronouncements of many mystics. But it's always difficult to hold on to the insight. *This is a major problem: That "break" into the beyond may affect one deeply for a short time, but, without an internal supporting structure providing the context of what one is doing and why, it can fade away or develop into an illusory sense of self-improvement or power, or even cause serious trauma.*

In a "small-world" network, most points have few connections to others, and are generally not many connections away from any other point in the network. This mode produces the efficient, if limited, communication necessary for the mundane orderly quick-thinking and the automatic reactions needed, to check on everyday life events, crossing the street, driving, and the like.

The psychological shift to what neuroscientists call a "random graph" architecture in which each point has more or less of an equal probability of being connected directly to every other one, is an expansion from the everyday brain's workings. Connections that were behind barriers are now open, so understanding can "ascend" to a higher level. This second mode of consciousness moves beyond beliefs, along a continuum connecting to a direct experience or perception of what some have called "God" — the transcendent experience of prophets and spiritual teachers.

FOR FURTHER READING

The Eureka Factor: Aha Moments, Creative Insight, and the Brain, John Kounios and Mark Beeman, Penguin, 2015.

The Way of the Sufi, Idries Shah, Jonathan Cape, 1971.

New World New Mind: Moving Toward Conscious Evolution, Robert Ornstein and Paul Ehrlich, Malor Books, 2011.

13

Toward A New Spiritual Literacy

THE PEARL

A raindrop, dripping from a cloud,
 Was ashamed when it saw the sea.
'Who am I where there is a sea?' it said.
When it saw itself with the eye of humility,
A shell nurtured it in its embrace.

— SAADI OF SHIRAZ[1]

The Virtue of Virtues

All religious and ethical systems that we know of counsel being virtuous. They encourage people to practice humility, charity, forgiveness and generosity; to sacrifice for others, feel empathy and treat others with compassion; and to focus on gratitude for what one has instead of envy of what others possess. These systems all encourage being thankful, being honest, offering service to others, practicing altruism, developing patience and tolerance, and reducing one's desires.

Being virtuous, and seeing others in our orbit as virtuous, is undoubtedly helpful in maintaining a healthy group or society. Certainly, virtuous behavior makes a stable society possible by reducing conflict, maintaining social cohesion and enhancing trust and cooperation.

So it's not surprising that all three Abrahamic religions emphasize being cooperative, courteous and amenable to the likes and dislikes of others. That's part of what makes a society a society rather than a brawling, inchoate rabble. Everybody is for virtue. *"By the One who holds my soul in His hand, a man does not believe until he loves for his neighbor or brother what he loves for himself,"* said Muhammad (Hadith 13). The same idea is found in Matthew 7:12 [NIV], where Jesus says, *"Do to others what you would have them do to you, for this sums up the Law and the Prophets."* Hillel makes one of the clearest claims for virtue as part of a religious/spiritual life: *"That which is hateful to you, do not do to your fellow. **That is the whole Torah; the rest is the explanation; go and learn.**"* [emphasis ours].*

Although *God 4.0* centers on the three Abrahamic religious traditions, every religion and moral tradition, with almost no exception, counsels these same virtues — from the Vedas through Confucius, all the way up to the Mormon creed, which encourages all of us "to practice the Savior's Golden Rule."

This is not an accident; the deeper reason for it — that's often neglected, forgotten or misunderstood — relates to our neurobiology and the development of a wider understanding and approach to the experience of God.

What these different virtues — humility, generosity, empathy, patience, compassion, forgiveness, honesty, etc. — all have in common is that they each draw attention away from a focus upon the self. They push toward "ego reduction" and a personal decentration; in other words, they encourage us not to see

---

*Babylonian Talmud, Shabbat 31a

ourselves as the center of everything. This is an internal, psychological process that mirrors the changes — initiated by Copernicus — in the scientific understanding of humanity's place in the universe. Practicing virtues draws the brain's operational mechanics away from the area that situates our self, our space, our place and our role in the mundane world, and takes a step toward timelessness and placelessness — to a "higher" more comprehensive consciousness. One can understand, then, why such a move away from self-centeredness is held, in many spiritual traditions, to be the groundwork upon which one can begin to prepare for this shift.

It's important to examine what is going on inside the brain during virtuous actions. But because this is a new area of research, only a few of the virtues listed above have been studied in individuals who have undergone stimulation and/or deactivation of a specific area of the brain (with the resulting loss of function) through stroke or injury.

Forgiveness is one virtue for which the concomitant brain functions have been measured. A study of individuals with traumatic brain injury suggests that forgiveness is related to decreased RPL functioning. You'll recall that decreased RPL functioning leads to decreased focus on oneself, and this seems to be experienced, in turn, as a diminished sense of the perceived wrong to the self, and that leads to an increase in forgiveness, gratitude and empathy.[2] Different amounts of RPL functioning produced different amounts of forgiveness. The greater the decrease in parietal function, the greater was the forgiveness expressed. The same results occur in people without brain injuries when using new techniques such as electric current to deactivate the RPL.[3]

It's important to understand that *deactivating* this area of the brain that controls self, time and space enhances virtues such as forgiveness, and allows us to take a "higher" view of life. As one sage put it: "My humility which you mention is not there for you to be impressed by it. It is there for its own reason."[4] There are virtues, and there is a "hidden" virtue in being virtuous.

So the injunction to act virtuously, which is found in all traditions, is as a "means of travel," intended to move consciousness away from our ordinary, self-centered mode to a greater vision — as do other "ego-reduction" techniques. All of this clarifies why spiritual experiences are described as "selfless," "timeless," "placeless," "thing-less" and "higher," and why they are nonverbal and so difficult to talk about — and, if talked about, confuse the listeners and sometimes even put them off.

While new understanding in the fields of psychology and neurobiology give new impetus to this view, it seems that many people — not just the famous and great figures in religious life — have reached the understanding that virtues are a basis of spirituality. Consider this statement:

> In judging our progress as individuals we tend to concentrate on external factors such as one's social position, influence and popularity, wealth and standard of education. These are, of course, important in measuring one's success in material matters and it is perfectly understandable if many people exert themselves mainly to achieve all these. But internal factors may be even more crucial in assessing one's development as a human being. Honesty, sincerity, simplicity, humility, pure generosity, absence of vanity, readiness to serve others — qualities which are within easy reach of every soul — are the foundation of one's spiritual life.[5]

These are not the words of an Abrahamic teacher, or Confucius or Martin Luther, but the words of Nelson Mandela, writing from his cell in South Africa's Robben Island prison.

"Be In the World but Not Of the World"

The above proverb from the Middle East emphasizes an important point: Developing an extended perception of reality isn't suited to a monastic life. Many spiritual traditions have noted this; you'll recall that James the brother of Jesus, strongly emphasized participation in the world. Monasteries, unless prescribed by a teacher for a limited time and purpose, tend to rely on generalized repetitive practices and uniformity, which tends to produce automatism and conditioned-response behavior.

'Are you prepared to leave the world as you know it and live in a mountain retreat on a very basic diet?' I signified that I was.

'You see,' he nodded his head regretfully, 'you still feel that to find knowledge you must seek a solitary life away from impure things. This is a primitive attitude and one satisfactory for savages. Do you not realise that a sophisticated path of development keeps pace with the requirements of the present day? Can you comprehend the uselessness of abandoning the world for the sake of your selfish development? . . . There is nothing 'impure' about reasonable worldly activity provided you do not allow it, nay invite it, to corrupt you. If you have enough skill you can actually harness the negative forces to serve you . . . but you must have enough skill.'[6]

But how to practically develop this capacity? Many of us have experienced the difficulty in successfully "giving up" doing something; too often, trying to give it up seems only to keep one focused on the forbidden object or enterprise — enhancing the desire rather than taming it. As I (RO) have written about extensively in other books,* the key is self-observation: You have to learn to observe yourself *as if you were another person*. Under the stimulus of self-observation, the mind begins to change, and the links between action and reaction loosen. One useful strategy is to realize that one has multiple selves that can be recognized and organized by "an observer" self. Once that self is stronger one can start to have a choice, and — to paraphrase the words of the Muskogee Creek Native American shaman,

---

*For example, *The Evolution of Consciousness, Multimind, The Psychology of Consciousness, MindReal*.

Bear Heart, whom we quoted at the beginning of this book —
you can let the "selves" that no longer serve you die. (Or at least,
you can move them aside when necessary).

Non-attachment is not, as many have assumed, detachment
from life. It is, rather, an attempt at a total present-centeredness
— an acceptance of what comes without "clinging" to it (as is
said in Zen). The key question to ask is: "Am I using it, or is it
using me?"

Apart from, or a Part of?

Almost by definition, being "a part" of something means that
you are connected to it, just as your arm is connected to the rest
of you. The connection provides unity, just as the body's limbs,
organs and skeleton — all separate entities — coalesce to form
one whole. We don't think of those parts as separate, unless we
have an injury or a disease.

Some individuals have "ascended" to a more unified level of
experience seemingly at random; some, as a result of serious life
changes or threatening life events. The experience of being "a
part of " surprised them, since they had not sought it. Here are
three more accounts, the first from a study on consciousness
and the second by the Russian author Leo Tolstoy:

> There was no separation between myself and the rest of the
> universe. In fact, to say that there was a universe, a self, or any 'thing'
> would be misleading — it would be an equally correct description
> to say that there was 'nothing' as to say that there was 'everything.'
> ... This knowingness is a deep understanding that occurs without
> words. I was certain that the universe was one whole and that it
> was benign and loving at its ground.[7]

> Old as I am I have discovered a new state of consciousness,
> that of eternal Goodness. It is not of imagination; it is a state of
> consciousness to reach which one clearly feels the changes as one
> passes from confusion and suffering to clarity and calm, just as
> one feels heat and cold.... and this is the essential thing — one

abandons the values of man for the values of God. If only I can keep this light within me until my death.[8]

And Edgar Mitchell, the Lunar Module Pilot of Apollo 14, expressed it this way:

> My view of our planet was a glimpse of divinity. . . . The biggest joy was on the way home, in my cockpit window every two minutes — the Earth, the Moon, the Sun, and a whole 360-degree panorama of the heavens. And that was a powerful, overwhelming experience. Suddenly I realized that the molecules of my body, and the molecules of the spacecraft, the molecules in the body of my partners, were prototyped and manufactured in some ancient generation of stars. And that was an overwhelming sense of oneness, of connectedness. It wasn't them and us, it was — that's me, that's all of it, it's one thing. And it was accompanied by an ecstasy, a sense of 'oh my god, wow, yes,' an insight, an epiphany.[9]

One Small First Step into a New Land and Its Challenges

The first experience of a "breakthrough" has almost always all the excitement and limitations of any initial and limited experience. It makes clear that the way one has experienced the world up to that point is not all there is. For some people, this experience is enough to relieve their depression or addiction, or to provide them with a lasting measure of peace. And it has changed the lives of others in the ways we've quoted.

However, it is just the first step in the way to a true insight on life, and is a bit like seeing those metaphorical stars, but not knowing how to navigate by them — or, to use another allegory, attaining freedom from jail after a long period of incarceration, but having no money, home or job.

While any glimpse beyond the "clouds" may not be a life-changing occurrence for most of us, the experience and understanding that "this is not the only way to see the world" is helpful in reducing one's worries, calming one's anxieties and the like. One of the subjects in the Good Friday study on the effects of psilocybin said:

> It left me with a completely unquestioned certainty that there is an environment bigger than one I'm conscious of. I have my own interpretation of what that is, but it went from a theoretical proposition to an experiential one. In one sense it didn't change anything, I didn't discover something I hadn't dreamed of, but what I had thought on the basis of reading and teaching was there. I knew it. Somehow it was much more real to me....I expect things from meditation and prayer and so forth that I might have been a bit more skeptical about before....I have gotten help with problems, and at times I think direction and guidance in problem solving.[10]

This glimpse is certainly beneficial, but it is not transcendent.

As we've said, when the brain operates in the second system of cognition, one perceives connections between objects and events that were formerly seen as unrelated, viewing that unity from a "higher" perspective. But, since this experience is inexpressible in language, it has been expressed in metaphors that are often equated with what we know as "religious" experience — "perceiving Divinity," "union with Truth," "seeing God" or "being in God." However, if we view the experience that these metaphors are attempting to describe as the activation of the mind's second system of insight and connection, this new land becomes a bit less foreign and, perhaps, worth further investigation. Again, *understanding the neurobiology of higher consciousness makes such an experience no less remarkable and does, hopefully, clear away some of the confusion, anachronistic religious terminology and literal distortions.*

When you see "God" and the higher consciousness perspective as a venue of connecting, then Love is a connection, Truth is connecting things together, and the statement "God is Love, God is Truth, God is Everywhere" makes sense since it is all about the unity of what might seem separate.

It is in the consciousness of the connectedness of things that we, in perceiving that we are part of "everywhere," experience the first glimpse of "knowing god."

Beyond Belief – to Unity

> Do not like; do not dislike; all will then be clear.
>
> — AN 8TH-CENTURY CHINESE ZEN MASTER

To briefly recap our story so far, spirituality — the search for transcendence — is at the basis of human society. It's commonly thought that before our ancestors developed agriculture, they settled in a place and then "put down roots," and that this social stability provided the platform for further spiritual experiences. I (RO) subscribed to this view when I wrote about it previously.[11] But, as we said earlier, the opposite appears to be true: An analysis of the plantings about 30 kilometers (18.6 miles) away from Göbekli Tepe, the "first Temple" in Turkey, strongly suggests that coming together for spiritual worship necessitated the development of agriculture.

There's a psychology of higher experience: We have an almost innate sense of associating things "high" with good and even with "holy." Certain places, whether natural or specially constructed, stimulate awe in us, which, as we saw in Chapter 5, decreases our tolerance for uncertainty and increases our belief that there is a purpose in everything. Extremes of behavior, such as fasting and other forms of self-deprivation, and extreme events such as accidents — all break up the normal fog of life and can allow us to perceive beyond it.

Modern brain studies have identified several parts of an internal second network that stimulate an extended cognition. It's not simple, it isn't a single part of the brain (that dongs or pings), it isn't some great entity outside; it is not primary as are vision and hearing. It is a secondary system that is usually idling in the background and which can be brought to the fore by different routines, practices, rituals and events, some of which we've mentioned. It is a state of consciousness, produced by the same brain process that yields other insights and creative breakthroughs.

This system has proven useful in the development of human civilization, so if it is indeed a "workaround" as we've suggested, then our normal mode of cognition has been "worked around" for millennia, all over the world. Almost every society on Earth has found and activated it. It has deep roots in our bipedalism and the resulting development of farsightedness: the ability to see beyond our current surroundings, both physically into the distance and temporally into the future; and beyond ourselves to connect with and understand others; and beyond that to a higher perception. In activating this second system, we shift from the "small world" of daily life, which is a necessarily limited, detailed and fine-grained world, to a more comprehensive, overall "global view."

This happens under different circumstances, as we've described, and gives us a glimpse of a greater understanding. But that is all it is: a glimpse. To go further — to develop an intuitive, more comprehensive, transcendent understanding that can inform our everyday life — requires guidance and education, much as becoming a professional at anything may begin with an interest but will always require considerable effort, work, learning and mentoring.

Consider the understanding of these fairly imprecise terms — transcendence, mysticism, spirituality — in another way. As we've mentioned, we all share many abilities that are built upon our universal inheritance: three-dimensional color vision; fine-motor dexterity; the ability to speak and understand language, and to count — among many others. These are basic and innate. But some people can develop beyond counting to learn algebra, and some can even go beyond that, to learn differential equations. Many, but not all, people go beyond speaking and hearing language to learn to read and write, and an advanced few can produce beautiful poetry and fiction.

The ability to develop consciousness follows the same pattern. Most people have a basic intuitive, perceptual ability to develop insights about complex daily events. Thousands evinced "gifts" in their own realms: artists, writers and composers, inventors and innovators in all fields. At the far end of this continuum are those extraordinary individuals, spiritual teachers and prophets — Moses, Muhammad, Jesus, Hillel, Rumi, Saadi and others.

Over the centuries, many of the myths surrounding these exceptional people have become misunderstood and ossified. As a result, many ordinary religious people are conditioned into believing in someone else's interpretation of their original insight and the circumstances surrounding it — scribed, codified, reduced and modified over the course of millennia. At best, only "homeopathic-size doses" remain.

This dilution is described in another classic tale about the notorious folk hero Nasrudin:

> A kinsman came to see Nasrudin from the country, bringing a duck as a gift. Delighted, Nasrudin had the bird cooked and shared it with his guest. After this, one countryman after another started to call, each one 'the friend of the friend of the man who brought you the duck.' No further presents were forthcoming.
>
> At length Nasrudin was exasperated. One day yet another stranger appeared. 'I am the friend of the friend of the friend of the friend of the relative who brought you the duck.'
>
> He sat down, like all the rest, expecting a meal. Nasrudin handed him a bowl of water.
>
> 'What is this?'
>
> 'That is the soup of the soup of the soup of the soup of the duck which was brought by my relative.'[12]

The longer analysis we have provided here might show the way to change that.

Again, it's important to note that while the underlying neurobiology describes what happens physiologically, the experience is individual and dependent upon capacity and preparedness.

The Sufi poet Saadi once said, "If dust ascends to the skies, it is not made more precious."

End of Daze

Some literalist followers of Christian doctrine depict the "end of days" as a scenario in which the whole world is going to (somehow and in some way) suddenly explode, and the "heathens" will be blown to pieces all over the place, while the righteous believers will be in Paradise. But "the end of days" or "the last days," originally meant that, through the work of the prophet or teacher, the present evil age would come to an end. It meant there would be a time when war and hatred would be banished (so, the end of these awful days), and then a time would follow when *the earth shall be full of the knowledge of the Lord, as the waters cover the sea*" (Isaiah 11:9 [NIV]).

While this wish seems almost as unrealistic as awaiting the mega-blowup that will end life on Earth, it is a worthy aspiration toward real spirituality — which could begin with an emphasis on developing our second system of consciousness.

The myths, legends, sayings and metaphors of our religious traditions make this second system seem far away from our normal lives. But, as we've tried to show, it is close to home and natural — and, in fact, its development is based on the way everyone's brain works to transcend or "bypass" ordinary waking consciousness. It's a journey that any one of us can take. Nothing from the outside has to intervene, and nobody has to literally die, for you to develop it.

Until now, we haven't had a modern language to describe it, one that's free of such terms as "angels," "devils" and "God's wrath," and unconnected to weird beliefs, deliberate violations of the norm, and the supposition of miracles. The terms religious people previously used — especially the positive ones — were the best available at the time to describe the experience of a comprehensive "higher" state of conscious awareness, one in which events and objects usually seen as separate and independent are perceived as a unified whole.

For many people, especially scientists, the existence of these archaic terms and their often incoherent adherents on the other side of the barrier spectrum automatically suggests that there's nothing of value in spirituality, transcendence or higher consciousness. But this logic is wrong. Again, believing that thunderstorms are displays of God's anger, that meteors are chunks of metal hurled down from heaven by the gods, and that earthquakes are caused by a subterranean demon doesn't abolish the storms, the meteors or the earthquakes. This reality—that the brain can switch to a "higher" and more comprehensive form of perception—is not antithetical to science (nor to common sense).

Similarly, the fact that our churches, mosques and synagogues use archaic language about transcendence doesn't preclude that there can be a development of consciousness and a new language to describe it, a sense that the brain is operating whether one is aware of this or not, and can operate in a different mode — one that fleetingly gives us insight and can be developed.

It's clear that the world needs to change and to become more united on a new basis. If this potential for human development is understood, communicated and promulgated, we might begin to dissolve the barriers between peoples — the exclusive religious, tribal and cultural biases — and usher in a new era based on a development of consciousness, a new "spiritual literacy."

We need to move beyond beliefs, to perception.

Imagine, then, a second system of knowing, one that resides quietly within us. It involves restraining the part of the brain that places us in space and time, and deactivating the DMN so that more connections are possible. Again, the resulting insight may simply show you how to fettle an uncooperative widget or it may give you a new religious/spiritual vision — with everything in-between.

We are a problem-solving animal. We evolve both physically and mentally in response to challenges, and the most important thing we inherit is our ability to go beyond our inheritance.

Our Paleolithic ancestors survived almost insurmountable odds 35,000 years ago; our problems today, though entirely different, are equally challenging and equally consequential. To solve them, we need to understand and advance a new view of humanity. Our species is certainly capable of rationality, and we are possessors of sequential reasoning ability and thought, but with an added dimension that humanity has evolved and can develop: the ability and insight to see things whole, and to perceive ourselves as one part of the greater whole. Transcending the norm in this way is at the heart of our humanity.

Part of our responsibility today, as human beings, is to en-courage this. You read earlier in this book about the innate moral endowment that we are born with and that infants demon-strate; and no one can have failed to remark on the natural creativity of very young children. What happens in an individ-ual's development is that certain talents get emphasized by an early education in which certain ideas and attitudes are favored over others.

Instead of identifying with tribes or families, we need to bring up our children to identify with humanity itself. Our schools need to include a new curriculum in which understanding ourselves becomes at least as important as math, geography and the like. We need to understand our human nature — not only its weaknesses and how to overcome them, but also its enormous potential and how to cultivate that. I (RO) have expanded at length on this in previous works.[13] We need to update our education continually — in schools, at home and in the news media — and teach the latest understandings.

Instead of focusing on our own specific countries, we need to understand that we all live on one globe, and to communicate that to our children — especially to adolescents, who are "making up their adult minds" about their role in the culture. We need a global patriotism instead of a local one. Instead of the news focusing only on specific, exciting stories, a greater focus on the broader, continuing problems we face, and their potential solutions, could help increase people's understanding and perspective.*

We now need to emphasize a diverse basic education that fosters individual curiosity, where both the arts and the sciences can provide a platform for creative ways of looking at problems and coming up with solutions. This would encourage an openness to our innate intuitive capacities and allow them to develop and be experienced naturally.

Teaching stories selected and written for children by Idries Shah have become quite popular in schools, and are a useful addition to early education.[14] In my own research (RO), I found that this genre of story activates the right side of the brain much more than does reading ordinary prose.[15] Recall that the right side of the brain provides context, the essential function of putting together the different components of experience. The brain's left side provides the "text," or the individual pieces, such as the words in a sentence, the elements in a drawing, or the unassembled pieces of a bicycle kit. The right hemisphere puts

---

*Paul Ehrlich and I (RO) wrote more about this in *New World New Mind*, Malor Books, 2011.

the bicycle together. These teaching stories foster the ability to ride the bike and the knowledge of where and when to ride it.*

Again, if the ability to develop a second mode of knowing were acknowledged and taught as a skill as are math or writing, this second mode could take hold, and individuals could attain an extension of their normal consciousness, and then be able to make the choices and decisions that would assist all of humanity.

We hope this new vision of the experience that some traditions label "God" will jump-start your thinking about transcending ordinary consciousness. What is needed now is a new view, to reassess and reform the concept of "God": It is the experience of going beyond the norm to achieve insight as to how life events are connected on a "higher" level. We now have an idea of how that process happens in the brain and, importantly, how to develop this innate potential in today's world. This knowledge could be the first small step toward finding the common ground for us to stand on as we work toward achieving a new spiritual literacy.

One short book on the nature of transcendence, beyond science and sects, certainly won't solve that much. But gaining such an understanding could be a first step toward a unity of different approaches to knowledge and the world. We all have the natural capacity for connecting up and perceiving the unity beyond diversity. And we can build on this to begin a long-term process of rapprochement and unity for humanity. At least, we hope so.

It is time to combine the scientific and the traditional, and to enter a new era — God 4.0 — together.

Afterword

A Contemporary Way

Remember that perception and illumination will
not at first be of such a character that you can say of
them 'This is perception' or 'This is illumination.'[1]

—BAHAUDIN NAQSHBAND

The Teaching Story: Observations on the Folklore of our "Modern" Thought by Idries Shah*

There is no nation, no community without its stories. Children are brought up on fairy tales, cults and religions depend upon them for moral instruction. They are used for entertainment and for training. They are usually catalogued as myths, as humorous tales, as semi-historical fact, and so on, in accordance with what people believe to be their origin and function.

---

*Reprinted from *Point*, Number 4 (Winter 1968-69), pp. 4-9. Visit ishk. net/traditional-psychology for an audio recording of this, read by David Wade, and for downloadable audio editions of Idries Shah's lectures given in San Francisco. Visit idriesshahfoundation.org for the complete works of Idries Shah.

But what a story can be used for is often what it was originally intended to be used for. The fables of all nations provide a really remarkable example of this, because, if you can understand them at a technical level, they provide the most striking evidence of the persistence of a consistent teaching, preserved sometimes through mere repetition, yet handed down and prized simply because they give a stimulus to the imagination or entertainment for the people at large.

There are very few people nowadays who are able to make the necessary use of stories. Those who know about the higher level of being represented by stories can learn something from them, but very little. Those who can experience this level can teach the use of stories. But first of all we must allow the working hypothesis that there may be such a level operative in stories. We must approach them from the point of view that they may on that level be documents of technical value: an ancient yet still irreplaceable method of arranging and transmitting a knowledge which cannot be put in any other way.

In this sense such stories (because *all* stories are not technical literature), such stories may be regarded as part of a curriculum, and as valid a representation of fact as, for instance, any mathematical formula or scientific textbook.

Like any scientific textbook or mathematical formula, however, stories depend for their higher power upon someone to understand them at the higher level, someone who can establish their validity in a course of study, people who are prepared to study and use them, and so on.

At this point we can see quite easily that our conditioning (which trains us to use stories for amusement purposes) is generally in itself sufficient to prevent us from making any serious study of stories as a vehicle for higher teaching. This tendency, the human tendency to regard anything as of use to man on a lower level than it could operate, runs through much of our studies, and has to be marked well.

Yet traditions about stories do in fact linger here and there. People say that certain stories, if repeated, will provide some sort of "good luck"; or that tales have meanings which have been forgotten, and the like. But what would be called in contemporary speech the "security aspect" of stories is almost complete in the case of the genre which we call "teaching stories" because of another factor.

This factor is the operation of the law that a story, like a scientific industrial formula, say, can have its developmental or teaching effect only upon a person correctly prepared for its understanding. This is why we must use stories in a manner which will enable us to harvest their value for us in a given situation.

There is another problem which has to be appreciated when dealing with stories. Unlike scientific formulae, they have a whole series of developmental effects. In accordance with the degree of preparation of an individual and a group, so will the successive "layers" of the story become apparent. Outside of a proper school where the method and content of stories is understood, there is almost no chance of an arbitrary study of stories yielding much.

But we have to go back to an even earlier stage in order to ground ourselves, prepare ourselves, for the value of the story. This is the stage at which we can familiarise ourselves with the story and regard it as a consistent and productive parallel or allegory of certain states of mind. Its symbols are the characters in the story. The way in which they move conveys to the mind the way in which the human mind can work. In grasping this in terms of men and women, animals and places, movement and manipulation of a tale, we can put ourselves into a relationship with the higher faculties possible to the mind, by working on a lower level, the level of visualisation.

Let us examine a story or two from the foregoing points of view. First, take a story of the "Elephant in the Dark":

A number of blind people, or sighted people in a dark house, grope and find an elephant. Each touches only a part; each gives to his friends outside a different account of what he has experienced. Some think that it was a fan (the ears of the animal); another takes the legs for pillars; a third the tail for a rope, and so on.

This has actually been published as a children's book. It appears in the books of Rumi and Sanai. We have made it the subject of a commercial film, *The Dermis Probe*. This story, on the lowest possible level, makes fun of the scientists and academics who try to explain things through the evidence which they *can* evaluate, and none other. In another direction, on the same level, it is humorous in as much as it makes us laugh at the stupidity of people who work on such little evidence. As a philosophical teaching it says that man is blind and is trying to assess something too great for assessment by means of inadequate tools. In the religious field it says that God is everywhere and everything, and man gives different names to what seem to him to be separate things, but which are in fact only parts of some greater whole which he cannot perceive because "he is blind" or "there is no light."

The interpretations are far and high as anyone can go. Because of this, people address themselves to this story in one or more of these interpretations. They then accept or reject them. Now they can feel happy; they have arrived at an opinion about the matter. According to their conditioning they produce the answer. Now look at their answers. Some will say that this is a fascinating and touching allegory of the presence of God. Others will say that it is showing people how stupid mankind can be. Some say it is anti-scholastic. Others that it is just a tale copied by Rumi from Sanai — and so on. Because none of these people can taste an inner content, none will even begin to imagine that one exists. As I say these words the ordinary mind will easily be able to dispose of them by thinking that this is just someone who has provided a sophisticated explanation for something which cannot be checked.

But we are not here to justify ourselves. We are here to open the door of the mind to the possibility that stories might be technical documents. We are here to say that there is a method of making use of these documents. Especially we are here to say that the most ancient and most important knowledge available to man is in part contained in these documents. And that this form, however primitive or old-fashioned it may seem, is in fact almost the only form in which certain teachings can be captured, preserved and transmitted. And, too, that these stories are conscious works of art, devised by people who knew exactly what they were doing, for the use of other people who knew exactly what could be done with them.

It may take a conventional thinker some time to understand that if he is looking for truth and a hidden teaching, it may be concealed in a form which would be the last, perhaps, which he would consider to be applicable to his search.

But, in order to possess himself of this knowledge, he must take it from where it *really is*, not from where he imagines it might be.

There is plenty of evidence of the working of this method, that of the story deliberately concocted and passed down, in all cultures. We do not have to confine ourselves to Eastern fables. But it is in stories of Eastern origin that we find the most complete and least deteriorated forms of the tradition. We therefore start with them. They lead us, naturally, to the significant documents in the Western and other branches of the tradition.

In approaching the study of stories, then, we have to make sure that we reclaim the information that stories contain, shall we say, a message. In this sense we are like people whose technology has fallen into disuse, rediscovering the devices used by our ancestors as we become fitted for it. Then we have to realise that we have to familiarise ourselves with certain stories, so that we can hold them in our minds, like memorising a formula. In this use, the teaching story resembles the mnemonic or formula which we trot out to help us calculate something: like saying: "one kilo equals 2.2 pounds in weight"; or even "thirty days hath September."

Now we have to realise that, since we are dealing with a form of knowledge which is specific in as much as it is planned to act in a certain way under certain conditions, those conditions must be present if we are to be able to use the story coherently. By coherently I mean here, if the story is to be the guide whereby we work through the various stages of consciousness open to us.

This means that we must not only get to know certain tales; we must study them, or even just familiarise ourselves with them, in a certain order. This idea tends to find opposition among literate people who are accustomed to doing their own reading, having been led to believe that the more you read the more likely you are to know more. But this quantitative approach is absurd when you are dealing with specific material. If you went to the British Museum library and decided to read everything in it in order to educate yourself, you would not get very far. It is only the ignorant, even in the formal sense, who cannot understand the need for particular kinds of specialisation. This is well exemplified by the club porter who once said to me, in all seriousness "You are a college man, Sir, please explain football pool permutations to me."

It is in order to get some possibility of right study that I continually say things like "Let us get down out of the trees and start to build."

So far, however, we have not been saying much more than this:

1. A special, effective and surpassingly important teaching is contained in certain materials. In this case the materials are stories.
2. We must accept the possibility before we can begin to approach the study of this knowledge.
3. Having accepted, even as a working hypothesis, the foregoing contentions, we have to set about the study in an efficient manner. In the case of the tales, the efficient manner means to approach the right stories, in the right manner, under the right circumstances.

Failure to adhere to these principles will make it impossible for us to function on the high level needed. If, for example, we settle for merely knowing a lot of stories, we may become mere raconteurs or consumers. If we settle for the moral or social teaching of the story, we simply duplicate the activities of people working in that domain. If we compare stories to try to see where the higher level is, we will not find it, because we do not know unless guided which are the ones to compare with each other, under what conditions, what to look for, whether we can perceive the secret content, in what order to approach the matter.

So the story remains a tool as much as anything else. Only the expert can use the tool, or produce anything worthwhile with it.

Having heard and accepted the above assertions, people always feel impatience. They want to get on with the job. But, not knowing that "everything takes a minimum time," or at any rate not applying this fact, they destroy the possibility of progress in a real sense.

Having established in a certain order the above facts, we have to follow through with a curriculum of study which will enable us to profit by the existence of this wonderful range of material. If you start to study what you take to be teaching stories indiscriminately, you are more than likely to get only a small result, even with the facts already set out. Why is this?

Not only because you do not know the conditions under which the study must take place, but because the conditions themselves contain requirements of self-collection which seem to have no relationship to the necessities for familiarising oneself with a literary form.

We must, therefore, work on the mind to enable it to make use of the story, as well as presenting it with the story. This "work" on the mind is correctly possible only in the living situation, when certain people are grouped together in a certain manner, and develop a certain form of rapport. This, and no other, is the purpose of having meetings at which people are physically present.

If read hurriedly, or with one or other of the customary biases which are common among intellectuals but not other kinds of thinkers, the foregoing two paragraphs will be supposed to contain exclusivistic claims which are not in fact there.

This is itself one of the interesting — and encouraging — symptoms of the present phase of human intellectual folklore. If a tendency can readily be seen manifesting itself, whether in physics, scholasticism or metaphysics, one may be approaching its solution. What is this tendency?

The tendency is to demand a justification of what are taken to be certain claims *in the language in which the demand is made.* My stressing, for instance, that meetings at which people are present who have been grouped in a certain manner, may easily (and incorrectly) be supposed to state that the kind of learning to which I am referring can take place in no other manner. The intention of the paragraph, however, was simply to refer to one concrete manner in which what I have called "a living situation" can come about. A meeting of a number of people in a room is the only form of such a situation familiar to any extent to an average reader of such materials as this.

I have used the word "folklore" to refer to a state of mind of modern man closely similar to that of less developed communities. But there is a great difference between the two folklores. In what we regard as ingenuous folklore, the individual may believe that certain objects have magical or special characteristics, and he is more or less aware of what these are claimed to be.

In modern man's folklore, he believes that certain contentions must be absurd, and holds on to other assumptions, without being aware that he is doing so. He is motivated, in fact, by almost completely hidden prejudices.

To illustrate the working of such preconceptions, it is often necessary to provide a "shock" stimulus.

Such a stimulus occurs both in the present series of contentions about the teaching story (because, and only because, certain information about it is lost to the community being addressed) and exists equally strongly within the frameworks of such stories themselves, when one can view them in a structural manner.

This train of thought itself produces an illustration of the relative fragmentation of contemporary minds. Here it is:

Although it is a matter of the everyday experience of almost everyone on this planet, irrespective of his stage of culture or his community, that any one thing may have a multiplicity of uses, functions and meanings, man does not apply this experience to cases which — for some occult reason — he regards as insusceptible to such attention. In other words, a person may admit that an orange has colour, aroma, food value, shape, texture and so on; and he will readily concede that an orange may be many different things according to what function is desired, observed or being fulfilled. But if you venture to suggest that, say, a story has an equal range of possible functions, his folkloric evaluating mechanism will make him say: "No, a story is for entertainment," or else something almost as byzantine: "Yes, of course. Now, are you talking about the psychological, social, anthropological or philosophical uses?"

Nobody has told him that there are, or might be, categories of effective function of a story in ranges which he has not yet experienced, perhaps not yet heard of, perhaps even cannot perceive or even coherently discuss, until a certain basic information process has taken place in his mind.

And to this kind of statement the answer is pat and hard to combat. It is: "You are trying to be clever." This, you may recall is only the "yaaboo" reaction of the schoolchild who has come up against something which it cannot, at least at that moment, rationalise away or fully understand.

The Magic Horse*

This tale is of great importance because it belongs to an instructional corpus of mystical materials with inner content but — beyond entertainment value — without immediate external significance.

The teaching story was brought to perfection as a communication instrument many thousands of years ago. The fact that it has not developed greatly since then has caused people obsessed by some theories of our current civilizations to regard it as the product of a less enlightened time. They feel that it must surely be little more than a literary curiosity, something fit for children, the projection, perhaps, of infantile desires, a means of enacting a wish-fulfillment.

Hardly anything could be further from the truth of such pseudophilosophical, certainly unscientific, imaginings. Many teaching stories *are* entertaining to children and to naive

*From *Caravan of Dreams* by Idries Shah © The Estate of Idries Shah.

peasants. Many of them in the forms in which they are viewed by conditioned theorists have been so processed by unregenerate amateurs that their effective content is distorted. Some apply only to certain communities, depending upon special circumstances for their correct unfolding: circumstances whose absence effectively prevents the action of which they are capable.

So little is known to the academics, the scholars, and the intellectuals of this world about these materials, that there is no word in modern languages which has been set aside to describe them.

But the teaching story exists, nevertheless. It is a part of the most priceless heritage of mankind.

Real teaching stories are not to be confused with parables; which are adequate enough in their intention, but still on a lower level of material, generally confined to the inculcation of moralistic principles, not the assistance of interior movement of the human mind. What we often take on the lower level of parable, however, can sometimes be seen by real specialists as teaching stories; especially when experienced under the correct conditions.

Unlike the parable, the meaning of the teaching story cannot be unraveled by ordinary intellectual methods alone. Its action is direct and certain, upon the innermost part of the human being, an action incapable of manifestation by means of the emotional or intellectual apparatus.

The closest that we can come to describing its effect is to say that it connects with a part of the individual which cannot be reached by any other convention, and that it establishes in him or in her a means of communication with a non-verbalised truth beyond the customary limitations of our familiar dimensions.

Some teaching stories cannot now be reclaimed because of the literary and traditionalistic, even ideological, processing to which they have been subjected. The worst of such processes is the historicising one, where a community comes to believe that one of their former teaching stories represents literal historical truth.

This tale is given here in a form which is innocent of this and other kinds of maltreatment.

O nce upon a time — not so very long ago — there was a realm in which the people were exceedingly prosperous. All kinds of discoveries had been made by them, in the growing of plants, in harvesting and preserving fruits, and in making objects for sale to other countries, and in many other practical arts.

Their ruler was unusually enlightened, and he encouraged new discoveries and activities, because he knew of their advantages for his people.

He had a son named Hoshyar, who was expert in using strange contrivances, and another — called Tambal — a dreamer, who seemed interested only in things which were of little value in the eyes of the citizens.

From time to time the king, who was named King Mumkin, circulated announcements to this effect:

"Let all those who have notable devices and useful artifacts present them to the palace for examination, so that they may be appropriately rewarded."

Now there were two men of that country — an ironsmith and a woodworker — who were great rivals in most things, and each delighted in making strange contraptions. When they heard this announcement one day, they agreed to compete for an award, so that their relative merits could be decided once and for all, by their sovereign, and publicly recognized.

Accordingly, the smith worked day and night on a mighty engine, employing a multitude of talented specialists, and surrounding his workshop with high walls so that his devices and methods should not become known.

At the same time the woodworker took his simple tools and went into a forest where, after long and solitary reflection, he prepared his own masterpiece.

News of the rivalry spread, and people thought that the smith must easily win, for his cunning works had been seen before, and while the woodworker's products were generally admired, they were of occasional and undramatic use.

When both were ready, the king received them in open court.

The smith produced an immense metallic fish which could, he said, swim in and under the water. It could carry large quantities of freight over the land. It could burrow into the earth; and it could even fly slowly through the air. At first the court found it hard to believe that there could be such a wonder made by man: but when the smith and his assistants demonstrated it, the king was overjoyed and declared the smith among the most honoured in the land, with a special rank and the title of "Benefactor of the Community."

Prince Hoshyar was placed in charge of the making of the wondrous fishes, and the services of this new device became available to all mankind.

Everyone blessed the smith and Hoshyar, as well as the benign and sagacious monarch whom they loved so much.

In the excitement, the self-effacing carpenter had been all but forgotten. Then, one day, someone said: "But what about the contest? Where is the entry of the woodworker? We all know him to be an ingenious man. Perhaps he has produced something useful."

"How could anything possibly be as useful as the Wondrous Fishes?" asked Hoshyar. And many of the courtiers and the people agreed with him.

But one day the king was bored. He had become accustomed to the novelty of the fishes and the reports of the wonders which they so regularly performed. He said: "Call the woodcarver, for I would now like to see what he has made."

The simple woodcarver came into the throne-room, carrying a parcel, wrapped in coarse cloth. As the whole court craned forward to see what he had, he took off the covering to reveal — a wooden horse. It was well enough carved, and it had some intricate patterning chiseled into it, as well as being decorated with coloured paints but it was only ... "A mere plaything!" snapped the king.

"But father," said Prince Tambal, "let us ask the man what it is for ..."

"Very well," said the king, "what is it for?"

"Your majesty," stammered the woodcarver, "it is a magic horse. It does not look impressive, but it has, as it were, its own inner senses. Unlike the fish, which has to be directed, this horse can interpret the desires of the rider, and carry him wherever he needs to go."

"Such stupidity is fit only for Tambal," murmured the chief minister at the king's elbow; "it cannot have any real advantage when measured against the wondrous fish."

The woodcarver was preparing sadly to depart when Tambal said: "Father, let me have the wooden horse."

"All right," said the king, "give it to him. Take the woodcarver away and tie him on a tree somewhere, so that he will realise that our time is valuable. Let him contemplate the prosperity which the wondrous fish has brought us, and perhaps after some time we shall let him go free, to practise whatever he may have learned of real industriousness, through true reflection."

The woodcarver was taken away, and Prince Tambal left the court carrying the magic horse.

Tambal took the horse to his quarters, where he discovered that it had several knobs, cunningly concealed in the carved designs. When these were turned in a certain manner, the horse — together with anyone mounted on it — rose into the air and sped to whatever place was in the mind of the person who moved the knobs.

In this way, day after day, Tambal flew to places which he had never visited before. By this process he came to know a great many things. He took the horse everywhere with him.

One day he met Hoshyar, who said to him: "Carrying a wooden horse is a fit occupation for such as you. As for me, I am working for the good of all, toward my heart's desire!"

Tambal thought: "I wish I knew what was the good of all. And I wish I could know what my heart's desire is."

When he was next in his room, he sat upon the horse and thought: "I would like to find my heart's desire." At the same time he moved some of the knobs on the horse's neck.

Swifter than light the horse rose into the air and carried the prince a thousand days' ordinary journey away, to a far kingdom, ruled by a magician-king.

The king, whose name was Kahana, had a beautiful daughter called Precious Pearl, Durri-Karima. In order to protect her, he had imprisoned her in a circling palace, which wheeled in the sky, higher than any mortal could reach. As he was approaching the magic land, Tambal saw the glittering palace in the heavens, and alighted there.

The princess and the young horseman met and fell in love.

"My father will never allow us to marry," she said; "for he has ordained that I become the wife of the son of another magician-king who lives across the cold desert to the east of our homeland. He has vowed that when I am old enough I shall cement the unity of the two kingdoms by this marriage. His will has never been successfully opposed."

"I will go and try to reason with him," answered Tambal, as he mounted the magic horse again.

But when he descended into the magic land there were so many new and exciting things to see that he did not hurry to the palace. When at length he approached it, the drum at the gate, indicating the absence of the king, was already beating.

"He has gone to visit his daughter in the Whirling Palace," said a passer-by when Tambal asked him when the king might be back; "and he usually spends several hours at a time with her."

Tambal went to a quiet place where he willed the horse to carry him to the king's own apartment. "I will approach him at his own home," he thought to himself, "for if I go to the Whirling Palace without his permission he may be angry."

He hid behind some curtains in the palace when he got there, and lay down to sleep.

Meanwhile, unable to keep her secret, the Princess Precious Pearl had confessed to her father that she had been visited by a man on a flying horse, and that he wanted to marry her. Kahana was furious.

He placed sentries around the Whirling Palace, and returned to his own apartment to think things over. As soon as he entered his bedchamber, one of the tongueless magic servants guarding it pointed to the wooden horse lying in a corner. "Aha!" exclaimed the magician-king. "Now I have him. Let us look at this horse and see what manner of thing it may be."

As he and his servants were examining the horse, the prince managed to slip away and conceal himself in another part of the palace.

After twisting the knobs, tapping the horse and generally trying to understand how it worked, the king was baffled. "Take that thing away. It has no virtue now, even if it ever had any," he said. "It is just a trifle, fit for children."

The horse was put into a store-cupboard.

Now King Kahana thought that he should make arrangements for his daughter's wedding without delay, in case the fugitive might have other powers or devices with which to try to win her. So he called her to his own palace and sent a message to the other magician-king, asking that the prince who was to marry her be sent to claim his bride.

Meanwhile Prince Tambal, escaping from the palace by night when some guards were asleep, decided that he must try to return to his own country. His quest for his heart's desire now seemed almost hopeless. "If it takes me the rest of my life," he said to himself, "I shall come back here, bringing troops to take this kingdom by force. I can only do that by convincing my father that I must have his help to attain my heart's desire."

So saying, he set off. Never was a man worse equipped for such a journey. An alien, travelling on foot, without any kind of provisions, facing pitiless heat and freezing nights interspersed with sandstorms, he soon became hopelessly lost in the desert.

Now, in his delirium, Tambal started to blame himself, his father, the magician-king, the woodcarver, even the princess and the magic horse itself. Sometimes he thought he saw water ahead of him, sometimes fair cities, sometimes he felt elated, sometimes incomparably sad. Sometimes he even thought that he had companions in his difficulties, but when he shook himself he saw that he was quite alone.

He seemed to have been travelling for an eternity. Suddenly, when he had given up and started again several times, he saw something directly in front of him. It looked like a mirage: a garden, full of delicious fruits, sparkling and almost, as it were, beckoning him toward them.

Tambal did not at first take much notice of this, but soon, as he walked, he saw that he was indeed passing through such a garden. He gathered some of the fruits and tasted them cautiously. They were delicious. They took away his fear as well as his hunger and thirst. When he was full, he lay down in the shade of a huge and welcoming tree and fell asleep.

When he woke up he felt well enough, but something seemed to be wrong. Running to a nearby pool, he looked at his reflection in the water. Staring up at him was a horrible apparition. It had a long beard, curved horns, ears a foot long. He looked down at his hands. They were covered with fur.

Was it a nightmare? He tried to wake himself, but all the pinching and pummelling had no effect. Now, almost bereft of his senses, beside himself with fear and horror, thrown into transports of screaming, racked with sobs, he threw himself on the ground. "Whether I live or die," he thought, "these accursed fruits have finally ruined me. Even with the greatest army of all time, conquest will not help me. Nobody would marry me now, much less the Princess Precious Pearl. And I cannot imagine the beast who would not be terrified at the sight of me — let alone my heart's desire!" And he lost consciousness.

When he woke again, it was dark and a light was approaching through the groves of silent trees. Fear and hope struggled in him. As it came closer he saw that the light was from a lamp enclosed in a brilliant star-like shape, and that it was carried by a bearded man, who walked in a pool of brightness which it cast around.

The man saw him. "My son," he said, "you have been affected by the influences of this place. If I had not come past, you would have remained just another beast of this enchanted grove, for there are many more like you. But I can help you."

Tambal wondered whether this man was a fiend in disguise, perhaps the very owner of the evil trees. But, as his sense came back he realised that he had nothing to lose.

"Help me, father," he said to the sage.

"If you really want your heart's desire," said the other man, "you have only to fix this desire firmly in your mind, not thinking of the fruit. You then have to take up some of the dried fruits, not the fresh, delicious ones, lying at the foot of all these trees, and eat them. Then follow your destiny."

So saying, he walked away.

While the sage's light disappeared into the darkness, Tambal saw that the moon was rising, and in its rays he could see that there were indeed piles of dried fruits under every tree.

He gathered some and ate them as quickly as he could.

Slowly, as he watched, the fur disappeared from his hands and arms. The horns first shrank, then vanished. The beard fell away. He was himself again. By now it was first light and in the dawn he heard the tinkling of camel bells. A procession was coming through the enchanted forest.

It was undoubtedly the cavalcade of some important personage, on a long journey. As Tambal stood there, two outriders detached themselves from the glittering escort and galloped up to him.

"In the name of the Prince, our lord, we demand some of your fruit. His celestial Highness is thirsty and has indicated a desire for some of these strange apricots," said an officer.

Still Tambal did not move, such was his numbed condition after his recent experiences. Now the Prince himself came down from his palanquin and said:

"I am Jadugarzada, son of the magician-king of the East. Here is a bag of gold, oaf. I am having some of your fruit, because I am desirous of it. I am in a hurry, hastening to claim my bride, Princess Precious Pearl, daughter of Kahana, magician-king of the West."

At these words Tambal's heart turned over. But, realising that this must be his destiny which the sage had told him to follow, he offered the Prince as much of the fruit as he could eat.

When he had eaten, the Prince began to fall asleep. As he did so, horns, fur and huge ears started to grow out of him. The soldiers shook him, and the Prince began to behave in a strange way. He claimed that *he* was normal, and that *they* were deformed.

The councilors who had accompanied the party restrained the prince and held a hurried debate. Tambal claimed that all would have been well if the prince had not fallen asleep. Eventually it was decided to put Tambal in the palanquin to play the part of the prince. The horned Jadugarzada was tied to a horse with a veil thrown over his face, disguised as a serving-woman.

"He may recover his wits eventually," said the councilors, "and in any case he is still our Prince. Tambal shall marry the girl. Then, as soon as possible, we shall carry them all back to our own country for our king to unravel the problem."

Tambal, biding his time and following his destiny, agreed to his own part in the masquerade.

When the party arrived at the capital of the West, the king himself came out to meet them. Tambal was taken to the princess as her bridegroom, and she was so astonished that she nearly fainted. But Tambal managed to whisper to her rapidly what had happened, and they were duly married, amid great jubilations.

In the meantime, the horned prince had half recovered his wits, but not his human form, and his escort still kept him under cover. As soon as the feasting was over, the chief of the horned prince's party (who had been keeping Tambal and the princess under a very close watch) presented himself to the court. He said: "O just and glorious monarch, fountain of wisdom; the time has now come, according to the pronouncements of our astrologers and soothsayers, to conduct the bridal pair back to our own land, so that they may be established in their new home under the most felicitous circumstances and influences."

The princess turned to Tambal in alarm, for she knew that Jadugarzada would claim her as soon as they were on the open road — and make an end of Tambal into the bargain.

Tambal whispered to her, "Fear nothing. We must act as best we can, following our destiny. Agree to go, making only the condition that you will not travel without the wooden horse."

At first the magician-king was annoyed at this foible of his daughter's. He realised that she wanted the horse because it was connected with her first suitor. But the chief minister of the horned prince said: "Majesty, I cannot see that this is anything worse than a whim for a toy, such as any young girl might have. I hope that you will allow her to have her plaything, so that we may make haste homeward."

So the magician-king agreed, and soon the cavalcade was resplendently on its way. After the king's escort had withdrawn, and before the time of the first night-halt, the hideous Jadugarzada threw off his veil and cried out to Tambal:

"Miserable author of my misfortunes! I now intend to bind you hand and foot, to take you captive back to my own land. If, when we arrive there, you do not tell me how to remove this enchantment, I will have you flayed alive, inch by inch. Now, give me the Princess Precious Pearl."

Tambal ran to the princess and, in front of the astonished party, rose into the sky on the wooden horse with Precious Pearl mounted behind him.

Within a matter of minutes the couple alighted at the palace of King Mumkin. They related everything that had happened to them, and the king was almost overcome with delight at their safe return. He at once gave orders for the hapless woodcarver to be released, recompensed and applauded by the entire populace.

When the king was gathered to his fathers, Princess Precious Pearl and Prince Tambal succeeded him. Prince Hoshyar was quite pleased, too, because he was still entranced by the wondrous fish.

"I am glad for your own sakes, if you are happy," he used to say to them, "but, for my own part, nothing is more rewarding than concerning myself with the wondrous fish."

And this history is the origin of a strange saying current among the people of that land, yet whose beginnings have now been forgotten. The saying is: "Those who want fish can achieve much through fish, and those who do not know their heart's desire may first have to hear the story of the wooden horse."

The Story of Tea*

In ancient times, tea was not known outside China. Rumours of its existence had reached the wise and the unwise of other countries, and each tried to find out what it was in accordance with what he wanted or what he thought it should be.

The king of Inja ("here") sent an embassy to China, and they were given tea by the Chinese Emperor. But, since they saw that the peasants drank it too, they concluded that it was not fit for their royal master; and, furthermore, that the Chinese Emperor was trying to deceive them, passing off some other substance for the celestial drink.

The greatest philosopher of Anja ("there") collected all the information he could about tea, and concluded that it must be a substance which existed but rarely, and was of another order than anything then known. For was it not referred to as being a herb, a water, green, black, sometimes bitter, sometimes sweet?

In the countries of Koshish and Bebinem, for centuries the people tested all the herbs they could find. Many were poisoned, all were disappointed. For nobody had brought the tea-plant to their lands, and thus they could not find it. They also drank all the liquids which they could find, but to no avail.

In the territory of Mazhab ("Sectarianism") a small bag of tea was carried in procession before the people as they went on their religious observances. Nobody thought of tasting it: Indeed, nobody knew how. All were convinced that the tea itself had a magical quality. A wise man said: "Pour upon it boiling water, ye ignorant ones!" They hanged him and nailed him up, because to do this, according to their belief, would mean the destruction of their tea. This showed that he was an enemy of their religion.

---

*From *Tales of the Dervishes* by Idries Shah © The Estate of Idries Shah.

Before he died, he had told his secret to a few, and they managed to obtain some tea and drink it secretly. When anyone said: "What are you doing?" they answered: "It is but medicine which we take for a certain disease."

And so it was throughout the world. Tea had actually been seen growing by some, who did not recognize it. It had been given to others to drink, but they thought it the beverage of the common people. It had been in the possession of others, and they worshipped it. Outside China, only a few people actually drank it, and those covertly.

Then came a man of knowledge, who said to the merchants of tea, and the drinkers of tea, and to others: "He who tastes, knows. He who tastes not, knows not. Instead of talking about the celestial beverage, say nothing, but offer it at your banquets. Those who like it will ask for more. Those who do not, will show that they are not fitted to be tea-drinkers. Close the shop of argument and mystery. Open the teahouse of experience."

The tea was brought from one stage to another along the Silk Road, and whenever a merchant carrying jade or gems or silk would pause to rest, he would make tea, and offer it to such people as were near him, whether they were aware of the repute of tea or not. This was the beginning of the Chaikhanas, the teahouses which were established all the way from Peking to Bokhara and Samarkand. And those who tasted, knew.

At first, mark well, it was only the great and the pretended men of wisdom who sought the celestial drink and who also exclaimed: "But this is only dried leaves!" or: "Why do you boil water, stranger, when all I want is the celestial drink?" or yet again: "How do I know what this is? Prove it to me. Besides the color of the liquid is not golden, but ochre!"

When the truth was known, and when the tea was brought for all who would taste, the roles were reversed, and the only people who said things like the great and intelligent had said were the absolute fools. And such is the case to this day.

* * *

Drinks of all kinds have been used by almost all peoples as allegories connected with the search for higher knowledge.

Coffee, the most recent of social drinks, was discovered by the dervish sheikh Abu el-Hasan Shadhili, at Mocha in Arabia.

Although the Sufis and others often clearly state that "magical drinks" (wine, the water of life) are an analogy of a certain experience, literalist students tend to believe that the origin of these myths dates from the discovery of some hallucinogenic or inebriative quality in potations. According to the dervishes, such an idea is a reflection of the investigator's incapacity to understand that they are speaking in parallels. This tale is from the teachings of the Master Hamadani (died 1140), teacher of the great Yasavi of Turkestan.

The Tale of the Sands*

A stream, from its source in far-off mountains, passing through every kind and description of countryside, at last reached the sands of the desert. Just as it had crossed every other barrier, the stream tried to cross this one, but it found that as fast as it ran into the sand, its waters disappeared.

It was convinced, however, that its destiny was to cross this desert, and yet there was no way. Now a hidden voice, coming from the desert itself, whispered: "The Wind crosses that desert, and so can the stream."

The stream objected that it was dashing itself against the sand, and only getting absorbed: that the wind could fly, and this was why it could cross a desert.

"By hurtling in your own accustomed way you cannot get across. You will either disappear or become a marsh. You must allow the wind to carry you over, to your destination."

---

*From *Tales of the Dervishes* by Idries Shah © The Estate of Idries Shah.

But how could this happen?

"By allowing yourself to be absorbed in the wind."

This idea was not acceptable to the stream. After all, it had never been absorbed before. It did not want to lose its individuality. And, once having lost it, how was one to know that it could ever be regained?

"The wind," said the sand, "performs this function. It takes up water, carries it over the desert, and then lets it fall again. Falling as rain, the water again becomes a river."

"How can I know that this is true?"

"It is so, and if you do not believe it, you cannot become more than a quagmire, and even that could take many, many years; and it certainly is not the same as a stream."

"But can I not remain the same stream that I am today?"

"You cannot in either case remain so," the whisper said. "Your essential part is carried away and forms a stream again. You are called what you are today because you do not know which part of you is the essential one."

When he heard this, certain echoes began to arise in the thoughts of the stream. Dimly, he remembered a state in which he — or some part of him, was it? — had been held in the arms of a wind. He also remembered — or did he? — that this was the real thing, not necessarily the obvious thing, to do.

And the stream raised his vapour into the welcoming arms of the wind, which gently and easily bore it upwards and along, letting it fall softly as soon as they reached the roof of a mountain, many, many miles away. And because he had had his doubts, the stream was able to remember and record more strongly in his mind the details of the experience. He reflected, "Yes, now I have learned my true identity."

The stream was learning. But the sands whispered: "We know, because we see it happen day after day: and because we, the sands, extend from the riverside all the way to the mountain."

And that is why it is said that the way in which the Stream of Life is to continue on its journey is written in the Sands.

*   *   *

This beautiful story is current in oral tradition in many languages, almost always circulating among dervishes and their pupils.

It was used in Sir Fairfax Cartwright's *Mystic Rose from the Garden of the King*, published in Britain in 1899.

The present version is from Awad Afifi the Tunisian, who died in 1870.

FOR FURTHER READING

For additional titles by Idries Shah, visit the Idries Shah Foundation's website at idriesshahfoundation.org

Addendum

CHAPTER 3
A recent study by scientists from the University of Edinburgh suggests that one of the pillars (known as the Vulture Stone) found at Göbekli Tepe may contain a record of a comet striking the Earth about 12,800 years ago. This apocalyptic event may have triggered the sudden "mini" Ice Age known as the Younger Dryas, leading to great loss of human life and the demise of the woolly mammoth.

CHAPTER 4
One can find many violent and anachronistic tracts in the sacred books of the three major Abrahamic religions. Here are just a few, some of them shocking to modern sensibilities:

Qur'an (9:29): *"Fight against Christians and Jews until they pay the tribute readily, being brought low."*

Qur'an (5:51): *"Don't take Jews or Christians for friends. If you do, then Allah will consider you to be one of them."*

Qur'an (2:65-66): *"Christians and Jews must believe what Allah has revealed to Muhammad or Allah will disfigure their faces or turn them into apes, as he did the Sabbath-breakers."*

Exodus 21:7-8 (NLT): *"When a man sells his daughter as a slave, she will not be freed at the end of six years as the men are. If she does not please the man who bought her, he may allow her to be bought back again."*

II Kings 6:28-29 (NLT): "*But then the king asked, 'What is the matter?' She replied, 'This woman said to me: "Come on, let's eat your son today, then we will eat my son tomorrow." So we cooked my son and ate him. Then the next day I said to her, "Kill your son so we can eat him," but she has hidden her son.'*"

Leviticus 20:2 (NLT): "*Give the people of Israel these instructions, which apply both to native Israelites and to the foreigners living in Israel. 'If any of them offer their children as a sacrifice to Molech, they must be put to death. The people of the community must stone them to death.'*"

Deuteronomy 13:15-16 (KJV): [If anyone finds out that people are serving other gods:]"*Thou shalt surely smite the inhabitants of that city with the edge of the sword, destroying it utterly, and all that is therein, and the cattle thereof, with the edge of the sword. And thou shalt gather all the spoil of it into the midst of the street thereof, and shalt burn with fire the city, and all the spoil thereof every whit, for the Lord thy God: and it shall be an heap for ever; it shall not be built again.*"

Revelation 21:8 (KJV): "*But the fearful, and unbelieving, and the abominable, and murderers, and whoremongers, and sorcerers, and idolaters, and all liars, shall have their part in the lake which burneth with fire and brimstone: which is the second death.*"

A contrast between the standard of generosity expected of Christians today and that required of the early Church members is illustrated in this New Testament story: We are told that "*the multitude of them that believed were of one heart and soul: and not one of them said that ought of the things which he possessed was his own; but they had all things common.*" (Acts 4:32 [KJV]) Acts 5:1-11 expands on this further, telling of Ananias and his wife Sapphira who sold a house and gave most of the money to the community but kept some of it for themselves. When the apostle Peter questioned them, they admitted to keeping some of the money. Nevertheless, we're told that they both "*fell down dead*" as a punishment for not giving it all to the community.

Unsurprisingly, the narrator tells us *"Great fear seized the whole church and all who heard about these events."*

CHAPTER 5
Note #1
The situation of planet Earth is considerably more complex than its simple turning on its axis, although not so obviously relevant to daily life or social ritual. At the same time as the Earth is moving around the Sun at about 67,000 miles per hour, both the Sun and the Earth are moving together at about 44,000 miles per hour in roughly the direction of the bright star Vega, which is in the constellation of Lyra. And our solar system itself is moving at 515,000 miles per hour around the galaxy!

Note #2
Today, an average of less than one meteorite fall per year is reported globally, and not one has been noted in Egypt. An astounding event such as a meteor falling to Earth would almost certainly have been understood by early humans as a direct communication from the gods.

In 2009, researchers located thousands of iron fragments from a meteorite that fell 5,000 years ago in a desolate area of the southern Egyptian desert. It left a crater 45-meters (147 feet) wide that is now known as Gebel Kamil.[1] The Egyptian name for iron, *bia-en-pet*, can translate as *bia* for "thunderbolt" and "pet" for "Heaven," a clear indication that the early Egyptians considered it to be of celestial origin. Other meanings have been suggested, such as "metal of Heaven,"[2] as we mentioned. Predynastic iron beads that contain 7.5% nickel (indicating that their origin was in outer space) were discovered in Egypt in 1911.

A natural glass that is found in the western Egyptian desert (and is known locally as Dakhla glass) has been determined to be the product of a meteorite crashing there between 100,000 and 200,000 years ago — a time when that area was fertile. Such an event would have caused enough devastation — to all living creatures in the area — to hold a permanent place in people's collective memory and be assimilated into their oral tradition.

CHAPTER 6

Professor Vincent Walsh of the Institute of Cognitive Neuroscience and Department of Psychology at University College London is the architect of something called A Theory of Magnitude (ATOM for short). In ATOM, he proposes that time, space and quantity are part of a generalized magnitude system (bigger, faster, brighter and further in one domain, correlating with bigger, faster, brighter and further in another domain), and that the brain's right inferior parietal cortex is the locus of this system.

Walsh sets out to show that similarities in these domains of space, time and quantity which indicate common processing mechanisms, derive from our need — even at a very young age, before we've developed language — to learn about our environment by interacting physically with it. "The proposal is that we learn about space and time through action and associations between space, time and magnitudes relevant for action (such as size, speed and, under some conditions, luminance and contrast) will be made through action....the main function, of the many capacities of the parietal cortex is the need to encode information about the magnitudes in the external world that are used in action. In other words, the parietal cortex transformations that are often assumed to compute 'where' in space, really answer the questions 'how far, how fast, how much, how long and how many' with respect to action."[3]

CHAPTER 8

"People who develop states without preparation will experience all kinds of contaminated states, which is what generally happens with self-appointed experimenters. Sufis call the mystical state, where it is perceived as anything strange at all, the action of the higher impulses on the lower, unaltered and therefore unsuitable consciousness. 'States,' therefore, are regarded as prisons and vicissitudes: 'realised people' — as Hujwiri* says — are those who have escaped from having 'states,' mystical experiences. The true states, however, cannot be described, because they are an annihilation of speech." — Idries Shah.[4]

CHAPTER 11

Colin Humphreys, a British physicist who has made a study of religions in the ancient world, has determined that notable natural incidents and circumstances can explain all the major miracles of the Old Testament narrative of the Exodus. His research relocates Mount Sinai from the Sinai Peninsula — which is where the Exodus story was placed in the third century CE, about 1,500 years after the events were said to have occurred — to the much more plausible settlement of Midian, which is modern al-Bad' in Saudi Arabia.[5]

In the terrain around al-Bad', it is possible that a small volcanic vent under the famous "burning bush" produced the "flames of fire from within," so that "although the bush was on fire it did not burn up." (Exodus 3:2 [NIV]) Humphreys writes:

> The fact that the book of Exodus calls 'holy' the ground on which the burning bush stood, but not the burning bush itself, is consistent with my suggestion that the fire came from the ground (either due to natural gas or volcanic gases) and not from the bush itself.

Humphreys also notes that the sound made by gases when they are forced out through cracks in solid rock is very much like "a very loud trumpet blast." (Exodus 19:16[NIV])

Such dramatic natural events are often recorded by more than one tradition, or are passed on from one community to

---

*Ali b. Uthman al Jullabi al Hujwiri: Kashf al Mahjub (11th Century).

another, as in the story of the Flood. A Sumerian genesis flood dates from 2150 BCE; the Akkadian epic *Atra-Hassis* describes a massive flood, which dates to 1635 BCE; and the famous neo-Babylonian *Epic of Gilgamesh*, which has many parallels with the biblical story of the flood, was inscribed on tablets that date to 1150 BCE.

The geophysicists William Ryan and Walter Pitman, in their book *Noah's Flood: The New Scientific Discoveries about the Event that Changed History*, describe how, through the use of sound waves and coring devices, they probed the sea floor of what is today known as the Black Sea and came up with evidence that until about 7,600 years ago, this was a vast freshwater lake lying hundreds of feet below sea level. They write:

> It was an area that remained warm when the mountain flanks of the Fertile Crescent, the Negev highlands, and the Anatolian plateau chilled. It held vast volumes of fresh water when the lakes elsewhere shriveled to undrinkable salt ponds and marshes, and the Jericho spring dried up in the second Mini Ice Age.

Over a period of thousands of years, as glaciers and icecaps melted, sea levels rose, and the water of the Mediterranean eventually burst through the narrow Bosporus with a force estimated to have been 200 times that of Niagara Falls. This water poured into the waters below and flooded the settled areas around the freshwater lake described by Ryan and Pitman. The explorer Robert Ballard (best-known for having discovered the wreck of the Titanic) discovered what appears to have been an ancient wooden structure that was apparently flooded in an area of two submerged river beds under the Black Sea off the coast of northern Turkey, at a depth of 311 feet (95 meters), so perhaps this actual flood was the inspiration for the mythic tale of Noah's ark.

References

Introduction

1 Rumi, J., in *The Way of the Sufi*, Idries Shah, Octagon Press, 2004, p. 102.

2 Armstrong, K., *The Case for God*, Alfred A. Knopf, 2009, p. 10.

3 Shah, I., *The Way of the Sufi*, Octagon Press, 2004, p. 222.

4 Ibid., p. 14.

5 Ibid., p. 219.

6 For a comprehensive definition of the Sufi, see *The Sufis* by Idries Shah, Octagon Press, 1964, and "The Study of Sufism in the West" in *The Way of the Sufi* by Idries Shah, Octagon Press, 2004, p. 13. The Saadi quote is from *Knowing How to Know* by Idries Shah, Octagon Press, 2000, p. 217.

7 Haji Bahaudin, "Remembering" in *The Way of the Sufi* by Idries Shah, Octagon Press, 2004, p. 261.

Chapter 1:

1 Douthat, R., *Bad Religion: How we became a nation of heretics*, Free Press, 2012, p. 247.

2 Ibid.

3 Amis, M., *The Information*, Vintage (Random House), 1995, p. 91.

4   Pollan, M., "The Intelligent Plant: Scientists debate a new way of understanding flora," *The New Yorker*, Dec. 16, 2013, published in the print edition of the December 23 and 30, 2013, issue.

5   Bogen, J.E., "The other side of the brain: I.II.III.," *Bulletin of the Los Angeles Neurological Societies* 34:3 (1969).

6   Deglin, V.L. and Kinsbourne, M., "Divergent thinking styles of the hemispheres: How syllogisms are solved during transitory hemisphere suppression," *Brain and Cognition*, 31, 285-307 (1996).

7   Powell, J., Lewis, P.A., Roberts, N., García-Fiñana, M. and Dunbar, R.I.M., "Orbital prefrontal cortex volume predicts social network size: an imaging study of individual differences in humans," *Proceedings of the Royal Society B*. Published before print February 1, 2012, on royalsocietypublishing.org/doi/full/10.1098/rspb.2011.2574

8   "Brain size is bigger if you have more friends." New release from University of Oxford, February 1, 2012, ox.ac.uk/news/2012-02-01-brain-size-bigger-if-you-have-more-friends
    See also: Powell, J., Lewis, P.A., Roberts, N., García-Fiñana, M., and Dunbar, R.I. "Orbital prefrontal cortex volume predicts social network size: an imaging study of individual differences in humans," *Proceedings of the Royal Society B.*, 2012 Jun 7;279(1736):2157-62, doi.org/10.1098/rspb.2011.2574

9   Vaillant, G.E., "The neuroendocrine system and stress, emotions, thoughts and feelings," in Singh, A.R. and Singh, S.A. (eds.), "Brain, Mind and Consciousness: An International, Interdisciplinary Perspective," *Mens Sana Monographs*, 9, 1, 113-128 (2011).

10 Shah, I., *Caravan of Dreams*, Octagon Press, 1967, p. 7.

11 Bourguignon, E. and Evascu, T.L., "Altered states of consciousness within a general evolutionary perspective: A holocultural analysis," *Behavior Science Research*, Vol. 12, 3: 197-216 (1997), journals.sagepub.com

12 Bourguignon, E., "Possession and trance in cross-cultural studies of mental health," in Lebra, W.P. (ed.), "Culture-bound

syndromes, ethnopsychiatry, and alternate therapies," Vol. IV of *Mental Health Research in Asia and the Pacific*, an East-West Center Book, Honolulu: The University Press of Hawaii, 1976, p. 51.

13 Clottes, J. and Lewis-Williams, D., *The Shamans of Prehistory: Trance and Magic in the Painted Caves*, Harry N. Abrams, 1998, p. 12.

14 Meyer, M., "The Gospel of Thomas: Saying 113" in *The Gnostic Gospels of Jesus: Definitive Collection of Mystical Gospels and Secret Books about Jesus of Nazareth*, Harper Collins, 2005, p. 25.

15 *The Hadith: The Words of The Prophet Muhammad* (peace and blessings upon him), *A Collection of Hadith on Non-Violence, Peace and Mercy*, compiled and edited by Kabir Helminski from the reliable sources offered by Dr. M. Hafiz Syed.

16 James, W., *Pragmatism: A New Name for Some Old Ways of Thinking*. In *Popular Lectures on Philosophy*, Longmans, Green, and Co., New York, 1908, p. 12.

17 Huxley, A., *The Doors of Perception and Heaven and Hell*, Harper & Brothers, 1956, p. 8.

18 Ibn El-Arabi: "The Greatest Sheikh," in *The Sufis*, by Idries Shah, Octagon Press, 1964, p. 137.

19 Shah, I., *Neglected Aspects of Sufi Studies*, Octagon Press, 2002, pp. 38-39.

Chapter 2:

1 Armstrong, K., *The Case for God*, Knopf Doubleday Publishing Group, 2009, p. 9.

2 Ryan, R.E., *The Strong Eye of Shamanism*, Inner Traditions Intl., 1999, pp. 51-52. Quotes Herbert Kühn, *Auf den Spüren des Eiszeitmenschen* (Wiesbaden Germany: F.A. Brockhause, 1953, pp. 91-94,) as found in Campbell, J., *Historical Atlas of World Mythology*, Vol.1., "The Way of the Animal Powers," pp. 73-75.

3 Kühn, Herbert, *On the Track of Prehistoric Man*, transl. Alan Brodrick, Random House, 1955, pp. 108-110.

4 Leroi-Gourhan, A., *Treasures of Prehistoric Art*, Henry N. Abrams Pub., 1967, p. 164.

5 Lewis-Williams, D., *The Mind in the Cave: Consciousness and the Origins of Art*, Thames & Hudson, 2002, p. 195.

6 Snow, Dean R., "Sexual dimorphism in European Upper Paleolithic cave art," *American Antiquity*, 78(4), 2013, p. 746.

7 Tallavaara, M., Luoto, M., Korhonen, N., Järvinen, H. and Seppä, H., "Human population dynamics in Europe over the last glacial maximum," *Proceedings of the National Academy of Sciences*, July 7, 2015, 112 (27) 8232-8237.

8 Shah, I., *Thinkers of the East*, Octagon Press, 1982, p. 109.

9 Bear Heart, with Molly Larkin, *The Wind is My Mother: Life and Teachings of a Native American Shaman*, Berkeley Pub., 1998, p. 65.

10 Ibid., p. 129.

11 Wright, R., *The Evolution of God*, Little, Brown and Company, 2009, p. 19.

12 Lewis-Williams, D., *The Mind in the Cave*: Consciousness and the Origins of Art, Thames & Hudson, 2002, pp. 139-142.

13 Eliade, M., *Shamanism: Archaic Techniques of Ecstasy*, Princeton Univ. Press, 2004, p. 5.

14 Walsh, R., *The World of Shamanism: New Views of an Ancient Tradition*, Llewellyn Pub., 2007, p. 64.

15 Ryan, R.E., *The Strong Eye of Shamanism*, Inner Traditions Intl., 1999, p. 5.

16 Winkelman, M.J., *Shamanism: A Biopsychosocial Paradigm of Consciousness and Healing*, 2nd Ed., Praeger, 2010, p. 3.

17 Bourguignon E. "Possession and Trance," in Ember, C.R. and Ember, M. (eds.), *Encyclopedia of Medical Anthropology*, Springer, Boston, MA, 2004, pp. 137-145.
See also: Bourguignon, E., "A framework for the comparative study of altered states of consciousness," in Bourguignon, E. (ed.), *Religion, altered states of consciousness, and social change*, Ohio State University Press, 1973, pp. 3-38.

18 Marshack, A., *The Roots of Civilization: The Cognitive Beginnings of Man's First Art, Symbol and Notation*, McGraw-Hill, 1972, p. 133.

19 Milbrath, C. and Lightfoot, C. (eds.), *Art and Human Development*, Psychology Press, 2013, p. 30.

20 Lewis-Williams, D., *The Mind in the Cave*: Consciousness and the Origins of Art, Thames & Hudson, 2002, p. 194.

21 Lorblanchet, M., "Spitting images: replicating the spotted horses of Pech Merle," *Archaeology* 44(6), 25-31 (1991).

22 Lewis-Williams, D., *The Mind in the Cave: Consciousness and the Origins of Art*, Thames & Hudson, 2002, p. 149.

23 Ibid., p. 134.

24 Lewis-Williams, D. and Pearce, D., *Inside the Neolithic Mind: Consciousness, Cosmos and the Realm of the Gods*, Thames & Hudson, 2005, p. 83.

25 Eliade, M., *Shamanism: Archaic Techniques of Ecstasy*, Princeton Univ. Press, 2004, p. 510.

26 Ibid., p. 420.

27 Katz, R., *Boiling Energy: Community Healing Among the Kalahari !Kung*, Rev. Ed., Harvard Univ. Press, 1982, p. 116.

28 Gow, P., *An Amazonian Myth and Its History*, Oxford Univ. Press, 2001, p. 64.

29 Walsh, R., *The World of Shamanism: New Views of an Ancient Tradition*, Llewellyn Pub., 2007, p. 64.

30 Eliade, M., *Shamanism: Archaic Techniques of Ecstasy*, Princeton Univ. Press, 2004, p. 64.

31 Bear Heart, with Molly Larkin, *The Wind is My Mother: Life and Teachings of a Native American Shaman*, Berkeley Pub., 1998, p. x.

32 Ibid., p. 55.

33 Ibid., p. 53.

34 Clottes and Lewis-Williams, *The Shamans of Prehistory: Trance and Magic in the Painted Caves*, Harry N. Abrams, 1998, p. 14.

35 Ibid., pp. 16-17.

36 Clottes, J. and Lewis-Williams, D., "Upper palaeolithic cave art: French and South African collaboration," *Cambridge Archaeological Journal*, 2/1 (April 1996). (For article reprint, see cambridge. org)

37 Clottes and Lewis-Williams, *The Shamans of Prehistory*: Trance and Magic in the Painted Caves, Harry N. Abrams, 1998, pp. 28-29.

38 Van Pool, C.S., "The signs of the sacred: Identifying shamans using archaeological evidence," *Journal of Anthropological Archaeology*, 28 (2009), p. 177-190.

39 Sombrun, C., *Mon initiation chez les chamanes*, Paris: Albin Michel, 2004.

40 Flor-Henry, P., Shapiro, Y., and Sombrun, C., "Brain changes during a shamanic trance: Altered modes of consciousness, hemispheric laterality, band systemic psychobiology," *Cogent Psychology* 4: 1313522 (April 24, 2017).

41 Ibid.

See also: Tsakiris, M., Costantini, M., and Haggard, P., "The role of the right temporo-parietal junction in maintaining a coherent sense of one's body," *Neuropsychologia*, 46, (2008), pp. 3014-3018.

42 Pollan, M., "The Trip Treatment," *The New Yorker*, Feb. 9, 2015, writing about Patrick Mettes, a cancer patient in the N.Y.U. psilocybin trial, 2010. Volunteers were required to write a narrative of their experience soon after the treatment.

43 Lewis-Williams, D. and Pearce, D., *Inside the Neolithic Mind: Consciousness, Cosmos and the Realm of the Gods*, Thames & Hudson, 2005, p. 82.

44 Smith, D., Schlaepfer, P., Major, K., Dyble, M., Page, A.E., Thompson, J., Chaudhary, N., Salali, G.D., Mace, R., Astete, L., Ngales, M., Vinicius, L., and Migliano, A.B., "Cooperation and the evolution of hunter-gatherer storytelling," *Nature Communications*, 8/1853 (Dec. 5, 2017).

45 Weber, M., Gerth, H.H., and Wright Mills, C. (eds.), *From Max Weber: Essays in Sociology*, Oxford University Press, 1958, p. 287.

46 Sanderson, S. K., *Religious Evolution and the Axial Age: From Shamans to Priests to Prophets, Scientific Studies of Religion, Inquiry and Explanation*, Bloomsbury Publishing, Kindle Edition, 2018, location 1841.

47 Sweatman, M.B., and Coombs, A., "Decoding European Paleolithic art: Extremely ancient knowledge of precession of the equinoxes," *The Athens Journal of History*, Vol. 5, Issue 1 (January 2019), pp, 14 -30.

48 Breuil, Abbe H., *Four Hundred Centuries of Cave Art*, transl. Mary E. Boyle, realized by Fernand Windels, Paris, France (1952), p. 176.

Chapter 3:

1 Quoted in Kolbert, E., "Ice memory," *The New Yorker*, February 7, 2002.

2 Lewis-Williams, D. and Pearce, D., *Inside the Neolithic Mind: Consciousness, Cosmos and the Realm of the Gods*, Thames & Hudson, 2005, p. 167.

3 Ibid, pp. 103-108.

4 Hodder, I., *The Leopard's Tale: Revealing the Mysteries of Çatalhöyük*, Reprint Ed., Thames & Hudson, 2011, p. 198.

5 Watkins, T., "The Neolithic revolution and the emergence of humanity: a cognitive approach to the first comprehensive world-view." An abstract of his paper is available online: academia.edu/270175

6 Bear Heart, with Molly Larkin, *The Wind is My Mother: Life and Teachings of a Native American Shaman*, p. 186.

7 Krajick, K., "The scientific detectives probing the secrets of ancient oracles, geological features, toxic fumes, and visions of the future," *Atlas Obscura*, May 17, 2018. atlasobscura.com/articles/where-are-the-greek-oracles

8   Hale, J.R., (Prof.), University of Louisville, "Exploring the Roots of Religion, Part 2," The Teaching Company DVD, 2009.

9   de Boer, J.Z. and Hale, J.R., "The geological origins of the Oracle at Delphi, Greece," in McGuire, W.G., Griffiths, D.R., Hancock, P.L. and Stewart, I.S. (eds.), *The Archaeology of Geological Catastrophes*, Geological Society, London, Special Publications, 171, pp. 399-412 (2000).

10 Hale, J.R., (Prof.), University of Louisville, "Exploring the Roots of Religion, Part 2," The Teaching Company DVD, 2009.

11 Wright, R., *The Evolution of God*, Little, Brown and Company, 2009, p. 75.

12 Spar, I., "Mesopotamian Deities," Department of Ancient Near Eastern Art, The Metropolitan Museum of Art, April 2009.

13 Jacobsen, T., *The Treasures of Darkness: A History of Mesopotamian Religion*, Rev. Ed., Yale University Press, 1976, p. 21.

14 Ibid, p. 7.

15 Ibid., p. 14.

16 Ibid., p. 161.

17 Armstrong, Karen, *The Case for God*, Random House, 2010, p.18.

Chapter 4:

1   Armstrong, Karen, *A History of God*, Random House Publishing Group, 1993, p. 54.

2   Boyce, M., *Zoroastrians: Their Religious Beliefs and Practices*, Routledge (Taylor & Francis), 1979, 2001, p. 29.

3   Doane, T.W., *Bible Myths, and their Parallels in other Religions*, Amazon Createspace, 2007. Also available in print form of 1882 edition from Cosimo Classics Reprint, 2007.

4   Armstrong, K., *The Case for God*, Random House, 2010, p. 34.

5   Meyer, M. (ed.), *The Nag Hammadi Scriptures: The Revised and Updated Translation of Sacred Gnostic Texts Complete in One Volume*, Saying 8, HarperOne, 2009.

6 Whiston, W. (transl.), *The Complete Works of Flavius Josephus*, "Antiquities of the Jews," 18:3.3., Thomas Nelson Publishers, 1998.

7 Ibid., "Wars III," 4.1.1.9.

8 Anonymous, *The Marketing of Christianity: The Evolution of Early Christian Doctrine*, Institute for Cultural Research, London, 2000.

9 Pagels, E., *The Gnostic Gospels*, Vintage Books, 1979, p. xx.

10 The Gospel of Thomas 11-32, 10-51, 28, translated by Thomas O. Lambdin, from *The Nag Hammadi Library, Revised Edition: The definitive new translation of the Gnostic scriptures, complete in one volume*, 14, pp. 126-138 (James M. Robinson, General Editor).

11 Pagels, E., *Beyond Belief: The Secret Gospel of Thomas*, Knopf Doubleday Publishing Group, Kindle Edition, 2004, Chapter 2, p. 57.

12 Pagels, E., *The Book of Thomas the Contender*, 138.7-19, in *The Nag Hammadi Library*, 189, as quoted in *Beyond Belief: the Secret Gospel of Thomas* by Elaine Pagels, ibid.

13 Lambdin, T.O. (transl.), "The Gospel of Thomas," from *The Nag Hammadi Library, Revised Edition: The definitive new translation of the Gnostic scriptures, complete in one volume*, 14, p. 128 (James M. Robinson, General Editor).

14 Spong, J.S., *The Sins of Scripture*, HarperOne, Kindle Edition, 2009, Chapter 22, pp. 197-198.

15 Sanderson, S.K., *Religious Evolution and the Axial Age: From Shamans to Priests to Prophets, Scientific Studies of Religion, Inquiry and Explanation*, Bloomsbury Publishing, Kindle Edition, 2018, location 1716-1731.

16 Armstrong, Karen, *The Case for God*, Random House, 2010, p. 115.

17 Irenaeus of Lyon, *Against Heresies*, 3:11:8.

18 MacDonald, D.R., "Early Christian Literature," in *The Oxford Study Bible – Revised English Bible with the Apocrypha*, edited by

M. J. Suggs, K.D. Sakenfeld and J.R. Mueller, Oxford University Press, 1992, p. 116.

19 Borg, M. and Crossan, J.D., *The First Christmas: What the Gospels Really Teach About Jesus's Birth*, Harper Collins, 2009, p. 38.

20 Ibid., p. 192.

21 Vermes, G., *The Nativity: History and Legend*, Penguin, 2006, p. 38.

22 Spong, J.S., *The Fourth Gospel: Tales of a Jewish Mystic*, reprint edition, HarperOne, 2014, p. 185.

23 Morinelli, T.D., *Reason and Doctrine: Time for Christians to Rethink What They Believe*, Algora Publishing, 2016, p. 43.

24 See *Tales of the Dervishes* and other titles by Idries Shah, ISF Publishing, idriesshahfoundation.org

25 Spong, J.S., *The Fourth Gospel: Tales of a Jewish Mystic*, Reprint edition, HarperOne, 2014, p. 17.

26 Ehrman, B.D., *How Jesus Became God: The Exaltation of a Jewish Preacher from Galilee*, HarperOne, 2014. Quoting the translation from J.N.D Kelly, *Early Christian Creeds*, 3rd ed., Longman Group, London, 1972, p. 350.

27 Meeks, W., *The Writings of St. Paul*, Vol. 4, p. 398.

28 Sanderson, S.K. *Religious Evolution and the Axial Age: From Shamans to Priests to Prophets, Scientific Studies of Religion, Inquiry and Explanation*, Bloomsbury Publishing, Kindle Edition, 2018, location1813-1841.

29 Ehrman, B.D., *The Triumph of Christianity: How a Forbidden Religion Swept the World*, Simon & Schuster, 2018, p. 266.

30 Clark, G., *Christianity and Roman Society*, Cambridge University Press, 2004.

31 Ehrman, B.D., *The Triumph of Christianity: How a Forbidden Religion Swept the World*, Simon & Schuster, 2018, p. 139.

32 Armstrong, K., *Muhammad: A Prophet of our Time*, HarperOne, 2007, p. 28.

33 Ibid., Kindle Edition, location 2452.

34 Ibid., Harper Edition, pp. 67, 205.

35 Shah, I., *The Sufis*, Octagon Press, 1964, p. 375.

36 Ibn Ishaq, Sirat Rasul Allah, 143, in *Guillaume, Life of Muhammad*, taken here from K. Armstrong, *Muhammad: A Prophet of our Time*, Kindle Edition, location 409.

37 Armstrong, Karen, *The Case for God*, Alfred A. Knopf, 2009, p. 100.

38 Shah, I., *The Sufis*, Appendix 1: Esoteric Interpretation of the Qur'an, Octagon Press, 1964, p. 401.

39 Aslan, R., *No God But God: The Origins, Evolution, and Future of Islam* (Updated Edition), Random House Publishing, 2011, p. 47.

40 Armstrong, K., *Muhammad: A Prophet of our Time*, HarperOne, 2007, p. 28.

41 Ibid, p. 82, quoting Muhammad ibn Jarir at-Tabari, *Ta'rikh ar Rasul wa'l Muluk*, 2210, in Bamyeh, M.A., *Social Origins of Islam: Mind, Economy, Discourse*, University of Minnesota Press, 1999, pp. 144-145.

42 Donner, F. M., *Muhammad and the Believers: At the Origins of Islam*, Harvard University Press, 2010.

43 Alsan, R., *No God but God: The Origins, Evolution, and Future of Islam*, Random House, 2005, p. 12.

44 Boyce, M., *Zoroastrians: Their Religious Beliefs and Practices*, Routledge (Taylor & Francis), 1979, 2001, p. 29.

45 Donner, F. M., *Muhammad and the Believers: At the Origins of Islam*, 2010, Harvard University Press.

46 Donner, F., *Narratives of Islamic Origins: The Beginnings of Islamic Historical Writing*, Darwin Press, Inc., 1998, pp. 82-84.

47 Shah, I., *Caravan of Dreams*, Octagon Press, 1967, p. 25.

48 Shah, I., *The Sufis*, Appendix 1: Esoteric Interpretation of the Qur'an, Octagon Press, 1964, p. 401.

49 Shah, I., *The Sufis*, Octagon Press, 1964, p. 27.

50 Al-Khalili, Jim, *The House of Wisdom*, Penguin Publishing Group, 2010, p. 26.

51 Shah, I., *Caravan of Dreams*, "Sayings of the Prophet," Octagon Press, 1967, p. 19.

52 Ibid., p. 18.

53 Hyman, A. and J. J. Walsh, *Philosophy in the Middle Ages*, Hackett Publishing Group, Indianapolis, 1973, p. 204. Also cited in Josef W. Meri and Jere L. Bacharach (eds.), *Medieval Islamic Civilization*, Vol. 1, A–K, Index, 2006, p. 304.

54 newworldencyclopedia.org/entry/Al-Kindi

55 Nightingale, S., *Granada: A Pomegranate in the Hand of God*, Counterpoint Press, Berkeley, CA, 2015, p. 118.

56 Menocal, M.R., *The Ornament of the World*, Little, Brown and Company, 2002, p. 142.

57 Shah, I., *The Way of the Sufi*, Octagon Press, 2004, p. 52.

58 Shah, I., *The Sufis*, Octagon Press, 1964, p. 34.

59 Ibid., p. 25.

60 Ibid., p. 33.

Chapter 5:

1 James, W., *Varieties of Religious Experience, a Study in Human Nature*, "Lectures XIV and XVII: Mysticism," DigitalReads, Kindle Edition, 2011, p. 337.

2 Huxley, A., *The Doors of Perception and Heaven and Hell*, Harper & Brothers, 1956.

3 Previc, F.H., "Functional specialisation in the lower and upper visual fields in humans: its ecological origins and neurophysiological implications," *Behavioral and Brain Sciences*, 13, 3, 519-542 (1990).
See also: Previc, F.H. "The role of the extrapersonal brain systems in religious behavior," *Consciousness and Cognition*, 15, 500-539 (2006).

4 Tolaas, J., "Notes on the origin of some spatialization metaphors," *Metaphor and Symbolic Activity*, 6, 203-218 (1991).

5   Ibid.

6   Ponomarenko, V., "Kingdom in the sky – Earthly fetters and heavenly freedoms. The pilot's approach to the military flight environment," North Atlantic Treaty Organization: Research and Technology Organization, Neuilly-sur-Seine, France (2000).

7   Meier, B.P. and Robinson, M.D., "Why the sunny side is up: associations between affect and vertical position," *Psychological Science*, 15 (2004), pp. 243-247.

8   Meier, B.P. and Robinson, M.D., "Does 'feeling down' mean seeing down?: Depressive symptoms and vertical selective attention," *Journal of Research in Personality*, 40, 4 (2005), pp. 451-61.

9   Meier, B.P., Hauser, D. J., Robinson, M.D., et al. "What's 'up' with God?: Vertical space as a representation of the divine," *Journal of Personality and Social Psychology*, Vol. 93(5)(Nov 2007), p. 708.

10 Heschel, A. (Rabbi), quoted in "The Beginning of Wisdom," huffpost.com/entry/the-beginning-of-wisdom_b_4268656

11 Winfrey, O., as quoted in the article on: washingtonpost.com/national/religion/oprah-interview-stirs-debate-what-is-an-atheist/2013/10/21/21315f20-3a78-11e3-b0e7-716179a2c2c7_story.html

12 Freud, S., *The Future of Illusion*, Wilder Publications, 2011, p. 15-16.

13 Paneth F.A., "The frequency of meteorite falls throughout the ages," *Vistas in Astronomy*, Vol. 2, 1956, pp. 1681-1686.

14 Marchant J., "Iron in Egyptian relics came from space," *Nature*, 29 May 2013, doi.org/10.1038/nature.2013.13091, 86.

15 Keltner, D. and Haidt, J., "Approaching awe, a moral, spiritual, and aesthetic emotion," *Cognition and Emotion*, 17(2) (2003), pp. 297-314.

16 Fredrickson, L.M. and Anderson, D.H., "A qualitative exploration of the wilderness experience as a source of spiritual inspiration," *Journal of Environmental Psychology*, 19 (1999), pp. 21-39.
    See also: Ravizza, K., "Peak experiences in sport," Journal of Humanistic Psychology, 17 (1997), pp. 35-40. Vohs, K.D. and

Schmeichel, B.J. "Self-regulation and the extended now: Controlling the self alters the subjective experience of time," *Journal of Personality and Social Psychology*, 85 (2003), pp. 217-230.

17 Parker, J., "The Beauty and Horror of Blue Planet II," *The Atlantic*, April 2018.

18 Ponomarenko, V., "Kingdom in the sky – Earthly fetters and heavenly freedoms. The pilot's approach to the military flight environment," North Atlantic Treaty Organization: Research and Technology Organization, Neuilly-sur-Seine, France (2000), p. 141.

19 Piff, P.K., Dietze, P., Feinberg, M., Stancato, D.M., and Keltner, D., "Awe, the small self, and prosocial behavior," *Journal of Personality and Social Psychology*, 108(6) (2015), pp. 883-899.

20 Rudd, M., Vohs, K.D. and Aaker, J., "Awe expands people's perception, alters decision making, and enhances well-being," *Psychological Science*, 23,10 (2012), pp. 1130-1136.

21 Valdesolo, P. and Graham, J., "Awe, uncertainty, and agency detection," *Psychological Science*, 25(1) (2014), pp. 170-178.

22 Sibley, C.G. and Bulbulia, J., "Faith after an earthquake: A longitudinal study of religion and perceived health before and after the 2011 Christchurch New Zealand earthquake," *PloS one* (Public Library of Science) 7(12) (2012), e49648.

Chapter 6:

1 Perroud, N., "Religion/spirituality and neuropsychiatry" in *Religion and Spirituality in Psychiatry*, Huguelet, P. and Koenig, H.G. (eds.), Cambridge Univ Press, 2009, p. 50.

2 Lingford-Hughes, A. and Kalk, N., "Clinical Anatomy," in *Core Psychiatry*, P. Wright and M. Phelan (eds.), Saunders, Ltd., 2011.

See also: Wendelken, C., "Meta-analysis: how does posterior parietal cortex contribute to reasoning?," *Frontiers in Human Neuroscience*, 8:1042 (2015), doi.org/10.3389/fnhum.2014.01042

3 Webb, W., "Organization of the nervous system," in *Neurology for the Speech-Language Pathologist*, 6th Ed., Mosby, 2017.

4 Bueti, D. and Walsh, W., "The parietal cortex and the representation of time, space, number and other magnitudes," *Philosophical Transactions of the Royal Society: Biological Sciences*, 264/1525 (2009), p. 1836.

5 Braithwaite, J.J., Watson, D.G., and Dewe, H., "Predisposition to out-of-body experience (OBE) is associated with aberrations in multisensory integration: Psychophysiological support from a 'rubber hand illusion' study," *Journal of Experimental Psychology: Human Perception and Performance*, 43(6) (2017), pp. 1125-1143.

6 Bardi, L., Six, P. and Brass, M., "Repetitive TMS of the temporoparietal junction disrupts participant's expectations in a spontaneous Theory of Mind Task," *Social Cognitive and Affective Neuroscience*, Volume 12, Issue 11, Nov. 1, 2017, pp. 1775-1782.

7 Bisiacchi, P.S., Cona, G., Schiff, S. and Basso, D., "Modulation of a fronto-parietal network in event-based prospective memory: an rTMS study," *Neuropsychologia*, 49(8), Pergamon, July 1, 2011, pp. 2225-2232.

8 Salillas, E., Semenza, C., Basso, D., Vecchi, T. and Siegal, M., "Single pulse TMS induced disruption to right and left parietal cortex on addition and multiplication," *Neuroimage*, Elsevier, Feb. 15, 2012.

9 Vallacher, R.R. and Wegner, D.M. *A Theory of Action Identification*, Hillsdale, NJ: Erlbaum, 1985.
See also: Liberman, N., Trope, Y., "The psychology of transcending the here and now," *Science*, 2008 Nov. 21; 322 (5905), pp. 1201-1205, doi.org/10.1126/science.1161958

10 Bueti, D. and Walsh, W., "The parietal cortex and the representation of time, space, number and other magnitudes," *Philosophical*

Transactions of the Royal Society: Biological Sciences, 264/1525 (2009), p. 1832.

11 Johnstone, B. and Glass, B.A., "Evaluation of a neuropsychological model of spirituality in persons with traumatic brain injury," *Zygon*, 43 (2008), pp. 861-74.

12 Ibid.

13 Johnstone, B., Bodling, A., Cohen, D., Christ, S.E., and Wegrzyn, A., "Right parietal lobe-related 'selflessness' as the neuropsychological basis of spiritual transcendence," *The International Journal for the Psychology of Religion*, 22, p. 279.

14 Ibid., p. 280.

15 Urgesi, C., Aglioti, S.M., Skrap, M. and Fabbro, F., "The spiritual brain: selective cortical lesions modulate human self-transcendence," *Neuron*, 65, 3 (2010), p. 310.

16 Ibid., p. 316.

17 Badcock, C., *The Imprinted Brain: How Genes Set the Balance Between Autism and Psychosis*, Jessica Kingsley Publishers, 2009, p. 152.

18 Torrey, E.F., "Schizophrenia and the inferior parietal lobes," *Schizophrenia Research*, 1 (2007), pp. 215-225.

19 Ibid., p. 106.

20 Jaspers, K., *General Psychopathology*, Manchester University Press, 1963 (English-language edition), quoted on p. 296.

21 Schreber, D.P., *Memoirs of My Nervous Illness*, New York Review Books, 2000, p. 197.

22 Badcock, C., *The Imprinted Brain: How Genes Set the Balance Between Autism and Psychosis*, Jessica Kingsley Publishers, 2009, p. 95.

23 Bogdashina, O., *Autism and the Edges of the Known World: Sensitivities, Language and Constructed Reality*, Jessica Kingsley Publishers, 2010, p. 39.

24 Saitoh, O. and Courchesne, E., "Magnetic resonance imaging study of the brain in autism," *Psychiatry and Clinical Neurosciences*, 52 (1998), pp. S219-222.

25 Egaas, B., Courchesne, E. and Saitoh, O., "Reduced size of corpus callosum in autism," *Archives of Neurology*, 52/8 (1995), pp. 794-801.

26 Farias, M., Underwood, R., Claridge, G., "Unusual but sound minds: mental health indicators in spiritual individuals," *British Journal of Psychology*, 104 (2013), p. 377.

27 Lieberman, M.D., *Social: Why Our Brains are Wired to Connect*, Crown Pub. (Random House), 2013, p. 21.

28 Brewer, J.A., Worhunsky, P.D., Gray, J.R., Tang, Y-Y., Weber, J. and Kober, H., "Meditation experience is associated with differences in default mode network activity and connectivity," *Proceedings of the National Academy of Sciences*, 108 (50), Dec. 13, 2011, 20254-20259.

29 Raichle, M.E., MacLeod, A.M., Snyder, A.Z., Powers, W.J., Gusnard, D.A., and Shulman, G.L., "A default mode of brain function," *PNAS* 98 (2001), pp. 676-682.

30 Hove, M.J., Stelzer, J., Nierhaus, T., Thiel, S.D., Gundlach, C., Margulies, D.S., Van Dijk, K.R.A., Turner, R., Keller, P.E., and Merker, B., "Brain network reconfiguration and perceptual decoupling during an absorptive state of consciousness," *Cerebral Cortex*, 137, 10.1093 (2015), p. 1.

31 Glucklich, A., *Sacred Pain: Hurting the Body for the Sake of the Soul*, Oxford Press, 2001.

32 Alshelh, Z., Marciszewski, K.K., Akhter, R., Di Pietro, F., Mills, E.P., Vickers, E.R., Peck, C.C., Murray, G.M., and Henderson, L.A., "Disruption of default mode network dynamics in acute and chronic pain states," *NeuroImage:Clinical*, 2018/17 (2015), pp. 222-231.

33 van Elk, M., Arciniegas-Gomez, M.A., van der Zwaag, W., van Schie, H.T., and Sauter, D., "The neural correlates of the awe experience: Reduced default mode network activity during feelings of awe," *Human Brain Mapping*, 2019/40, pp. 3561-3574, doi.org/10.1002/hbm.24616

34 Carhart-Harris, R.L., et al., "Neural correlates of the psychedelic state as determined by fMRI studies with psilocybin," *Proceedings*

of the National Academy of Sciences 109, no. 6 (2012), pp. 2138-2143, doi.org/10.1073/pnas.1119598109

35 Ibid.

Chapter 7:

1 Bolte Taylor, J., *My Stroke of Insight: A Brain Scientist's Personal Journey*, Viking (Penguin Books), 2008, p. 3.

2 Ibid., p. 41.

3 Ibid., p. 42.

4 Ibid., pp. 49-50.

5 Ibid., p. 67.

6 Ibid., p. 68.

7 Ibid., p. 54.

8 Ibid., p. 70.

9 Ibid., pp. 134-135.

10 From an anonymous contributor's online chat room account (2012). Cited in Alasdair Coles. "Temporal lobe epilepsy and Dostoyevksy seizures: Neuropathology and spirituality," Royal College of Psychiatrists, rcpsych.ac.uk/docs/default-source/members/sigs/spirituality-spsig/spirituality-special-interest-group-publications-alasdair-coles-temporal-lobe-epilepsy-and-dostoyevsky-seizures.pdf?sfvrsn=bf258b2f_2

11 Dylan, B. in November 19, 2004, interview "60 Minutes with Ed Bradley," alldylan.com/bob-dylan-the-classic-60-minutes-interview-with-ed-bradley-19-november-2004-video/

12 Taylor, S., *Out of the Darkness: From Turmoil to Transformation*, Hay House UK, 2011, p. 54.

13 Ibid., pp. 74-75.

14 Red Hong (pseud.), "Expansion of Self in the Antarctic: The Archives of Scientists' Transcendent Experiences," in Tart, C., Collected Archives, Submission No. 00001 (1999). See also: aapsglobal.com/1999/03/07/expansion-of-self-in-the-antarctic/

15 Smith, A., "My Experience of Cosmic Consciousness," in Tart, C., ibid., Submission No. 00004 (1999).
    See also: aapsglobal.com/1999/03/07/4-my-experience-of-cosmic-consciousness/

16 Elliot, T.S., excerpt from *Burnt Norton* (No. 1 of "Four Quartets").

17 Rumi, J., excerpt from "I am the Life of My Beloved," *The Sufis* by Idries Shah, ISF Publishing, Kindle Edition, 2015, Location 1510.

Chapter 8:

1 Quoted in Newberg, A., et al., *Why God Won't Go Away*, Random House, 2001, p. 104.

2 *The Lankavatara Sutra: A Mahayana Text*, transl. by D. T. Suzuki. Dev Publishers & Distributors, 2020, Chapter VIII, sacred-texts.com/bud/bb/bb15.htm

3 Hilton, W., *The Scale of Perfection*, Burnes & Coates, London, 1953, p. 205.

4 Shapiro, D.H., "Adverse effects of meditation: A preliminary investigation of long-term meditators," *International Journal of Psychosomatics*, 39(Nos. 1-4) (1992). See also a more recent review: Van Dam, N.T., et al., "Mind the hype: A critical evaluation and prescriptive agenda for research on mindfulness and meditation," *Perspectives on Psycholological Science* 13(1), January 2018, pp. 36-61, doi.org/10.1177/1745691617709589

5 Lindahl, J.R., Fisher, N.E., Cooper, D.J., Rosen, R.K., and Britton, W.B., "The varieties of contemplative experience: A mixed-methods study of meditation-related challenges in Western Buddhists," *PLoS ONE* 12(5) (2017), doi.org/10.1371/journal.pone.0176239

6 Shah, I., *Knowing How to Know*, The Estate of Idries Shah, 1998, p. 192.

7 Gebauer, J.E., et al., "Mind-body practices and the self: Yoga and meditation do not quiet the ego but instead boost self-enhancement," *Psychological Science* 29(8) (2018), p. 1299.

8   Farias, M. and Wikholm, C., *The Buddha Pill: Can Meditation Change You?*, Watkins Publishing, 2015, p. 143.

9   Ibid., p. 152.

10   Varela, F.J. (ed.), *Sleeping, Dreaming, and Dying: An exploration of consciousness with the Dalai Lama*, Wisdom Publications, Somerville, MA, 1997.

11   Hall, E., "The Sufi Tradition: An Interview with Idries Shah," *Psychology Today*, July 1975.

12   Armstrong, Karen, *The Case for God*, Alfred A. Knopf, 2009, p. 111.

13   Samorini, G., "The oldest representations of hallucinogenic mushrooms in the world," en.psilosophy.info/the_oldest_representations _of_hallucinogenic_mushrooms_in_the_world.html

14   Pahnke, W.M., "Summary of the Thesis: Drugs and Mysticism — An analysis of the Relationship between Psychedelic Drug Experience and the Mystical State of Consciousness," 1963 (Unpublished).
See also: maps.org/images/pdf/books/pahnke/walter_pahnke_ drugs_and_mysticism.pdf

15   Doblin, R., "Pahnke's 'Good Friday Experiment': A long-term follow-up and methodological critique," *The Journal of Transpersonal Psychology*, 23(1) (1991), p. 14.

16   Ibid.

17   Griffiths, R.R., Richards, W.A., Johnson, M.W., McCann, U.D., and Jesse, R. "Mystical-type experiences occasioned by psilocybin mediate the attribution of personal meaning and spiritual significance 14 months later," *Journal of Psychopharmacology*, 22(6), March 30, 2008, pp. 621-632.

18   Watts, R., Day, C., Krzanowski, J., Nutt, D., and Carhart-Harris, R., "Patients' accounts of increased 'connectedness' and 'acceptance' after psilocybin for treatment-resistant depression," *Journal of Humanistic Psychology*, 57(5), June 19, 2017, p. 528.

19   Pollan, M., *How to Change Your Mind*, Penguin Publishing Group, Penguin Books, Kindle Edition, 2018, p. 6.

20 Huxley, A., *The Doors of Perception and Heaven and Hell*, Harper & Brothers, 1956, p. 35.

21 Michaud, R. and Michaud, S., *Afghanistan* (English Translation), Harry N. Abrams, Inc., 2002, p. 12.

22 Maimonides (Moses Ben Maimon, 12th Century, Cordoba), as quoted by Dupuis, C.F., *Origine de tous les Cultus ou la Réligion Universelle / Origin of Religious Belief*, 1795, and by Doane, T.W., in *Bible Myths and Their Parallels in Other Religions*, 4th Edition, Truth Seeker Company, 1889, p. 100.

23 Shah, I., *The Dermis Probe*, ISF Publishing, Kindle Edition, 2016, location 1812.

24 Shah, I., *The Sufis*, Octagon Press, 1964, p. 119.

25 Hall, E., "The Sufi Tradition: An Interview with Idries Shah," *Psychology Today*, July 1975, p. 31.

26 Shah, I., *Caravan of Dreams*, Octagon Press, 1967, pp. 96-97.

27 Shah, I., *The Pleasantries of the Incredible Mulla Nasrudin*, "The High Cost of Learning," Jonathan Cape, Ltd., 1968, p. 82. See also: idriesshahfoundation.org

Chapter 9:

1 Paul, G., "The chronic dependence of popular religiosity upon dysfunctional psychosociological conditions," *Evolutionary Psychology* 7(3) (2009), pp. 398-441.

2 Zuckerman, P., *Society Without God: What the Least Religious Nations Can Tell Us About Contentment*, New York University Press, 2008, p. 210.

3 Evans, J., "U.S. adults are more religious than Western Europeans," Pew Research Center (2018), pewresearch.org/fact-tank/2018/09/05/u-s-adults-are-more-religious-than-western-europeans/

4 "Jesus Christ's Return to Earth," Pew Research Center, July 14, 2010, pewresearch.org/fact-tank/2010/07/14/jesus-christs-return-to-earth/

5 Diener, E., Tay, L., and Myers, D. G., "The religion paradox: If religion makes people happy, why are so many dropping out?," *Journal of Personality and Social Psychology*, 101 (2011), pp. 1278-1290.
   See also: Tay, L., Li, M., Myers, D., and Diener, E., "Religiosity and subjective well-being: An international perspective," in Kim-Prieto, C. (ed.), *Religion and Spirituality Across Cultures*, Vol. 9, Springer, 2014, pp. 163-175.

6 Brenan, M., "Religion considered important to 72% of Americans," Gallup Poll (2018), news.gallup.com/poll/ 245651/ religion-considered-important-americans.aspx

7 Diener, E., *et al.*, "The religion paradox: If religion makes people happy, why are so many dropping out?," *Journal of Personality and Social Psychology*, 101 (2011), pp. 1278-1290.

8 Ibid., p. 1278.

9 Zuckerman, P., *Society Without God: What the Least Religious Nations Can Tell Us About Contentment*, New York University Press, 2008, p.13.

10 Ibid., pp. 8-9.

11 Fahmy, D., "Key findings about God in America," Pew Research Center (2018), pewresearch.org/fact-tank/ 2018/04/25/key-findings-about-americans-belief-in-god/

12 Kraemer, J.L., *Maimonides: The Life and World of One of the Civilization's Greatest Minds*, Doubleday, 2008, p. 362.

13 Bragg, M. and guests: Sir Anthony Kenny, philosopher and former Master of Balliol College, Oxford; Anne Hudson, Emeritus Professor of Medieval English at the University of Oxford; and Rob Lutton, Lecturer in Medieval History at the University of Nottingham, discuss the life, times and legacy of the great Jewish medieval philosopher, Maimonides, youtube.com/watch?v=J-Wt2g7D9ks

14 Feynman, R., interview published in *Superstrings: A Theory of Everything?*, edited by Paul C. W. Davies and Julian R. Brown, Cambridge University Press, 1988, pp. 208-209.

15 Inzlicht, M., McGregor, I., Hirsh, J.B., and Nash, K. "Neural markers of religious conviction," *Psychological Science*, 20 (2009), pp. 385-392.

16 Kossowska, M., Szwed, P., Wronka, E., Czarnek, G., and Wyczesany, M., "Anxiolytic function of fundamentalist beliefs: Neurocognitive evidence," *Personality and Individual Differences*, Volume 101 (October 2016), pp. 390-395.

17 Norenzayan, A. and Lee, A. "It was meant to happen: explaining cultural variations in fate attributions," *Journal of Personality and Social Psychology* 98, no. 5 (2010), p. 702.

18 Routledge, C., Abeyta, A.A., and Roylance, C., "We are not alone: The meaning motive, religiosity, and belief in extraterrestrial intelligence," *Motivation and Emotion*, 41 (2017), pp. 135-146.

19 Calvin, J., *Institutes of the Christian Religion*, Philadelphia: Westminster John Knox Press, 2006, p. I.3.1.

20 Antonovsky, A., *Unraveling the Mystery of Health: How People Manage Stress and Stay Well*, Jossey-Bass, 1987.

21 Ibid., p. 19.

22 Eriksson, M. and Lindstrom, B., "Antonovsky's sense of coherence scale and its relation with health: A systematic review," *J Epidemiol Community Health*, 60 (2006), pp. 376-381.

23 Abdel-Khalek, A.M., *et al.*, "Religiosity, health and happiness: significant relations in adolescents from Qatar," *International Journal of Social Psychiatry* (2014).

24 Whitson, J.A. and Galinsky, A.D., "Lacking control increases illusory pattern perception," *Science*, 322 (2008), pp. 115-117.

25 Morford, M., "The Sad, Quotable Jerry Falwell," *SF Gate*, May 18, 2007, updated February 11, 2012.

26 Merritt, J., "Some of the most visible Christians in America are failing the coronavirus test," *The Atlantic*, April 24, 2020.

27 Fischer, R., Callander, R., Reddish, P., and Bulbulia, J., "How do rituals affect cooperation?: An experimental field study comparing nine ritual types," *Human Nature*, 24 (2013), pp. 115-125.

28 Atran, S. and Norenzayan, A., "Religion's evolutionary landscape: Counterintuition, commitment, compassion, communion," *Behavioral and Brain Sciences*, 27, (2004), pp. 713-730.

29 Boyer, P. and Ramble, C., "Cognitive templates for religious concepts: cross-cultural evidence for recall of counter-intuitive representations," *Cognitive Science*, 25/4 (2001), pp. 535-564.

30 Shah, I., *The Sufis*, Octagon Press, 1964, p. 26.

31 Atran, S. *In gods we trust: The evolutionary landscape of religion.* Oxford University Press, 2002. *See also*, Atran, S. and Norenzayan, A., "Religion's evolutionary landscape: Counterintuition, commitment, compassion, communion," *Behavioral and Brain Sciences*, 27, (2004), pp. 713-730.

32 Shariff, A.F. and Norenzayan, A., "God is watching you: priming God concepts increases prosocial behavior in an anonymous economic game," *Psychological Science*, Volume 18, Number 9 (2007), pp. 803-809.

33 Bering, J.M., McLeod, K., and Shackelford, T.K., "Reasoning about dead agents reveals possible adaptive trends," *Human Nature*, 16 (2005), pp. 360-381.

34 Bateson, M., Nettle, D., and Roberts, G., "Cues of being watched enhance cooperation in a real-world setting," *Biology Letters*, 2(3) (2006), pp. 412-414.

35 Ernest-Jones, M., Nettle, D. and Bateson, M., "Effects of eye images on everyday cooperative behavior: A field experiment," *Evolution and Human Behavior*, 32 (2011), pp. 172-178.

36 Letter from Thomas Jefferson to Peter Carr, with Enclosure, 10 August, 1787.

37 gened.fas.harvard.edu/if-there-is-no-god

38 theconversation.com/morality-requires-a-god-whether-youre-religious-or-not-42411

39 Wright, R., *The Moral Animal*, Vintage Books, 1995.

40 Biedrzycki, M.L. and Bais, H.P., "Kin recognition: another biological function for root secretions," *Plant Signaling & Behavior*, Volume 5, Issue 4 (2010), pp. 401-402.

41 Murphy, G.P. and Dudley, S.A., "Kin recognition: competition and cooperation in impatiens (Balsaminaceae)," *American Journal of Botany Evolution and Phylogeny*, 96(11) (2009), pp. 1990-1996.

42 Bais, H.P., "Shedding light on kin recognition response in plants," *New Phytologist*, 205(1), (2015), pp. 4-6.

43 Flack, J.C. and de Waal, F.B.M., "'Any animal whatever': Darwinian building blocks of morality in monkeys and apes," *Journal of Consciousness Studies*, 7:1-2 (2000), pp. 1-29.

44 Church, R., "Emotional reactions of rats to the pain of others," *Journal of Comparative & Physiological Psychology*, 52, 2 (1959), pp. 132-134.

45 Masserman, J.H., Wechkin, S., and Terris, W., "'Altruistic' behavior in rhesus monkeys," *American Journal of Psychiatry*, 121 (1964), pp. 584-585.

46 de Waal, F., *Our Inner Ape: A Leading Primatologist Explains Why We Are Who We Are*, Penguin, 2006, p. 2.

47 Melis, A.P., Warneken, F., Jensen, K., Schneider, A., Call, J., and Tomasello, M., "Chimpanzees help conspecifics obtain food and non-food items," *Proceedings of the Royal Society* B 27, Oct. 2010.

48 Hamlyn, J.K., Wynn, K., and Bloom, P., "Social evaluation by preverbal infants," *Nature*, 450/7169), Nov. 22, 2007, pp. 557-559.

49 Hamlyn, J.K. and Wynn, K., "Young infants prefer prosocial to antisocial others," *Cognitive Development*, 26 (2011), pp. 30-39.

50 Dunfield, K.A. and Kuhlmeier, V., "Intention-mediated selective helping in infancy," *Psychological Science*, 21 (2010), pp. 523-527.

51 Vaish, A., Carpenter, M., and Tomasello, M., "Young children selectively avoid helping people with harmful intentions," *Child Development*, 81, 6 (2010), pp. 1661-1669.

52 de Waal, F., *The Bonobo and the Atheist: In Search of Humanism Among the Primates*, Norton, 2009, p. 17.

53 Iacoboni, M., "Imitation, empathy, and mirror neurons," *Annual Review of Psychology*, 60 (2009), pp. 666-667.

Chapter 10:

1 Nuevo, R., Chatterji, S., Verdes, E., Naidoo, N., Arango, C., and Ayuso-Mateos, J.L., "The continuum of psychotic symptoms in the general population: a cross-national study," *Schizophrenia Bulletin*, 38(3), May 1, 2012, pp. 475-485.

2 Harrison, A. and Singer, J., "Boundaries in the mind: historical context and current research using the boundary questionnaire," *Imagination, Cognition and Personality*, 33 (1-2) (2013-2014), pp. 205-215.

3 Hartmann, E., Harrison, R., and Zborowski, M., "Boundaries in the mind: past research and future directions," *North American Journal of Psychology*, 3 (1989), p. 361, pp. 347-368.
   Hartmann, E., "Boundaries of dreams, boundaries of dreamers: thin and thick boundaries as a new personality measure," *Psychiatry Journal of the University of Ottawa*, 14, 4 (1989), pp. 557-560.
   Hartmann, E. and Kunzendorf, R.G., "The central image (CI) in recent dreams, dreams that stand out, and earliest dreams: relationship to boundaries," *Imagination, Cognition and Personality*, 25(4) (2005), pp. 383-392.

4 Luhrmann, T.M., as quoted in "To Dream in Different Cultures," *The New York Times*, May 13, 2014.

5 Luhrmann, T.M., *When God Talks Back: Understanding the American Evangelical Relationship with God*, Knopf, 2012, p. 197.

6 Luhrmann, T.M., Nusbaum, H., and Thisted, R., "The absorption hypothesis: learning to hear God in evangelical Christianity," *American Anthropologist*, 112, 1 (2010), pp. 66-78.

7 Tellegen, A. and Atkinson, G., "Openness to absorbing and self-altering experiences ('absorption'), a trait related to hypnotic susceptibility," *Journal of Abnormal Psychology*, 83, 3 (1974), 268-277.

8 Ibid.

9 Luhrman T.M., *When God Talks Back: Understanding the American Evangelical Relationship with God*, Alfred A Knopf (2012), pp. 196-197.

10 Bradshaw, M. and Ellison, C.G., "Do genetic factors influence religious life?: Findings from a behavior genetic analysis of twin siblings," *Journal for the Scientific Study of Religion*, 47, 7 (2008), p. 539, pp. 529-544.

11 Ludeke, S., Johnson, W., and Bouchard, Jr., T., "Obedience to traditional authority: A heritable factor underlying authoritarianism, conservatism and religiousness," *Personality and Individual Differences*, 55 (2013), pp. 375-380.

12 Steger M.F., Bundick M.J., and Yeager D., "Meaning in life," in Levesque, R.J.R. (ed.), *Encyclopedia of Adolescence*, Springer Pub., 2011.

13 Farias, M., Underwood, R., and Claridge, G., "Unusual but sound minds: mental health indicators in spiritual individuals," *British Journal of Psychology*, 104 (2013), p. 377, pp. 364-381.

14 Saucier, G. and Skrzypin, K., "Spiritual but not religious?: Evidence for two independent dispositions," *Journal of Personality*, 74:5, October 2006.

15 Farias, M., Underwood, R., and Claridge, G., "Unusual but sound minds: mental health indicators in spiritual individuals," *British Journal of Psychology*, 104 (2013), p. 377, pp. 364-381.

16 Feather, N.T., "Conservatism, traditionalism, cleanliness, more disgust, needing order value correlates of conservatism," *Journal of Personality and Social Psychology*, 37(9) (1979), pp. 1617-1630.

17 Bouchard, Thomas J., Jr., "Authoritarianism, Religiousness, and Conservatism: Is 'Obedience to Authority' the Explanation for Their Clustering, Universality and Evolution?," in *The Biological Evolution of Religious Mind and Behavior*, Voland, E. and Schiefenhövel, W. (eds.), Berlin Heidelberg: Springer, 2009, pp.165-180.

18 McCrae, R.R. and Costa, P.T. Jr., *Personality in Adulthood: A Five-Factor Theory Perspective*, 2d ed., Guilford Publications, 2003.

19 Wink, P., Ciciolla, L., Dillon, M., and Tracy, A., "Religiousness, spiritual seeking, and personality: Findings from a longitudinal study," *Journal of Personality*, 75 (2007), pp. 1051-1070.

20 Diener, E., Tay, L., and Myers, D. G., "The religion paradox: If religion makes people happy, why are so many dropping out?," *Journal of Personality and Social Psychology*, 101 (2011), pp. 1278-1290.
    See also: Tay, L., Li, M., Myers, D., and Diener, E., "Religiosity and subjective well-being: An international perspective," in Kim-Prieto, C. (ed.), *Religion and Spirituality Across Cultures*, Vol. 9, Springer, 2014, pp. 163-175.

21 Pizzagalli, D., Lehmann, D., and Brugger, P., "Lateralized direct and indirect semantic priming effects in subjects with paranormal experiences and beliefs," *Psychopathology*, 34 (2001), pp. 75-80.

22 Mohr, C., Bracha, H.S., and Brugger, P., "Magical ideation modulates spatial behavior," *Journal of Neuropsychiatry and Clinical Neuroscience*, 15, 2 (2003), pp. 168-174.

23 Brugger, P., "Tracking a Finer Madness: Many believers in psychic phenomena are also inventive — a fact that may help bridge the gap between creative genius and clinical insanity," *Scientific American Mind*, October/November 2007, p. 77.

24 Anscombe, G.E.M., *Metaphysics and the Philosophy of Mind: The Collected Philosophical Papers of G.E.M. Anscombe*, Vol. 2, Basil Blackwell, 1981, p. 20.

25 Grossman, C.L., "Richard Dawkins to atheist rally: 'Show contempt' for faith," *USA Today*, March 25, 2012.

26 Cornwell, J., *Darwin's Angel: An Angelic Riposte to "The God Delusion,"* Profile Books, 2009, p. 145.

27 Mukherjee, S., "A Failure to Heal," *New York Times*, November 28, 2017.

28 Rosenberg, L., "Searching for the Dark," *Scientific American*, January 2018.

29 NASA press release Oct. 13, 2016.

30 Camerer, C.F., et al., "Evaluating the replicability of social science experiments in nature and science between 2010 and 2015," *Nature Human Behaviour*, August 27, 2018.

Chapter 11:

1 Schonfield, H., *The Passover Plot: New Light on the History of Jesus* (40th Anniv. Ed.), Disinformation Co., Ltd., 2005, p. 184.

2 Cox, D. and Jones, R.P., "Few Americans see natural disasters as a sign from God," PRRI, March 24, 2011, prri.org/research/few-americans-see-earthquakes-floods-and-other-natural-disasters-a-sign-from-god-2/

3 Pew Research Center, "U.S. Public Becoming Less Religious," November 3, 2015, pewforum.org/2015/11/ 03/u-s-public-becoming-less-religious/

4 upi.com/Health_News/2013/12/22/US-belief-in-God-down-belief-in-theory-of-evolution-up/24081387762886/

5 Shah, I., *A Perfumed Scorpion*, Octagon Press, 1978, p. 139.

6 Condon, R.J., *Our Pagan Christmas*, American Atheist Press, 1989, p. 2.

7 Shah, I., *Thinkers of the East*, Octagon Press, 1971, p. 127.

8 Humphreys, C., *The Miracles of Exodus: A Scientist's Discovery of the Extraordinary Natural Causes of the Biblical Stories*, Harper Collins, 2004, p. 320.

9 Spong, J.S., *The Fourth Gospel: Tales of a Jewish Mystic*, reprint edition, HarperOne, 2014, p. 205.

Chapter 12:

1 Quoted in Shah, I., *The Way of the Sufi*, Octagon Press, 2004, p. 267.

2 Shah, I., "The King Spoke to Me," *The Pleasantries of the Incredible Mulla Nasrudin*, ISF Publishing, eBook Edition, (p. 172).

3 Kounios, J., and Beeman, M., *The Eureka Factor: Aha Moments, Creative Insight, and the Brain*, Penguin Books, Kindle Edition, 2015, location 1279.

   Kounios, J., and Beeman, M., "The Aha! moment: The cognitive neuroscience of insight," *Curr. Dir. Psychol. Sci.* 18(4) (2009), pp. 210-216.

   Kounios, J., and Beeman, M., "The cognitive neuroscience of insight," *Annu. Rev. Psychol.*, 65 (2014), pp. 71-93.

4   Mayseless, N. and Shamay-Tsoory, S.G., "Enhancing verbal creativity: Modulating creativity by altering the balance between right and left inferior frontal gyrus with tDCS," *Neuroscience*, 291 (2015), pp. 167-176.

5   Shamay-Tsoory, S.G., Adler, N., Aharon-Peretz, J., Perry, D., and Mayseless, N., "The origins of originality: The neural bases of creative thinking and originality," *Neuropsychologia* 49, (2011), pp. 178-185.

6   Aberg, K.C., Doell, S.S., and Kristoffer, C., "The 'Creative Right Brain' revisited: Individual creativity and associative priming in the right hemisphere relate to hemispheric asymmetries in reward brain function," *Cerebral Cortex* 27(10), October 1, 2017, p. 4946.

7   Howard-Jones, P.A., Blakemore, S-J., Samuel, E.A., Summers, I.R., and Claxton, G. "Semantic divergence and creative story generation: An fMRI investigation," *Cognitive Brain Research* 25(1) (2005), pp. 240-250.

8   Rozin, P., Moscovitch, M., and Imada, S., "Right:Left :: East:West — Evidence that individuals from East Asian and South Asian cultures emphasize right hemisphere functions in comparison to Euro-American cultures," *Neuropsychologia*, Volume 90, September 2016, pp. 3-11.

Chapter 13:

1   Shah, I., *The Way of the Sufi*, Octagon Press, 2004, p. 83.

2   Shamay-Tsoory, S. G., Tomer, R., Berger, B. D., Goldsher, D., and Aharon-Peretz, J., "Impairment in cognitive and affective empathy in patients with brain lesions: Anatomical and cognitive correlates," *Journal of Clinical and Experimental Neuropsychology*, 26, 8 (2004), pp. 1113-1127.

3   Sellaro, R., Nitsche, M.A., and Colzato, L.S., "The stimulated social brain: effects of transcranial direct current stimulation on social cognition," *Annals of the New York Academy of Sciences*, 1369(1), May 20, 2016.

4 Shah, I., quoting the 11th century Persian poet Fakruddin As'ad Gurgani in *The Way of the Sufi*, Octagon Press, 2004, p. 31.

5 Mandela, N., *Conversations with Myself*, Picador Reprint Edition, Kindle Edition, 2011, location 29.

6 Lefort, R., *The Teachers of Gurdjieff*, Malor Books, 2014, pp. xi-xii.

7 Smith, A.L. and Tart, C.T., "Cosmic consciousness experience and psychedelic experiences: A first-person comparison," *Journal of Consciousness Studies*, 5(1) (1998), pp. 97-107.

8 Tolstoy's Diary, 14 October 1897, reproduced in *The King's Son: Readings in the Traditional Psychologies and Contemporary Thought on Man*, compiler Cecil, R., 1980, Octagon Press, p. 61.

9 Mitchell, Edgar, from "In the Shadow of the Moon" DVD, Channel 4 Studio, 2008.

10 Doblin, R., "Pahnke's 'Good Friday Experiment': A long-term follow-up and methodological critique," *The Journal of Transpersonal Psychology*, 23(1) (1991), pp. 14-15.

11 Ornstein, R., *The Evolution of Consciousness*, Prentice Hall Press, 1991, Malor Books, 2021.

12 Shah, I., *The Sufis*, Octagon Press, 1964, p. 61.

13 Ornstein, R., *The Psychology of Consciousness*, *The Evolution of Consciousness*, and *Multimind*, Malor Books, 2021.

14 For examples of these children's stories by Idries Shah visit: Hoopoe Books at hoopoebooks.com

15 Ornstein, R., *The Psychology of Consciousness*, Malor Books, 2021.

See also: Ornstein, R., "Teaching Stories and the Brain" video of a lecture at the Library of Congress, 2002, RobertOrnstein.com/video

Afterword:

1 Shah, I., "Counsels of Bahaudin," in *Thinkers of the East*, The Estate of Idries Shah, 2002, p. 188.

Addendum:

1   Broad, W.J., "Black-Market Trinkets From Space," *New York Times*, April 4, 2011.

2   Wainwright, G.A., "Letopolis," *The Journal of Egyptian Archaeology*, Volume: 18:1, May 1, 1932, pp. 159-172.

3   Walsh, V. , "A theory of magnitude: common cortical metrics of time, space and quantity," *Trends in Cognitive Sciences*, (2003) 7, 11, 483-488.

4   Shah, I., *Knowing How to Know*, Octagon Press, 1988, p. 304.

5   Humphreys, C., *The Miracles of Exodus: A Scientist's Discovery of the Extraordinary Natural Causes of the Biblical Stories*, Harper Collins, 2004, pp. 44-47.

Index

Lightning Source UK Ltd.
Milton Keynes UK
UKHW011102020622
403848UK00005B/260

9 781949 358992